RON SCHARA'S
Minnesota Fishing Guide

WALDMAN HOUSE PRESS
Minneapolis, Minnesota

Waldman House Press
519 North Third Street
Minneapolis, Minnesota 55401

Printed in the United States of America
First Printing, April 1978
Library of Congress Catalog Number: 78-54246
International Standard Book Number: 0-931674-01-8

Illustrations by Ken Haag
Cover Design by Michael Carroll

To Simone and Laura,
Whose fishing days lie ahead.

Introduction/Let Us Wet A Line . . .

Part I/Basics Briefly

Part II/Whatchacatchin?

Part III/Gone Fishing

Acknowledgments

The fishing expert who wrote this book is not me.

I am more like a sponge in a leaky fishing boat, soaking in the skills and techniques, the lessons and tribulations of my many fishing partners. So it is they who really filled these pages.

My memory is good but it's awfully short. Surely I've drifted a lake or waded a river's pool with many kind anglers whose names have floated away but whose contributions can be found between these covers.

But here are a few, a lineup of some of the greatest fishermen and people I know:

Dad, my first partner; Joe Ball, of boyhood trout streams and catfish holes; Uncle Bob Dickens, catcher of trout; Conservation Officer Ray Lakso, basics of steelheading; Dick Knapp, magic of muskies; Ron Weber, fishing is his business; Dan Gapen, loves those rivers; Tony Herbert, Mille Lacs owes him nothing; Al and Ron Lindner, piscatorial thinkers; Bud and Ted Burger, try this rod; Dick Sternberg, knows what he catches; Bob Taintor, eye for a fly; Lee Rudsenske, defeat at Spider Lake; Ted Capra, I've got a secret; Gary Roach, good and rotten; and to Minnesota's many dedicated Area Fisheries Managers whose sole ambitions are to help all fishermen get a bite.

P.S. With apologies to fisherpersons ... the use of such masculine words as fisherman inadequately describe the interest and contributions that women have given to the sport. Please blame the language. To have used fisherperson or he/she in every reference to anglers in the following pages would have been awkward and possibly unnecessary. My Grandma always said she was a "better fisherman" than Grandpa.

Besides that, she was.

Ron Schara
March, 1978

Let Us Wet a Line . . .

In Minnesota, those folks that don't fish dig worms for those that do.

Fishing is what we're about. If baseball is the National Pastime, Minnesota ought to secede. No other state can match in name, reputation or natural assets, what the Dakota Indians so appropriately called "Minisota" — meaning sky-tinted waters.

We don't win Super Bowls and our politicians are only vice-presidents. We may be second in sugar beet production or even third in milk cows. But if Izaak Walton was the godfather of sport fishing, Minnesota is the Holy Land. Our common bond consists of fishing tackle, mosquito dope and a good walleye chop. Holidays in Minnesota are: Christmas, New Years Eve and Opening Day.

More than one million of the state's 3.8 million residents buy fishing licenses every year. Another 550,000 residents don't legally need a license because they're either too young or too old. And still others undoubtedly believe that being legal can spoil a fishing trip.

Nor do Minnesotans fish alone. Between 400,000 and 500,000 visiting fishermen from all corners of the world annually seek out our sky-tinted waters. No other state attracts such angling hordes.

What we catch is varied, of course. After all, fishing is fishing. Even in Minnesota. But none of us — resident or visitor — can ever complain about the amount of sky-tinted water on hand.

Our waters were formed by glaciers, dams and beavers.

There is so much of it, the muskrats are still exploring. Even our license plates with the famous "10,000 Lakes" slogan are wrong. The latest estimate is about 12,000 lakes of 10 acres or more in size. Nobody yet has accurately counted the smaller ones.

If you poured it all in one spot, the water would cover some 4,900 square miles, or more than 3 million acres. That's without using Minnesota's portion of Lake Superior.

Not every puddle holds fish, of course. The ducks need a home, too. But about 65 per cent or 2 million acres supports catchable fish life. That means there'd be one acre of exclusive fishing water for every man, woman, and child if we all — resident and non-resident anglers — decided to wet a line at the same time.

Enough. Let's get to the nitty-gritty. You can pour water into a bath tub, too, but you won't catch anything. So Minnesota has the water. Does it have the fish?

I wasn't around 100 years ago. Or 50. But I suspect the boys who fished during the "good old days" filled a horse wagon every time. That's the way the stories go, anyway.

You can't do that today. For one thing, there are legal limits. For another, horse wagons are scarce. I've had bad luck and good luck. Maybe, once or twice, could have filled a wagon. Many times, I gave up with a drowned minnow and a dry stringer.

But never could I blame my piscatorial failures on a fish shortage. Of course, our rivers and lakes no longer teem with hook-happy fish — if they ever did. There are more of us fishing today. And more of us catching. No lake, no river bend is too remote to reach. Fishing frontiers have gone the way of nickel beers, gold strikes and passenger pigeons.

Still there are fish to be caught. It's proven every day in Minnesota. A summer or two ago, the walleyes on Mille Lacs Lake started committing suicide at a rate the old timers said they'd never seen. Blame it on poor memory, if you want. Yet, year after year, no lake gets pounded for its walleye riches like Mille Lacs. Still, Mille Lacs managed to satisfy our angling desires. And tell me, was the angler of yesteryear somehow more delirious with a limit of three pound walleyes or bass than the angler who did the same thing last week?

That's not to say that Minnesota is some kind of angling utopia. There are problems. Fishing pressure — sheer numbers of anglers — has had an impact on the state's walleye stocks. The business of fish management in Minnesota is under-financed and has been possibly for decades. Pollution, too, has destroyed some of our fishing grounds. We have scum, low forms of life that spear spawning fish in the spring, that snag trout, that take more than what our rules permit.

Still, there's fish to catch.

But if you disagree, you've come to the right place. That's what this book is about — for the angling brethren who find something lacking in their angling days and fishless nights. Sometimes sunsets and loon calls are not enough. They can be enjoyed without holding a fishing rod.

Fishing, they say, is a contemplative endeavor. Relax. While away the hours to the sleepy music of lapping water. If you catch something fine, if not, well ... baloney. If I must contemplate, let me do it with a taut line and bended rod. Fishing is a lot of things, fellowship and suntans, scenery and solitude. But most of all it is catching. Otherwise we wouldn't use hooks.

That's why this book is about catching — how to and where. For the true joy of fishing, the magnetism and endless appeal of the sport is dependent on one's ability to experience the joy of catching ... to occasionally do everything right, to master the unseen world underwater and fool its inhabitants.

Not every time. There's no such thing. Getting skunked over water is as natural as getting wet in water. We need it. We have a right to get skunked. If we never got skunked, if fishing no longer delivered surprises, mysteries and humiliations, then fishing would no longer exist.

Yet fishing entices us to seek perfection. Mankind has been around about two million years now. We've invented a jillion hooks and umpteen new ways to fool a fish. We've got hipboots, racy boats and float planes. We've made ball-bearing reels, space-age fishing lines and electronic underwater eyes. And lordy, we still get skunked.

That's why this how-to book is not written in stone. It is written, however, in the spirit of the chase ... to help us find more joy in fishing through the joy of catching. Lest you think that contradictory, allow me to explain. I have watched consistently mediocre fishermen become sometimes proficient. In doing so, they catch more but they keep less. Complete novices keep every fish for fear they'll never see another one. Therefore, the struggle to improve angling skills also is the key battle for conserving our fishing resources.

If, by chance, you think the battle already is lost, if you believe there are no fish to be caught, then grab the nearest shovel, please.

And dig me some worms.

Part I Basics Briefly

Tools of the Game

Minnesota's style of fishing isn't much different from other places.

Some of us talk funny because "dat's de vey dey lernt from de oldt kontry."

We chose the walleye as the official State Fish but we call it the "pike".

When the water freezes, we'll fish through the ice, a practice not accepted, appreciated or believed south of the Mason-Dixon Line.

For fishing, we use rods, reels and weather predictions by Grandma's lumbago to help fill our stringers. Our fish know both how to open their jaws like a starved wolf or clamp them tighter than a shoemaker's vice.

We have about 3,000 lakes, which provide most of our fishing. None of them are alike and they each act differently every day.

We have evil weather, known as cold fronts. When a cold front passes through, the fish sulk and seal their lips in silence, while the fisherman flaps his to deliver excuses — and drink beer.

But beyond that, we're normal, I "tink."

While it may help to hold your eyes right or salivate on your hook to catch fish in Minnesota, expensive preparations are unnecessary. It's possible to justify buying and using a different fishing rod for each game fish species in the state. But I'm not about to. Whatever you own now in the way of basic fishing gear will be sufficient to catch something in Minnesota. After all, there are about 145 different fish species living within the state's borders. Some of them never are caught by conventional angling methods.

Basically, most of us fish for only a few of those 145 species, mainly the gamefishes. A goodly number of them can be caught with one style of fishing rod and one style of reel. Others simply require techniques so specialized that different gear becomes a piscatorial necessity, not spendthrift advice. So — let's take a look:

Rods and Reels

First decide what you most like to fish for and in which way. In Minnesota, that usually means you'll fish for walleyes, northern pike and panfish. You'll use live bait most of the time, occasionally pitching an artificial lure or two. That also means you can get by with one rod, maybe two.

If you're the type who's looking for a good walleye rod that you can also use during the winter months, while you're vacationing in the Florida Keys, I'd suggest you buy one of everything. You can afford it.

But if I had but one rod to choose for Minnesota, it would include these credentials: It would be made of fiberglass or graphite. The rod's action, as classed by rod manufacturers, would be medium to light-medium. (The action of a rod is based largely on its spine and flex. A stout rod, one with a stiff tip end, is classed as a "heavy" action rod; the opposite extreme is an ultra-light or light action, one with flexibility of a bull whip.)

Medium action rods normally are designed to handle lures or weights ranging from ¼-ounce to ½-ounce. And that about covers everything you'd cast for walleyes, bass or northern pike. The light lures and baits used to catch panfish might not cast with absolute ease. But most of us use bobbers for such fish. And since we often use bobbers

10-times bigger than we need, you'll have no problem casting tiny lures with a medium action rod.

At least you're in business with such a rod choice. It will adequately handle the majority of your fishing needs for most of what Minnesota has to offer.

But then there are those special occasions. If you want the most fun and efficiency when you're fishing bluegills, crappies, perch, white bass and any other fish that tend to be scrappy but lightweight, an ultra-light outfit — rod and reel — is a must.

Ultra-lights, outfitted with 2 or 4-pound test line, could cast a housefly 30 feet if it would stay on the hook. They're ideal for flicking light lures and small spinners. If you thrill to the sight of a fully-arched fishing rod, the ultra-light will bend double on a ½-pound crappie. Don't use such a rod for muskies, however, unless you've never seen a rod tied into an overhand knot.

Speaking of muskies, a do-it-all medium action rod won't be worth a hoot on these monsters, either. Pool cues are preferred. You need a heavy or extra-heavy action rod to toss most of the conventional muskie-fooling plugs. If you don't use big plugs, you'll still need a stout rod to set the hooks in a muskie's jaws. 'Course, you can always take your chances. But muskies are elusive enough without knowingly chopping your odds. You don't climb mountains with a stepladder.

And then there's stream fishing for steelhead trout on Minnesota's North Shore. Again, if you want to give yourself a chance, steelhead catching requires investing in a long, stout flyrod. Not to fish with artificial flies, but to use much like a cane pole. Come to think about it, a cane pole would work. Until a steelhead hit and converted it to toothpicks.

A special rod might also be necessary if you choose to stalk the brook trout streams that wind through the jungles of Minnesota's Northeast. In that case, you might want an extremely short rod with a reel on one end and a fly swatter on the other to win bug attacks.

Otherwise, the best-equipped angler on Minnesota's lakes and streams need not own a sporting goods store.

Ted and Bud Burger do own sporting goods stores in Minneapolis and their first choice for most situations is a 7-7½-foot medium action rod. "You can only use one at a time anyway," said Bud. "Yeah," Ted added, "and if you can't catch fish, it won't matter what kind of rod you use."

Nor does it really matter what kind of reel you use. There are three basic styles — spinning, spin-cast and casting. Each has advantages and shortcomings. What is important is to choose the reel type that you can handle best.

Stick with brand names and buy top models. That goes for rods, too. Expensive gear alone won't make you a better fisherman, but it won't stop you from being one, either.

Some of my earliest memories of fishing frustrations were made by a casting reel, which was the cheapest model sold by a cheap reel company. It wouldn't cast with 10 sinkers unless I swung the rod sidearm like a double-bit axe.

Lines and Knots

To paraphrase W. C. Fields, there never was a man so bad at tying knots he couldn't serve as a good example.

Allow me to volunteer.

I once was stricken with inept knot-tying disease and still suffer occasional relapses. I know what it's like to tie on a new lure, heave it towards fishy-looking waters and watch it sail out of sight. We all could blame the line if it wasn't for the pigtail on the end, indisputable evidence of knot disease.

For Minnesota's fishing demands there's no excuse. The knots any angler needs to know to keep lures and fish on the end of the line are simple to learn and easy to tie.

Here are six knots that ought to serve your every knot tying wish:

Improved Clinch Knot The basic knot for tying on lures, hooks, flies or snaps. **1.** Pass the end of the line through the hook eye or swivel. Double back and make five or more twists of the line end around the standing line. **2.** Holding the coils, bring the end back through the first loop formed between the coils and the hook eye and then back through the big loop as shown. **3.** Hold onto the end and standing line and pull up tight. Clip off excess.

Palomar Knot Another basic knot for tying on hooks, lures, swivels. You may find it easier to tie than the Improved Clinch Knot. Properly tied it's just as strong. **1.** Pass line through eye of hook and return through eye making a 3″ or 4″ loop as shown. **2.** Hold line and hook eye with one hand and use other hand to tie a loose overhand knot in doubled line. Do not tighten. **3.** Hold loose overhand knot and pull loop over hook, swivel or lure. **4.** Pull on doubled line to draw knot up making sure loop does not hang up in hook eye or swivel. Pull both line ends to tighten. Clip off end about ⅛″ from knot.

Pull all four ends uniformly
to draw knot tight

Surgeon's Knot For tying a leader to a line end, where the diameters are unequal. **1.** Overlap ends of lines for several inches. Tie a simple overhand knot treating both strands as one. **2.** Pass the two strands through the loop again. Pull up tight. Trim ends.

Blood Knot The best knot for tying line to line when the diameters of the two are the same or nearly so. Makes a strong, small joint that slips through most rod guides easily. **1.** Overlap the ends of the two lines for several inches. Hold at the middle of the overlap and twist one end around the other line five or more turns. Bring end back and through strands as shown. **2.** Still holding the lines, turn other end around line the same number of turns in the opposite direction. Bring end back and pass between lines from opposite direction of first end. **3.** Tighten by pulling up slowly on both lines. Clip off short ends.

Spider Hitch Creates a double line with the full strength of unknotted line. **1.** Double-up length of line desired and form a loop. Hold loop between thumb and forefinger with thumb slightly extended past finger. **2.** Wrap doubled line five or more times around thumb and loop so that wraps lie evenly and parallel on your thumbnail. **3.** Pass end of doubled line through loop and slowly draw wraps one at a time off thumb. Pull ends and doubled line alternately to tighten. Clip off excess.

Surgeon's End Loop Quick, easy and strong. Tie it at the end of line, leaders or snells. **1.** Double up line end for a few inches. Form loop in doubled line, holding it in place between thumb and forefinger. **2.** Pass end of doubled line through loop twice. (For greater strength pass doubled line through loop four times.) Pull doubled end up tight to form final loop.

For many of us, monofilament line — the most popular and practical fishing line in use today — sometimes acts like a necessary evil. It tangles, twists, breaks or flies off our reels in professional overruns, otherwise known as a backlash.

Monofilament troubles are more deeply rooted with the user than the line, however. Again, for Minnesota fishing, you'll be in the ballpark by using line no lighter than 6-pound test and no heavier than 12-pound test. Most reels perform better with line sizes between those ranges.

Except for muskies, when you'll need heavier line, and trout, when you'll want finer monofilament, line tests of 6, 8, 10 or 12 will handle about any fish in Minnesota's freshwater.

Some fishermen insist on arming themselves with the heaviest line possible, say 20-pound test, just in case that trophy fish hits. It usually doesn't.

Excessively heavy line causes more problems than it's worth. Most spinning and spin-cast reels won't function properly; finely balanced lures won't swim right; casting distance is severely limited.

If you're uncertain about selecting the proper test line, make your mistake on the lighter side. Your reel and casting performance won't suffer. And it's already been proven that you can land any fish, no matter what size, on light line if you know the art of fighting a fish and have a reel with a working drag.

Sometimes monofilament does go haywire, however. Or seems to. A curly or twisted line not only weakens the line but it turns many fishermen into nervous wrecks. Curls develop when the line has been coiled on a reel for a length of time. And twists develop as a result of a lure rotating. With spinning reels, twists also develop from cranking the reel handle, retrieving line. Free-turning swivels placed ahead of lures, such as spoons and spinners, will help reduce some of the twisting. But sooner or later, you'll get the twists and your line will curl up on itself and eventually make a nest any robin would be proud to own.

But such headaches are so easy to avoid. If you've got

twists only in the first few feet of line, hold your rod tip high, letting your lure dangle free. It will slowly unwind. When it quits turning, the twists will be gone.

If you've got a severe case of the twists, cut everything off the end of your line — snaps, swivels, lures. Hop in a boat or stand in a stream and let the line peel out behind the moving boat or current. Let out enough line to cover the twisted portion. The friction of the water against the monofilament works as a magical untwister. In minutes your line will be like new again. And your headache will be gone.

What else should you know about fishing line? Not much. Monofilament will fray or develop weak spots near the terminal end, that part closest to the hook. Check for them occasionally by running the line between your fingers. Or simply snip off 3 or 4 feet of line.

Monofilament line itself will last for years. It does tend to become brittle with age and improper storage. Keep line stored out of sunlight and excessive heat to make it last longer.

And please don't throw waste monofilament line overboard. It virtually will never rot underwater and it can get wrapped around outboard props, breaking costly oil seals.

Besides, fish don't need line, anyway. They just test them.

Cold Fronts, Wind and Other Excuses

If you hang around Minnesota's bait shops, boat docks or lakeside taverns, sooner or later you'll hear some piscatorial moaning about cold fronts.

"Catch anything?"

"Naw."

"Weren't biting, huh?"

"Naw. Think it was that danged cold front."

Cold fronts are the perfect excuse for any empty stringer. You can say the front just arrived or just left and be technically correct. Your listeners will gush with sympathy. They don't know what a cold front is but it sounds official.

Not that cold fronts don't count. Such weather will often put a stop to fishing action for days. But I'm not sure most of us know a cold front when we see one, particularly since cold fronts can happen without any drastic change in temperature.

I shall leave the technicalities to the weatherman, however.

What fishermen need to know is that cold fronts generally are associated with bright, cloudless, high blue skies. One of those beautiful days for making suntans, ice cream or hay.

But anglers generally will find little to cheer about. From the moment the front hits, the fishing action will begin to falter, reaching rock bottom usually on the day after the front passes. Depending on the strength of the weather pattern, the action often begins to pick up by the second or third day.

Why cold fronts effect the fish and fishing is not clearly understood. Not that that matters. As they say, we can't do anything about the weather.

What's more the effect is widespread, touching everything from schools of bait fish to muskies longer than oars. Occasionally the persistent fisherman may improve his luck during a cold front by changing his objectives. That is, switching from bass to bluegills. Perch, for example, seem to bite all the time, although they may be less aggressive, too.

If you're stubborn, if your fishing weekend started with a high, blue sky and chilly breezes, then you have no choice but to face the catching difficulties born by a cold front.

Ron and Al Lindner, a pair of fish-thinking brothers and co-producers of the *In'Fisherman,* have confronted the bad odds of cold fronts. In their guiding days, the times of their worst luck were under the influence of cold fronts.

But they discovered a few last resorts.

"Generally we fished deeper water or the heaviest cover during cold fronts," Ron explained. "Our luck wasn't always phenomenal but we did catch something while other fishermen didn't.

"And we went to live bait ... for everything. The guy who throws artificials to bass during the effects of a cold front can forget it.

"I do think that walleyes are less affected by cold fronts than say bass. But still you should fish deeper and SLOWER. That's the key."

Minnesota has its share of wind, too. Some of it flows from politicians and some of it ripples fishing water. Both winds may pertain to the fisherman, but that which roils the waters is probably more meaningful.

Although angling poems have been written about wind direction — "wind from the east, fish bite the least" ... and so forth — the wind's intensity may do more to make or break your fishing luck. After all, the wind's direction is dependent on the location of pressure systems and frontal movements. Fish, indeed, may bite the least with an east wind, but the culprit is the weather phenomenon, not the wind's direction.

The wind's velocity is something else again. Winds that whip up dangerous boating conditions need no explanation. Fishermen shouldn't be out on big waters on those stormy occasions. I was once or twice and my fingerprints are still imbedded on the gunwales of the boat.

No, I'm referring to winds that are safe but affect your fishing success. For example, largemouth bass, roaming in bulrush shallows, are almost impossible to catch when the bulrushes are buffeted by wind and waves. The answer, of course, is to find those bassy-looking weedbeds that are out of the wind.

Walleye fishermen are always hoping for a "walleye chop," a brisk breeze that ripples the waters or forms light whitecaps. Such a wind does two things: reduces sunlight penetration for the light-sensitive walleyes, thereby often triggering a feeding binge. In addition, the steady winds are convenient for drifting while you fish, a popular walleye-catching technique.

There is a point, however, when the winds become a detriment to a drifting walleye fisherman. For he begins to drift too fast to control the boat or the bait. You'll know it when that happens. It's best then to anchor or seek quieter waters.

The important thing to remember is that wind does affect most gamefishes in Minnesota. And it can hamper or help your fishing techniques, the way your bait is presented, your ability to detect strikes, etc. Thus, be versatile. Count wind as a factor. There may be times when you'll intentionally want to fish in wind-rumpled waters. Then again, your best success may be waiting in quieter places ... lakeshores, islands, points on the leeward side.

And if your luck still is bad, blame it on a cold front. No one will be the wiser.

Using Your Eyes To The Bottom

Hundreds and hundreds of Minnesota's fishing lakes have been charted into hydrographic maps, showing depths, drop-offs, islands, vegetation and so forth.

These lake maps are invaluable aids to the fishermen who venture to strange waters. If you know how to read them. (See Illustration)

Remember that almost all fish like to be near something — boat docks, weed patches, brushy shores. These things are visible. But of course there are "objects" underwater that also attract and hold fish. These objects we cannot see. That's where the maps help. They'll show sunken islands, drop-offs, underwater points and bars. More importantly, the maps also show where the bottom is rather uninteresting, flat, boring. Chances are you'll find very little fish action in such places, unless there are features the maps don't show, such as emergent vegetation, a fish attractant.

Thus, you must use both your eyes and a hydrographic map.

And an electronic depth finder. also known as fish locators, sonars.

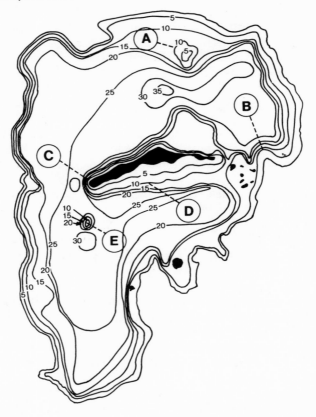

A typical lake map Note contour lines, which show depths, islands, points, bays. **(A)** Indicates underwater hump. **(B)** Shows how point extends underwater with fast drop-off outside of point; note small islands are in rather dull water. **(C)** Shows very sharp drop-off. The closer the contour lines the sharper the drop-off. As compared to **(D)** which shows contour lines farther apart, indicating a gradual increase in water depth. **(E)** Shows typical sunken island with 10-feet of water over top of the island.

A free list of mapped lakes is available from the Documents Section, Department of Natural Resources, Centennial Building, St. Paul, Minnesota 55155.

Individual maps may be purchased from the Documents Section. Resorts and bait shops often have maps available of lakes in their particular area.

These devices give instantaneous readings of the bottom. And if you've read the instructions properly or are an experienced user of depth finders, the machines are capable of indicating bottom type (rock, sand, mud). And most will show fish and underwater weed beds.

Do not use your electronic eyes to find fish, however. More often than not, such an exercise is a waste of time. Use the depth finders to locate where fish may be — the drop-offs, points and other haunts.

Generally, the hydrographic maps will give you a good idea of where to start fishing on a lake and the depth finder will give an exact location of where to drop your fishing line.

You'll also find that the maps are not always exact or accurate. That's why the smart fisherman with a depth finder will turn it on the minute he leaves the dock. You'll never know when — enroute to a spot marked on the map — you'll cross an underwater hump or some other fishy-looking structure that's not on the map. That doesn't mean it's not worth fishing. Try it. You may find that "secret" hotspot we all dream about.

Hiring A Guide

Minnesota is blessed with a number of skilled anglers who go fishing for hire. Some are more skilled than others, however.

Since it's your money, choose a guide based on what he's done, not what he says he'll do. Obtain references for guides through tackle shops, bait stores, resorts. Resorts particularly are concerned about the guides they suggest. For if you have a lousy time with a guide (regardless of what is caught), you're apt to blame the resort.

Make sure you understand what the guide will or will not furnish so there are no surprises when it's time to pay.

Check the guide's equipment. If he's professional, his boat will be in good shape and safely adequate for the waters you will be fishing.

Ask about his fishing style before you make a reservation. If you like to cast for northern pike and the guide you hire is a trolling specialist, you're not going to have a fun day. It's also unfair to ask a guide to fish your way. You're paying him for his experience and expertise, so get the most out of it. So — if you like to cast for bass, choose a guide who likes to do the same thing. In that way, the guide will be at his best and you'll learn and have a good time. And you might even catch lots of fish.

Guide fees vary. Make sure you know what the charges are and how many rods (people) are included. Don't hire one guide and expect to put the grandpa, two kids and Aunt Eva in the same boat.

Launch fishing is different, of course. Most launches can handle 20 or more fishermen at a time. In most cases, you can rent the whole launch and the captain or pay a certain amount per angler.

Again, inquire about how much time you're buying on a launch and what is provided (baits, rods, refreshments, life jackets, etc?).

In Minnesota, launch fishing is available on most of the state's big walleye lakes, such as Mille Lacs, Leech, Winnibigoshish and Lake of the Woods.

Charter boats are available on Lake Superior. They operate similarly with rates for half-day or full-day with a maximum number of guests or rods.

Keeping Minnows Happy

As Izaak Walton once wrote, "A dead worm is but a dead bait, and like to catch nothing, compared to a lively, stirring worm."

While Walton's wisdom speaks for itself, I might add that a dead minnow or a mushy nightcrawler represents the most expensive rotten meat you've ever bought. I once figured that nightcrawlers, selling for $1 a dozen, comes out at about $32 per pound. The point being, if you don't take care of your live bait, you'd be better off going to the fish market where walleyes only sell for about $3 or $4 a pound.

Before you can keep your live bait healthy, it first must be purchased in that condition. Look before you buy. A bait shop owner who runs a sloppy business can't hide the fact. If his minnows are dying in his tanks, you can be sure they'll roll over in your bucket.

When buying nightcrawlers, a reputable bait dealer won't mind if you first open the carton and take a look. Touch a few of the crawlers. They should react. If not, they're probably ready to die. Healthy 'crawlers also are plump like a short, fat cigar. Pick one up. If it looks like a shoestring, chances are you couldn't feed it to a robin much less a walleye. Never buy a carton of nightcrawlers that contains one dead member. The rest will be dead, shortly.

Of all live bait, leeches are the easiest to judge. Again, check the carton. Dead leeches turn white or gray. So make sure you're buying a lively dozen.

Once the bait is out of the store, it's up to you to keep it alive and active. I've already mentioned that live bait is expensive stuff. But as Walton said a dead worm is apt to catch nothing. Same with minnows, leeches, frogs, salamanders or whatever you use. Good bait is important for good fishing. Sure, you can grind up a nightcrawler and still feed it to bluegills or perch. And sun-ripened minnows will attract catfish for 15 miles. But for walleyes, crappies, northern pike, muskies and other fish, you'll want active bait.

John Vados of Spring Lake Park, Minnesota has been a long time catcher and keeper of live bait. He's seen all the mistakes and probably made a few of them.

Here's what Vados recommends

Minnows

1. The best way to transport minnows successfully is to use an ordinary styrofoam bucket with a good lid. Styrofoam buckets keep water fresh much longer than metal. Don't buy too many minnows each time and overcrowd your bucket. The more oxygen, the better the fishing!

2. Put 8-10 ice cubes in your bucket when transporting minnows long distances. If the ice cubes are made with ordinary tap water and contains chlorine, put them in a plastic bag first. Remember, keep the lid on!

3. Don't buy more minnows than you plan to use in a week's time. Minnows quickly grow stale in an unnatural environment and aren't nearly as effective as when fresh.

4. When it's necessary to change minnow water (usually when all the minnows come topside for oxygen) re-fill only half the bucket each time. A whole new bucket of lake water could likely cause shock and shorten minnow life. Any new water added to minnows should not change the temperature more than 10 degrees higher or lower than the water being replaced. Fresh water from a lake or well should be used.

5. When you take fish home in your minnow bucket be sure to wash it real good before it's used for minnows again. Slime remaining in the bucket after fish are removed contains bacteria that use up valuable oxygen. Wash your bucket with regular baking soda for best results.

Nightcrawlers and Worms

1. Nightcrawlers and worms usually are packaged in a special bedding material, which includes food as well as habitat. There is enough food in each box to last 3-4 weeks and keep nightcrawlers and worms as fresh as if in

their natural environment. Do not add moisture; packages contain just the right amount.

2. Nightcrawlers and worms should be kept within a temperature range of 40-60 degrees. A styrofoam bucket is ideal for traveling. Just put a few ice cubes in a plastic bag, place in the bucket and you've got a great refrigerator for one or several boxes. Between fishing trips you can keep them in your refrigerator at home.

3. Boxes of nightcrawlers or worms should never be left in areas exposed to direct sunlight. While fishing be sure to keep them shaded beneath a boat seat. Boxes exposed for less than 10 minutes to direct sunlight can result in dead nightcrawlers and worms.

Leeches

1. Keep leeches cool. To store, change water daily and refrigerate. No feeding is necessary.

Miscellaneous Baits

1. Grubs, wax worms, mousies should be kept refrigerated (about 60 degrees) between fishing trips.

Fileting: No Bones About It

One of the best fish cleaners I ever met was Danny Stott. And he was about 11 years old at the time. Just goes to show you don't have to be some grizzled old timer to cut out boneless filets. Danny's secret was plenty of experience. Everyday he'd wait on the dock at his father's Rainbow Inn resort to collect the walleyes coming in on the launch from Mille Lacs Lake.

As they say, practice makes perfect. That plus equip yourself with a decent filet knife. Decent mean two things: sharp and sharp. Having a filet knife with a flexible blade and comfy handle is fine and dandy. But if the blade isn't

How To Filet A Fish

1. Make first cut just behind the gills. Slice down to the bone, then, without removing blade, turn it and slice straight along backbone . . .

2. . . . to the tail. Note that the fillet has been cut away from the rest of the fish. After slicing fillet off at tail, turn fish over and repeat procedure on the other side.

3. With both sides removed, you have cut away both fillets without disturbing fish's entrails. This is the neatest and fastest way to prepare fish. Now to finish the fillets . . .

4. Next step is to remove the rib section. Again, a sharp, flexible knife is important to avoid wasting meat. Insert blade close to rib bones and slice entire section away. This should be done before skin is removed to keep waste to a minimum.

5. Removing the skin from each fillet is simply a matter of inserting knife at tail and "cutting" meat from the skin. With the proper knife, it's easily done.

6. Here is each fillet, ready for the pan, or freezer. Note there is no waste. Remember not to overwash fillets. This will preserve tasty juices and keep meat in its firm natural state.

7. Cutting out the "cheeks" is the next important step. Few fishermen know that cheeks are the filet mignon of the fish. Though small, they're tasty and well worth saving.

8. Slice into cheek where indicated then "scoop out" meat with blade, peeling away skin. Repeat on the other side. Many fishermen save cheeks until they have accumulated enough for a real gourmet's delight.

9. Here are all parts of the fish after you've finished. Note fish head, entrails, spine, tail and fins stay intact. This is the neatest way to prepare most game fish and, once you've mastered these few steps, the easiest.

Provided by the Normark Corp., Minneapolis

sharp or won't hold an edge, you'd do a better job with a machete.

There are several ways to skin a cat and filet a fish. But the method illustrated here works as good as any. By the way, almost any Minnesota fish can be fileted, except catfish and bullheads. These two bewhiskered fishes are best skinned and gutted, preferably by somebody other than yourself.

In northern pike, there are troublesome "Y-bones", which are not eliminated by usual fileting methods. So extra steps are necessary. Filet as usual, except do not remove the skin. With the filet flesh-side up, make an angular cut along the "lateral" line, which runs length-wise in the middle of the filet. Fold over the flap of flesh, containing the Y-bones (you can feel them with a finger) and make another cut, removing the flap. That should eliminate every bone in the filet. Then, remove the skin. Again practice makes perfect.

Legal Lines

If the sport of fishing is worth doing, then it is worth preserving and protecting.

That's what Minnesota's fishing laws are about.

Basically, a Minnesota fisherman needs to know three things: if he needs a valid license; the open seasons and the daily and possession fishing limits.

From there it gets more complicated. If you own or use a boat, familiarize yourself with Minnesota boating regulations, particularly the licensing requirements and required safety equipment, such as life saving devices. (One Coast Guard approved life jacket is required for each person onboard.)

If you plan to fish for trout, be aware that at certain times some portions of trout streams are off-limits. In some cases, multiple hooks are prohibited.

Minnesota is bounded by four states and Canada. On the border lakes or rivers, the fishing seasons and limits often are different from Minnesota's inland waterways.

Non-residents share all of the fishing privileges enjoyed by residents with one exception: nonresidents are not allowed to spear.

There is only one size limit in Minnesota, but a very important one. Muskies must be 30 inches or longer to be legally kept.

A synopsis of Minnesota's fishing laws, covering the various seasons and limits, is available annually at places that sell fishing licenses, such as county auditor offices, sporting goods stores, hardware stores, bait shops and some resorts.

Following are Minnesota's general license requirements and common restrictions:

Minnesota License Requirements
Residents

Resident Licenses may be issued only to U.S. citizens who have maintained a legal residence in Minnesota for a period of 60 days immediately preceding the date of application for a license, except as provided below.

Residents under the age of 16 years are not required to have an angling, spearing, or netting license.

A License to take fish shall be issued to any citizen of Minnesota who is a recipient of supplemental security income for the aged, blind, and disabled, without charge.

Residents Serving in the U.S. military or naval forces, or the reserve components thereof, who are stationed outside the state may fish without a license in Minnesota on regularly granted leave or furlough, provided they have the proper leave or furlough papers on their person.

A Permanent License to take fish shall be issued at the prevailing fee for an individual resident license to any citizen of Minnesota, 16 years of age or older, who is mentally retarded and whose parent or guardian furnishes satisfactory evidence of the disability to the county auditor or a sub-agent of the county auditor.

Permanent License to take fish shall be issued to Minnesota veterans who have a 100% service-connected disability.

Residents Who have attained the age of 65 years may take fish by angling and spearing without a license. However, they must have on their person evidence of their age and proof of Minnesota residency.

Patients of a U.S. veteran's Administration Hospital may fish without obtaining a license as long as they are patients. Also, patients or inmates of a State mental or correctional institution may be permitted to fish without obtaining a license as long as they are patients, subject to written consent of the superintendent of such institution.

Nonresidents:

A Nonresident under the age of 16 years is not required to have an angling license if his parent or legal guardian has obtained a nonresident angling license and provided the child's fish are included in the daily and possession limit of the parent or legal guardian. However, a nonresident under 16 may purchase a license and thereby be entitled to his own limit of fish.

Nonresidents in the Military or naval forces of the U.S., or in any reserve or component of the military or naval service, who have officially transferred to and are stationed in Minnesota, are eligible for resident fishing licenses.

Nonresident Full-time Students at public or private educational institutions who reside in Minnesota during the full term of the school year may purchase a resident fishing license from the county auditor upon presenting proof of their status as students.

GENERAL RESTRICTIONS
IT IS UNLAWFUL:

• For persons 16 years through 64 years of age to fish unless they have an angling license on their person ready for inspection, or to spear from a dark house unless they have a dark house spearing license in addition to an angling license.

• To be on board watercraft without a readily accessible personal floation device of the type approved by the U.S. Coast Guard.

• To deposit any refuse, poisonous substances, or chemicals injurious to fish life in any waters of the state.

• To buy or sell game fish, except fish taken under a commercial or private hatchery license.

• To take fish by means of explosives, drugs, poisons, lime, medicated bait, fish berries, or other deleterious substances, or by nets, traps, tip-ups, trotlines, set lines, wires, springs, ropes, cables, snaghooks or snaglines, except as expressly authorized.

• To operate any unregistered boat (except duck boats during the duck hunting season and rice boats during the harvest season).

• To stock fish in any waters or transfer fish from one body of water to another without written permit from the Director or his authorized agents.

• To take minnows from designated trout waters, except under special permit.

• To drive a motor boat through a posted spawning bed or fish preserve. (Note — Riparian landowners or lessees adjacent to such areas may use route doing least damage to vegetation to and from their property through such areas, provided they operate their motors at the slowest possible speed.)

- To drag boat anchors or other weights with a motor propelled boat through aquatic vegetation, except as authorized by law or by Commissioner's order.

- To fish in designated trout waters except during the trout season.

- It is unlawful to deposit garbage, rubbish, offal, in public waters or on the ice, or on public lands.

- To take fish by angling with a set or unattended line.

Floating Right

Today's modern fishing boats are the best in the history of boatmaking. Still, fishermen capsize and drown every year. In Minnesota, about 40 percent of all boating accidents involve fishermen. That probably says more about people than boats.

Minnesota has some mighty big water. Big enough to challenge the seaworthiness of many boats, not to mention the fishermen at the helm. I know. One unfortunate day on Mille Lacs, a storm hit without warning and tossed 23-foot boats around like corks. Two men in a smaller craft capsized and drowned.

That particular storm hit with very little warning. That's usually not the case. Most storms in Minnesota approach from the northwest, west or southwest. Whenever you're fishing keep an eye peeled in those directions. And don't take chances, particularly on big water. Give yourself enough time to arrive safely to shore. Be alert for a sudden change of wind direction. That usually means a weather change and it could be for the worse.

If you suspect bad weather later in your fishing day, try one of Minnesota's many smaller lakes instead of chancing ocean-size waves on big waters.

If you're a visitor and unfamiliar with Minnesota's weather signs, seek advice from local fishermen. Chances are if a local angler is skeptical about a lake's boating condition ("I wouldn't go out there if I were you") or the weather ("She looks nasty to the west") you'd be wise to heed the advice.

In addition, some lakes react differently to storms or strong winds, depending on their direction. For example, a gusty south wind on Lake X may not be dangerous to fishermen. However, the same wind from the west on Lake X could turn the water surface into a white froth.

Many of today's boats could handle such a white froth if today's fishermen all knew how to handle the boat. Whenever two or more fishermen head out, somebody invariably wants to ride in the bow seat. In my boat that's taboo in rough water. The key is to keep weight off the bow so that it can respond to the waves. Otherwise, the next thing you know water will be pouring in over the top.

Seats were placed in a boat for comfort under normal boating conditions. Rough waters are not normal. Don't hesitate to place your passengers on the deck or floor of the boat to ride out the bad water. Have them sit near the centerline of the boat to increase the craft's stability. Wise canoeists know the value of that lesson. For those who stand or ride high in a canoe will soon ride under.

So what's the perfect Minnesota fishing boat? That's a loaded question, which I shall refrain from triggering. I do have my opinions, of course. But it's important that each boat buyer determine where and how he intends to use the boat much of the time. Those fishermen who are in love with the state's giant lakes, such as Leech and Mille Lacs, should consider boats no smaller than 16-feet. If you fish some big waters, but mostly smaller lakes, then a 15-footer may be the best compromise. Of course there's a place for 12-foot johnboats, canoes, and other small cartoppers. They're handy and portable, ideal for fishing in that off-the-road hidden lake. But they do not belong on big water, unless you like trouble.

The amount of engine power is a personal thing and dependent on the boat being powered. However, the choice is critical for fishermen who like to troll for northern and muskies or backtroll (run the boat in reverse, stern-first) for walleyes.

Most fishermen tend to favor outboards in the lower horsepower ranges. Those small, 5 or 10 horse outboards will do just about anything a fisherman wants in the way of trolling speed. Other fishermen, of course, want to go somewhere fast. (The fishing is always better on the other side of the lake. Or is it?)

My personal choice for walleye fishing is somewhere in between — outboards of 25 or 35 horsepower. Both engine sizes will troll down nicely, yet have enough speed to push a fishing boat at a respectable clip. That's nice to have when storms may be approaching and you're on big water. On small lakes, the smaller outboards are more than adequate, however.

That doesn't mean you can't fish walleyes with a 50 horse outboard or a 120 horse inboard-outboard. However, the larger engines often "troll" too fast for walleyes, so you'll be limited to drifting or anchoring. Bass fishermen use big outboards but only for traveling speed. Bass anglers seldom troll; they cast. And when they want to move slowly, most bass anglers use small, quiet electric trolling motors, which are mounted on the bow.

Sometimes a fisherman has no choice of engine size. The kids may want to waterski. Since you can't afford two boats — one for fishing and one for waterskiing — you'll have to make certain concessions. But I haven't met a fish yet that was particular about the engine size on a fisherman's boat.

If you present the bait right, you'll catch fish.

If you don't, you won't.

Keeping Memories

There are only four things you can do with a fish: eat it, mount it, photograph it, release it. (Kinda makes you wonder why we try so hard to catch one, doesn't it?)

Still, we often botch up the four choices. It takes a terrible cook to ruin a frying pan of walleye or bluegill filets. But many of us average dudes take terrible photographs, ruin trophies for mounting and don't release enough fish to fight again another day.

Let's see if we can improve.

The key to interesting fish pictures is keep it simple.

Use a simple background, such as the sky. Get close to your subject, the fisherman and his catch. Don't add three limits and the neighbor's dog. An angler holding one or two fish makes a much better picture. The more fish added to a picture, the less fish actually noticed by the viewer.

Your fisherman model may want to look like Cary Grant and keep his sunglasses on. But have the glasses removed. Eyes are important for a picture. Also watch for harsh shadows across the face, made by hats and bright sun. Take the hat off or tilt it back or use a filler flash.

Action shots are fun to try, although you must keep your camera handy. But invariably, in the excitment of landing a fish, the camera will not be held evenly — and the horizon in the picture will appear like a mountain slope. And who's ever seen a lake tilted on its side? Concentrate on keeping the horizon level and hope that the action captured is what you wanted.

Also remember, it's the fisherman and his catch that are important. So get close to what's important. Why have George and his trophy walleye standing on the dock with half the lake and forty acres of trees also in the picture. Save that shot for scenics.

And take several pictures. Chances are if you only take one snap of George and his fish, George will have his eyes closed and his tongue out. Film is a cheap price to pay for fond memories.

Once-in-awhile, we each get lucky enough to catch a

fish worth putting on the wall, to treasure for a lifetime. Fine, so how do you get it safely to a taxidermist?

First, take several color photographs of the fish to give to the taxidermist. He'll use them to paint the fish and recapture its basic shape.

If you're close to a reputable taxidermist, deliver the fish as soon as possible. If not, freeze the whole fish in a plastic bag. Make sure the fins are folded back against the carcass. To protect the tail from breaking or splintering after it's frozen solid, place the tail between two pieces of cardboard and wrap securely before freezing.

When you first catch such a trophy, everybody and his brother will want to hold it, handle and show it to Uncle Louey. Avoid overhandling the fish, since some fish lose their scales easily. And missing scales will show up later, despite the best efforts of a taxidermist. By the way, you can expect to pay from $2.50 to $5 an inch (with minimums) to have your trophy mounted.

Of course you could have released that trophy alive. Huh? Few of us do, I know. But I think it's important that we think more about recycling our fish when appropriate. If you have a 10-pound walleye on the wall, why keep a 9-pounder if you have no plans to mount it also. The same reasoning should apply to bass, northern pike, muskies, you name it. By releasing a healthy fish, you could make another angler mighty happy.

I tossed a 6-pound walleye back into Mille Lacs one time in front of the disbelieving eyes of another fisherman.

"Say," he interrupted, "that was kind of a strange thing to do."

"Why?", I inquired.

"Well, some of us have been spending $200 a week to catch a fish like that," he said.

"I know," I replied. "Now at least you know there's one in there to catch."

The fisherman seemed satisfied. And pleased. But what did I want with another 6-pounder? I'd already had the fun of catching it. Why not let someone who's never caught a 6-pounder put the fish on the wall.

Of course, it would be foolish to release a fish that has

no chance of surviving. A fish that is bleeding after it's been hooked and landed probably won't live. But one that is hooked only in the lips and handled carefully (preferably released with little or no handling) will surely survive to bite again. A fish taken to the frying pan will not.

Something To Shoot For

Minnesota's fishing waters have yielded but one world record. A dandy fish, weighing 55-pounds, 5-ounces, caught by Frank Ledwein on Clearwater Lake near Annandale on July 10, 1952.

It was a carp.

It's buried someplace.

The big fish was put on display at the 1952 World's Fair in New York. When the fair ended, Ledwein said he didn't want the fish back. Nobody's seen it since.

Can't blame Ledwein. For catching a world record carp, he took enough ribbin' for three lifetimes. Too bad. That huge, ugly carp ought to be considered an asset. It shows Minnesota can grow big fish.

And the only one that's been caught so far is that carp. That means there's probably a bunch of other world records still swimming someplace in Minnesota.

Minnesota once claimed a former world's record muskellunge as its own state record, a 56-pound, 8-ounce giant caught by J.W. Collins on Lake of the Woods. That was a feather in everybody's hat until Jimmy Robinson, that sage historian of outdoor events in *Sports Afield* magazine, proved that Collins was fishing in Ontario's side of Lake of the Woods when the big fish struck.

So you can see the field is wide open for new Minnesota world records. Not to mention the listing of current state record fish.

Catching records isn't always so difficult. For example, Minnesota's record rainbow trout, 17-pounds, 6-ounces, was caught by Ottway "Red" Stuberud of Knife River. Red lives along the Knife River. He was doing a little ice fishing in his backyard when the lunker hit. Proves you don't always have to travel far to make the record books.

Minnesota's record brown bullhead was caught by an Iowan, Bill Meyer. Now that probably didn't surprise anybody. Iowans are known as infamous bullhead catchers, a reputation they may or may not deserve.

The trouble is, when Meyer tangled with that record 7-pound, 1-ounce bullhead he wasn't fishing in Minnesota's famed bullhead water around Waterville. No sir. Meyer had ventured to the land of pines and sky-blue waters around Grand Rapids, which prides itself as a fishing paradise for about everything, 'cept bullheads. In other words, when Waterville claimed the bullhead capital not one tourist promoter in northern Minnesota argued. Particularly Claude Titus, the head honcho of tourism in Grand Rapids. Claude always sought the big spenders of the angling fraternity, the folks who fished for walleyes and smallmouth bass or trout and muskies.

Bullhead fishing tourists are said to wear white shirts and carry $2 bills and not change either in a week.

But Meyer threw a wrench in all that when he caught that record bullhead smack-dad amidst the pines on Shallow Lake near Grand Rapids. Meyer said he was going to have his whiskered trophy mounted for display.

Titus, it's rumored, was willing to bury it.

Now tell me, who wouldn't like to see his or her name on the state record list. Not that you'd become rich or famous. But at least there'd be no need to brag anymore. Just tell 'em to "look it up in the records."

MINNESOTA'S LARGEST FISH TAKEN BY ANGLING

(Fish illustrated are most commonly known)

Species	Weight	Date	Where Caught	Angler
Illustrated Above				
1. Sturgeon (Lake)	236-0	1911	Lake of the Woods	Unknown
2. Mud Catfish	70-0	1970	St. Croix River	John Roberts
3. Channel Catfish	38-0	1975	Mississippi River	Terrence Fussy
4. Largemouth Bass	10-2	1961	Prairie Lake	Harold Lehn
5. Smallmouth Bass	8-0	1948	West Battle Lake	John Creighton
6. Black Crappie	5-0	1940	Vermillion River	Tom Christenson
7. Bluegill	2-13	1948	Lake Alice	Bob Parker
8. Perch	3-4	1945	Lake Plantaganette	Merle Johnson
9. Sauger	6-2½	1964	Mississippi River	Mrs. Wyles Larson
10. Brook Trout	9-0	1958	Ash River	Frank Hause
11. Rainbow Trout	17-6	1974	Knife River	Ottway (Red) Stuberud
12. Brown Trout	16-8	1961	Grindstone Lake	N. Lovgren
13. Walleye	16-11	1956	Lake of the Woods	Merrill Pullian
14. Lake Trout	43-8	1955	Lake Superior	G.H. Nelson
15. Northern Pike	45-12	1929	Basswood Lake	J.V. Schanken
16. Muskellunge	54-0	1957	Winnibigoshish	Art Lyons

Other Minnesota Record Fish Taken by Angling

Species	Weight	Where Caught	Date	Angler
17. Brown Bullhead**	7-1	Shallow Lake	1974	William Meyer
18. Burbot	14-4	Lake Vermillion	1976	Leo Krzychi
19. Ohrid Trout	6-6	Tofte Lake	1973	Jim Crigler
20. Splake	9-6	Pierz (Beaver) Lake	1971	Gerald Quade
21. Kokanee Salmon	2-15	Caribou Lake	1971	Lars Kindem
22. Chinook Salmon	20-0	Lake Superior	1977	Al Seckeuger, Jr.
23. Coho Salmon	10-6½	Lake Superior	1970	Louis Rhode
24. Dogfish	10-0	Lake Minnetonka	1941	R. Lehman
25. Sheepshead	30-0	Mississippi River	1960	D. Campbell
26. Mooneye	2-0	Mississippi River	1963	Unknown
27. Goldeye	1-8	St. Croix River	1948	Frank Bradac
28. White Sucker**	8-9	Mississippi River	1971	Leonard Krueger
29. Green Sunfish	14 oz.	Lake Charlotte	1974	Scott Hillman
30. Rock Bass	1-8	Mille Lacs	1973	P. Schultz
31. Tullibee	4-3	Big Sandy Lake	1974	Robert Graff
32. Carp*	55-5	Clearwater	1952	Frank Ledwein

* Minnesota's carp is the official world record for angling.
** Minnesota's white sucker and brown bullhead appear to be world records, but have not been officially recorded or accepted.

How To Catch A State Record

Please read carefully. This is important. You will note that there's no promise here to help you break a Minnesota record fish. But what's wrong with setting a new record?

Strangely, the Minnesota fish record record-keepers have missing records or none at all for a number of fish species caught by angling. Not all of them are as glamorous as a trout or muskie. But what's wrong with having your name behind the Minnesota State Record ... ahh ... Redhorse sucker?

Or what about the longnose gar? Or the shortnose gar? A decent fish anybody should be proud to claim. Right now, there isn't one. Or how about the white crappie, or the yellow or black bullhead?

None of these fish are represented on the list of angling records for Minnesota. There may be other fish species I've overlooked. Each fish must, however, be caught on hook and line, legally.

To report a possible record fish, contact a state conservation officer or an area fisheries manager. Have the weight recorded on a state-inspected scale with at least two witnesses. And have it weighed as soon as possible. A new walleye record was disqualified not long ago because the fish had been frozen before it was weighed, although it still weighed more than the current record. Nevertheless, a frozen fish could have been imported from outside of Minnesota. So the fish had to be disqualified.

If you insist on breaking an existing record, here's a tip. That 1-pound, 8-ounce rock bass is an insult. Who hasn't caught and tossed back larger "rockies" than that. The record's vulnerable, folks.

Have at it.

How To Starve Mosquitoes and Bugs

The bug experts say that each of us have a peculiar odor, which breaks down into two categories: the smell that mosquitoes love; the smell that mosquitoes can't stand.

So — if you smell bad you won't have to worry about losing blood to mosquitoes. But for you sweet-smellers, mosquitoes are capable of making you wish you stunk.

Fortunately, there are excellent insect repellents available in Minnesota for those people who think we have mosquitoes.

Occasionally, the natives will talk about black flies or no-see-ums. Some people believe these two blood-sucking bugs exist in Minnesota.

If you see them, use the same mosquito repellent and your blood count will rise.

If you don't see um, but you still feel like somebody is jabbing needles into your hide, then you're being attacked by no-see-ums. You can't see no-see-ums so just take my word for it. And spray more repellent.

Black flies look like miniature house flies. I've had them so thick around my head I thought I was dead and the flies were after my carcass.

Again spray yourself. The black flies then will keep a respectable distance away from you. About an inch.

How Fast They Grow

If Minnesota switched climates with Florida, the list of state record fish would be shattered. Our fish would become giants; muskies would be capable of smashing small boats. Fishing might even become a dangerous pastime. Kids couldn't swim in northern pike waters.

It's probably a good thing that Minnesota has long winters with cold water. Our fish can get big but they do it slower.

The growth rate of fishes is determined by a number of factors: water fertility, food supply, competition, species differences and individual differences. All rainbow trout may look alike but each is an individual.

But the overpowering control on growth rate of Minnesota's fishes is the cold water. Fish that live in warmer climates in warmer water grow the year around. In Minnesota that warm water is only available for a few months in every year. When the water cools, the fish's metabolism is greatly reduced. It eats less and grows less.

Minnesota still produces trophy fish, of course. That's because there's always a few fish that are smarter than most fishermen. They live long enough to become lunkers.

The age of most scaled fishes is determined by counting the annular rings on the scales, much like counting the growth rings on a tree to determine its age. In fish without scales, the age can be determined by counting the rings present in a cross-section of the backbone.

Minnesota fisheries biologist often collect scale samples from fish caught by anglers to monitor the growth rates of fishes from various lakes. If the rates aren't normal, for instance, biologists may be alerted to problems within the lake.

Rough estimates of a fish's age may be determined by measuring the length, however. The following chart, compiled by Minnesota's Department of Natural Resources, can be used as a guide. (See next page.)

You may be surprised at how many years are required to produce a lunker. No wonder it takes some luck to catch one.

Average total length in inches
of Minnesota fishes at the end of each year.

YEAR	1	2	3	4	5	6	7	8	9	10
Black crappie. .	2.4	4.8	6.8	8.3	9.5	10.5	11.6	12.3	12.8	13.5
Bluegill	1.9	3.4	4.9	6.1	7.1	7.8	8.3	8.6	9.1	9.6
Carp	6.8	15.6	17.8	21.6	25.8	28.9	29.4	31.4	—	—
Lake trout . . .	5.4	9.0	12.4	15.6	18.4	20.4	23.1	25.5	27.9	28.3
Largemouth bass	3.5	6.7	9.3	11.5	13.1	15.1	16.3	17.6	18.1	—
Muskellunge. .	6.9	12.5	17.1	21.5	25.8	29.0	33.4	39.1	41.8	43.5
Northern Pike .	7.8	13.2	17.7	21.1	24.2	26.8	29.0	31.1	33.3	35.1
Pumpkinseed .	1.7	3.1	4.4	5.5	6.4	7.2	7.7	8.1	8.5	—
Rainbow trout .	4.9	9.1	12.8	16.1	20.5	—	—	—	—	—
Rock bass . . .	1.6	3.0	4.5	5.9	7.1	8.3	9.1	9.6	10.1	10.5
Sauger	4.3	7.9	10.4	11.8	13.0	14.2	14.3	—	—	—
Smallmouth bass	3.9	7.3	10.0	12.2	18.2	20.5	—	—	—	—
Sucker	3.7	7.1	10.2	13.1	14.9	16.7	18.1	19.5	—	—
Tullibee.	3.9	6.8	9.3	11.3	13.0	14.3	15.4	16.3	17.1	18.1
Yellow perch .	2.6	4.5	6.0	7.3	8.4	9.3	10.0	10.8	11.3	—
Walleye	5.1	9.0	12.3	15.1	17.3	19.2	20.9	22.1	23.4	24.6
White bass . . .	3.7	6.6	9.2	11.0	12.3	—	—	—	—	—

Planning a Minnesota Fishing Trip

Fishing in Minnesota never ends.

No matter what time of year, there is always some kind of fishing sport available. Some times are better than others, of course.

I've done my share of fishing in other states. I know how the fishing always seem greener across the state lines ... until you get there. Then some wise ol' angler will tell you that you picked the wrong time. Like you should have been there last month or next month ... any time but now.

Visitors to Minnesota make the same mistakes. They show up in May for muskies or come in August and expect to slay walleyes. It doesn't work out that way very often.

First, decide what you really want to fish for and try to arrive in Minnesota when the fishing is best for the fish of your choice.

Here's a rough guide to go by:

Walleyes — Season opens mid-May. Opening week some-times can be sketchy. Fishing usually improves and holds steady from last days in May to first days in July. June is best month. Good catches are made in July but the action definitely starts to taper quickly as August nears. August walleye fishing is comparable to watching trees grow. Fishing picks up in mid-September and improves into October but bring long underwear. Best walleye ice fishing starts in mid-December and runs into mid-January. The latter days of January and early February are usually slow. The walleye season on inland lakes closes in mid-February. The border waters of Minnesota-Canada, such as Lake of the Woods, remain open for walleye fishing and the action usually is good until the season ends in mid-April. Walleye fishing on the Mississippi River is best in April and early May below the dams.

Northern Pike — Northern fishing tends to be sporadic from opening day (mid-May) until the warmer days of July. Top fishing is in August and September in all waters.

Largemouth Bass — The season opens usually in late May with often sketchy, often excellent results. Bass action improves in mid-June and continues through the summer into September, excluding daily ups and downs and occasional cold fronts. October can be excellent, depending on timing of Old Man Winter.

Smallmouth Bass — Action picks up in late May in the northern waters and continues often into early July. August tends to be slow but improves again in September. Rivers are good most any time, if water levels are near normal or low.

Panfish — (Bluegills, crappies, perch) Bluegills best starting in late June but August is the top for platter-sized 'gills. Fastest crappie action follows the departure of ice in April and continues into May or early June. Perch bite 365 days a year.

Muskellunge — Best times are August and September, spilling into October. July can be fair. Muskies taken in May and June normally run small ... to be released not mounted or eaten.

Trout — In stocked streams, trout are not planted until threat of spring floods is over. Usually May. Lake trout in inland lakes best when season opens in mid-May. Lake Superior trout and salmon good in July through September. Steelhead fishing on North Shore streams best from mid-April to mid-May.

Of course, don't forget to buy a fishing license. Nonresident fees are: season, $10; 3-day individual, $5; and season combination (husband and wife), $15. Licenses are sold at county auditor offices, bait shops, sporting goods stores, hardware stores and some resorts.

Minnesota's nights — even in mid-summer — can be cool. Bring a light to medium jacket and, of course, raingear. May or September fishing may require heavier clothing.

Bring your own fishing tackle. But don't worry about running low. Minnesota is a fishing state and tackle shops are never far away. Most bait stores also handle tackle in addition to such natural baits as: minnows, nightcrawlers leeches, earthworms. Some shops also carry crayfish, salamanders and frogs.

Most resorts have boats to rent or a boat is included in the rental price of a cabin. Most also rent outboard motors and provide Coast Guard approved life jackets. Many resorts and bait shops also will provide fishing guides for hire (see section: Hiring a Guide).

Minnesota is served by about a dozen regional and national commercial airlines. They are: Northwest Orient, North Central, Ozark, Air New Ulm, Mesaba, United, Air Wisconsin, Braniff, Western, Allegheny, Midstate and Eastern.

North Central Airlines, based in Minneapolis, offers special packages to northbound fishermen. Ask a travel agent.

Choosing a place to stay during your fishing visit can be confusing. Preferably, choose the lake first, one that harbors whatever species of fish you're seeking. Use the list of lakes in this book as a guide.

After you've picked the lake, select the accommodations that fit your needs on or nearby the waters you intend to fish. For resort information, contact the tourism region of your choice by writing to the following addresses:

Minnesota Tourism Regions

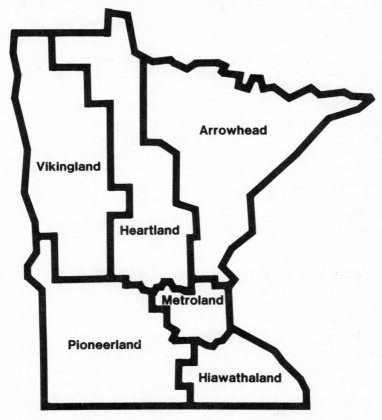

Minnesota
Arrowhead
Association
Hotel Duluth
Duluth, MN 55802
(218) 722-0874

Heartland, Inc.
P.O. Box 443
411 Laurel Street
Brainerd, MN 56401
(218) 829-1615

Hiawathaland
212 - 1st Ave. S.W.
Rochester, MN 55901
(507) 288-8970

Metroland
c/o Northern Dakota
County Chamber of
Commerce
Suite 101, 33 W. Wentworth
West St. Paul, MN 55118
(612) 222-5889

Pioneerland
Box 999
Mankato, MN 56001
(507) 345-4517

Viking-Land, USA
Box 545
Battle Lake, MN 56515
(218) 864-8181

If you plan to combine a fishing-camping trip in Minnesota, information on public campgrounds is available from the Department of Natural Resources, Parks and Recreation Division, 320 Centennial Building, St. Paul, Minnesota 55155. Or a listing of privately-owned campgrounds open to the public is available from the Minnesota Association of Campground Operators, Box 344G, Elk River, Minnesota 55330.

For additional tourist information, relating to scenic and historic sites, calendar of events, tours and so forth, write: Minnesota Tourist Information Center, 480 Cedar Street, St. Paul, Minnesota 55101.

Fishing information about specific lakes can be obtained by writing the Department of Natural Resources, Section of Fisheries, 320 Centennial Building, St. Paul, Minnesota 55155. Or a listing of privately-owned camp- located in Bemidji, Grand Rapids, Rochester, Brainerd, New Ulm and St. Paul.

But what you catch in Minnesota is up to you.

Where Fishermen Gather

The fellowship of the angling fraternity is no more evident than in Minnesota.

A number of organizations — fishermen all — have been formed to promote, protect and enhance the future of a particular fish. These anglers believe that fishing means more today than just buying a license. It means if there's going to be fishing tomorrow, fishermen must gather to fight pollution, fish habitat destruction and other threats. And they must contribute more time and money in boosting the fish and the sport so cherished.

And all of the organizations will welcome new members.

For more information, contact the clubs listed:

Minnesota's Muskies, Incorporated
1708 University Avenue
St. Paul, Minnesota 55104

Dedicated to promoting the sport of muskie fishing with emphasis on conservation and research. Operates its own muskie hatchery. More than 2,000 members. Chapters also in Wisconsin, Missouri, Illinois, North Dakota.

Lake Superior Steelhead Association
Box 6034
Duluth, Minnesota 55806

Dedicated to promoting the sport of steelhead (rainbow trout) fishing in Lake Superior and North Shore streams. Sponsors big trout and salmon fishing derby annually. Conducts fund-raising projects to finance development of trout spawning waters in North Shore streams; volunteers labor for stream litter clean-up campaigns.

Minnesota Bass Federation
1215 Lincoln Terrace
Minneapolis, Minnesota 55421

Dedicated to promoting the sport of bass fishing in Minnesota. Federation is composed of 19 bass fishing chapters scattered throughout the state, affiliated with the national *Bass Anglers Sportsman's Society* (BASS). Sponsors local and state bass fishing tournaments. Contributes funds for bass research in Minnesota.

In'Fisherman Fraternity of Twin Cities
Box 20316
Bloomington, Minnesota 55420

Dedicated to improving the angling art for all species. Represents fishermen in legislative issues. Affiliated with the national *In'Fisherman Society,* founded by Minnesotan Al Lindner.

out of the frying pan...

Out of the Frying Pan

Minnesota's contributions to the welfare of the country include iron ore, the Father of Waters and beer batter.

Iron rusts, the Mississippi floods but fish filets coated in beer batter have survived the tastes of time. Call it an intoxicating combination of the brewer's art from the land of sky blue waters and the fish that swim in it.

On football Sundays, the nation is intrigued with Minnesota's penchant for socializing under adverse climates, known as tailgating, wherein appropriate refreshments are concocted.

My friends, tailgating did not start in the stadium parking lots.

It was invented on the banks of Minnesota's lakes and rivers in the form of shore lunches. Rain or snow are mere inconveniences. The heat is supplied by driftwood; boulders and logs are tables and chairs.

And the frying pan contains the perfect definition of fresh fish, filets that were swimming while the butter was melting.

Lest you wonder how Minnesota happened to discover the finer things in life, meet Tom Collins.

Collins did not invent beer batter or shore lunches but he has sustained the art and added his own touch. Which is worth noting. Collins owns a restaurant on the main street of Walker. The cafe front has the trappings of a thousand other small town lunch counters that serve cheeseburgers and fries.

Collins offers elephant trunk or loin of lion. His skill in preparing wild fishes and fowl has attracted diners with delicate tastebuds throughout the North Country.

He has consented to share his own basic recipes, such as beer batter and breading. In addition, you'll find Collins' flare for cuisine ... even with bluegills.

Collins' Beer Batter

Ingredients

2 eggs, whole beaten
12 oz. beer
12 oz. flour
¼ tsp. salt
¼ tsp. pepper
¼ tsp. nutmeg
½ tsp. baking powder
Fish filets
Cornstarch (for dredging)

Here's How

1. Combine eggs and beer.

2. Add dry ingredients all at once. Mix smooth, adjust consistency as required. Moisture content of flour may vary. If the batter is heavy, adjust with a small amount of milk. If batter is too thin, adjust with cornstarch. Do not overmix.

3. **Frying Procedure**
   Dredge fish lightly in cornstarch. Shake off excess, dip fish in batter and immerse directly into deep fat. Fry at about 375°. Serve immediately with appropriate sauce.

Collins' Fish Breading

Ingredients

Commercial seasoned breading mix (available at supermarket)
Fish filets
2 raw eggs
2 oz. fresh milk
Salt and pepper
4 oz. melted butter
½ lemon
Cooking oil

Here's How

Whip the eggs lightly in a flat pan. Add 2 oz. milk and mix gently. Season the filet with salt and pepper, dip in egg wash, then bread very lightly. Be sure that your cooking oil (enough to completely cover the filets) is hot (375°). Fry the filet until golden brown. Do not overcook.

Brush with melted butter. Garnish with lemon wedge.

Baked Northern

Dress fish to be baked.
Clean and scale.
Remove head and fins (a "V"-shaped notch cut at each side of fins will remove bones.)
Rinse thoroughly in cold water, stuff fish cavity with stuffing of your choice and place cavity side down in a well-greased pan. Pour sauce over fish, cover with foil tent and bake until fork may be easily inserted in flesh (about 15-20 min. per lb. at 350°).

Basic Stuffing

Ingredients

12 oz. bread crumbs or commercial breading mixture
¼ cup celery, chopped
½ cup onions, chopped
2 oz. butter
⅛ tsp. poultry seasoning
¼ tsp. salt
¼ tsp. sage
1 tsp. parsley, chopped

Here's How

1. Trim bread, removing crust, cube. Soak in cold water. Drain. If commercial mix, follow directions.

2. Braise celery and onions in butter until lightly browned.

3. Combine celery and onions, seasonings and bread and toss to blend.

4. Stuff mixture lightly into cavity of fish to be baked.

This is a basic stuffing; you may add any variation of your own design.

Two sauces which may be used with Northerns for baking:

Tomato Sauce

Ingredients

⅛ tsp. garlic, chopped very fine
⅛ cup onions, chopped fine
⅛ cup celery, chopped fine
2 oz. melted butter
16 oz. canned tomato sauce
⅛ tsp. thyme, ground
¼ tsp. basil (sweet)
Dash powdered clove
Salt to taste
Pepper to taste
Cayenne to taste

Here's How

1. Braise in butter until golden brown the garlic, onions and celery.

2. Add tomato sauce and seasonings.

3. Simmer for 15 min.

4. Pour over fish to be baked.

Baste several times with sauce while baking.

Creole Sauce

Ingredients

1½ oz. salad oil
¼ cup onions, coarse diced
⅛ tsp. garlic, fresh crushed
¼ cup celery, cross cut ⅛" strips
12 oz. canned tomato, crushed
4 oz. tomato puree
Dash of thyme
1 bay leaf
Dash black pepper
Salt to taste
½ cup green peppers, medium diced
Cayenne to taste

Here's How

1. Heat oil in sauce pan. Add: onions, celery and garlic. Saute until golden brown.

2. Add: tomato puree and seasoning. Simmer at very low heat for 30 min.

3. Blanch green peppers in salted boiling water for 6 min. Drain.

4. When sauce is cooked remove bay leaf and add green pepper

5. Check seasoning for taste.

Baste several times with sauce while baking.

The Shore Dinner

For any freshly-caught fish, but particularly the panfish, trout, walleye and northern pike.

Panfish and smaller trout lend themselves readily to frying in the round or whole and are simply and tastefully prepared:

1. Remove entrails, head and fins, wash thoroughly.

2. Salt and pepper to taste.

3. Dredge with flour or cornmeal.

4. Pan fry in butter or corn oil.

Or

1. Filet fish to be cooked as described.

2. Prepare an egg wash — 2 eggs, 1 oz. milk, beat lightly to mix.

3. Season filet with salt and pepper to taste.

4. Dip filet in egg wash.

5. Apply a coating of cracker crumbs or any good commercial breading.

6. Fry in hot, deep cooking oil or butter until flesh is white and flaky.

Caution: Open fire is tricky: do not burn your fish, but do not overcook!

The Gourmet Touch
(Simplified Recipe for Broiling)

Amandine Sauce

1. 3 oz. butter
2. 1 tsp. of sliced almonds
3. 1 tsp. fresh lemon juice
4. Dash of Cayenne pepper

Dust filet with paprika — Broil

Here's How

Melt butter in sauce pan, add lemon, Cayenne and almonds.
Saute at medium heat until almonds are golden brown.
Spoon sauce hot over broiled or fried filet.

Sauce Grenobloise — Add capers while browning butter and almonds.

Maitre D'Hotel Butter — Melted butter and fresh lemon juice (lemon butter).

(Photo courtesy of Dan Gapen)

The classic shorelunch: freshly caught fish swimming in the frying pan.

Brook Trout, Meuniere

Ingredients

1 per person trout or any other pan fish
6 oz. milk
½ lb. flour
4 oz. butter
1 tsp. fresh parsley, chopped
1 tsp. fresh lemon juice

Here's How

1. Dress and wash trout. Dip in milk to which salt and coarse pepper have been added, then dip in flour.

2. Saute in butter until browned on both sides.

3. If fish are small, they may be completely cooked in this manner. If larger, place in well-greased pan and complete cooking in a moderate 325° oven until they are done.

4. Heat 4 oz. of butter in a hot sauce pan until it is browned.

5. Sprinkle fish with chopped parsley.

6. Mix lemon juice with browned butter, pour over fish.

The Business End of Fishing

Not all of Minnesota's fishing comes naturally.

The attraction of fishing in Minnesota is the backbone of the state's multi-million tourism industry. Aside from the waters and fishes, there are hundreds of resorts that cater to the needs of resident and visiting anglers.

Together we spend about $260 million annually in pursuit of the fishing sport in Minnesota. Nonresidents, alone, leave an estimated $78 million behind in return for the fish and memories they take home.

To maintain fishing, Minnesota spends only about $5 million annually via the Fisheries Section within the Department of Natural Resources.

There are about 200 full-time employees in the section, composed of fish research biologists, hatchery managers, lake survey specialists, regional fisheries supervisors, area managers, limnologists and so forth.

The Fisheries Section is responsible for the health of the fish resource, such as stocking, rough fish control, lake rehabilitation and habitat preservation.

Minnesota's state-owned hatcheries raise and stock more than 250 million fish a year. Most are walleyes, followed by northern pike, rainbow trout, lake trout, brown trout, brook trout, largemouth bass, bluegill, small-

(Photo courtesy of Minnesota Department of Natural Resources)

To help maintain fish populations, Minnesota stocks millions of fish every year.

mouth bass, muskie, crappie, catfish and a number of other lesser species.

Minnesota has 13 hatcheries that raise walleyes and muskies; five trout hatcheries, 18 walleye spawning stations (where eggs are collected); 7 muskie spawning stations, 190 walleye rearing ponds, 146 northern pike spawning areas and 15 muskie rearing ponds. There's one federal fish hatchery in the state at New London.

Every year more than six million pounds of rough fish, mostly carp, are removed from the state's fishing waters in an effort to control the populations of these pest fish.

Commercial fishing is permitted on Lake of the Woods, Namakan Lake, Lake Superior and parts of the St. Croix and Mississippi Rivers. The commercial catches are worth close to $500,000 annually. The net fishing is supervised to prevent damage to sport fishing, however.

The next time you catch a fish in Minnesota you might think about the dollars and manpower that went into that fish, regardless of size.

Considering the price of a fishing license, you got your money's worth.

(Photo courtesy of Minnesota Department of Natural Resources)

Minnesota is fishing water, fishing boats and an angler's sunrise.

What's Your Secret?

As they say, all fishermen are liars except you and me. You can't always believe what you see and little of what you hear about fishing. I trust you'll find this book an exception. It was written in the spirit of angling brotherhood to help others enjoy the Greatest Sport in the World.

How about you?

Consider this an invitation to help in the next edition of my Minnesota Fishing Guide. Send in your tips, suggestions and ... criticisms. We'll use your advice and give you credit if we don't think you're fibbin'. Or if you can think of ways to make this fishing guide more helpful, we'd like to know. Helping each other catch fish is almost as much fun as the actual catching.

So — send your tips and suggestions to:

Minnesota Fishing Guide
Waldman House Press
519 North Third Street
Minneapolis, Minnesota 55401

minnesota's filet mignon
walleyes

Part II Whatchacatchin

Walleyes/
Minnesota's Filet Mignon

If heaven were a walleye lake, most Minnesotans would die to get there.

Panfish may attract more anglers if you're counting numbers. But no fish is more intensively sought or more highly prized than a Minnesota walleye.

Its reputation as an Epicurean delight is unmatched among the freshwater fishes. Browned in butter or coated with beer batter, the white, firm, walleye filet has an exquisite taste of its own, not fishy, not mushy, not tough. It's absolutely . . . well, wait a minute.

The best tasting walleyes are the ones you've caught. Pardon the pun, but that's the catch. Wishing for walleyes is not enough. The walleye may be the "Royalty" of Minnesota's fishes; it may the official state fish; it may be abundant and highly desired. But nobody said they're always easy to catch.

Not even in Minnesota. But you've come to the right place. No matter where you roam in the state, you're not far from a walleye lake. Or at least a lake with walleyes in it. Minnesota leads the nation in hatching and stocking walleyes. But more than that, some of the state's largest lakes, such as Mille Lacs, Leech, Winnibigoshish, Lake of the Woods, Red Lake, are among the best natural walleye lakes in the world. These big waters rarely require stocking because the lakes have an abundance of natural spawning grounds with gravel sholes and rocky reefs. Nature, itself, supplies the walleye fishing on these and other lakes. Some state lakes will support walleyes but are incapable of maintaining their numbers naturally. These lakes then are stocked regularly or as needed.

Who, then, is this handsome fish with its golden sides, cream-white belly and glassy, pale blue eyes? The walleye is a member of the perch family, closely related to both the perch and the similar-looking sauger.

In fact, many anglers confuse the walleye and sauger, since both fishes often occupy the same waters, the same habitat and may be caught in the same ways. I might add the walleye and sauger are equally delicious. However, they are not the same fish. The walleye has a white marking on the lower tip of its tail; the sauger does not. Saugers usually have splotchy dark markings on their sides, which are much more defined than on a walleye. The spiny dorsal fin on the sauger's back also is quite speckled whereas the walleye's dorsal fin is rather opaque with a single black spot at the rear base of the fin.

In Minnesota, the walleye often is referred to as the "walleye-pike" or just "pike." Both names are technically incorrect, but . . . well, that's the way it is. In Canada, the walleye is known as the "pickerel." Of course that's a foreign country.

To impress your friends with trivia, the next time you discuss the walleye's sex life, advise them that the female walleye grows larger and faster than the male and lives longer, too. Males seldom reach sizes heavier than 3 to 5 pounds. If you're lucky enough to bag a trophy walleye, it is a "she," not a "he."

Walleyes also are meat-eaters, aquatic predators who prefer to attack prey that is alive or alive-acting. Their most common natural food consists of small, young-of-the-year perch. Or when eating-size perch aren't abundant, food studies have shown that walleyes will switch to larvae of aquatic insects, such as the mayfly.

Fortunately, walleyes also will inhale other things. Things with hooks. I've never met a walleye fisherman who was successful at using small perch to catch walleyes,

In Minnesota, happiness is a stringer of walleyes.

even though it's known that walleyes love perch meat. I'd guess the reason is competition. When walleyes really put the feedbag on for perch, there are so many perch available your odds are slim that your perch will be eaten. (By the way, it is legal to use perch or small bluegills for bait as long as they are caught by hook and line. It is illegal to seine gamefish, such as perch or bluegills, to use for bait.)

Of course, before you can feed some hooked morsel to a walleye, you've got to find them. That's the interesting part of the walleye fishing game.

Despite all of its attributes, the walleye never will be remembered as any great fighting fish. It does not leap like a smallmouth, attack like a muskie or roll like a northern pike.

Yet, the walleye is no slouch either. I've lost my share of walleyes "right at the boat" when the fish flopped, plunged or otherwise shook the hook. A hefty walleye when hooked will not tear madly about like a rainbow. Rather, it chooses to resist, making short but powerful runs back toward the depths and flopping its head back and forth. So, don't get the wrong idea. Walleyes may not win any fighting awards but neither do they surrender like a water-soaked log.

Nor is the appeal of walleye fishing strictly a meat-gathering tradition, although that certainly is a factor. While the sport of fishing, itself, is a form of hunting, the hunt for walleyes is a unique game all of its own.

Finding Walleyes

Too many fisherman with high hopes for walleyes always try to fight the system. They're the anglers who like bad odds. They think finding needles in haystacks is a beatable challenge. They also seldom win.

So what's the point? If you want to catch walleyes, go to a walleye lake. Not a lake with walleyes in it. No. Choose a lake with a reputation as a walleye producer. Granted, you've got a wide choice in Minnesota. But there's also a bunch of lakes that are not known walleye hotspots. Yet, invariably some poor soul will be out there trying to beat the odds, fishing walleyes in a danged good bass lake.

The good fishermen I know all have one skill in common: they know how to choose the best waters for the fish they're after. What's more, the state's better walleye bets are no secret. Certain lakes may go hot and cold as the seasons pass but generally the names and places remain the same. How do you find the better walleye lakes? Ask around. Ask local fishermen, ask the bait shop owner, ask state fisheries officials or resort operators. Or browse through the suggested walleye lakes in this book.

Starting out on a known walleye lake or river is at least half of the battle.

The other half is . . . well, a little more difficult. It's called fishing.

So where do you start fishing now that you've found the lake?

That depends on the time of year. Walleyes spawn in shallow water during April and early May in Minnesota. After spawning and as the weeks pass on into summer, the general rule is the walleyes gradually drop into deeper and deeper water.

There are exceptions, of course.

Under the cover of darkness, walleyes may move back into shallow water, say 6-feet or less, even in late summer. In many lakes, walleyes will actually spend their time in sunken weedbeds that are no deeper than 10 feet. Walleyes in weeds are often difficult to catch, since it is almost impossible to drop your bait without hooking weeds.

If you insist on fishing during the day, and saving your nocturnal hours for more normal pursuits, do not dismay. Walleyes can be caught under the luxury of sunlight. If you're in the right spot.

Walleyes tend to be clean bottom fish. That is, they prefer sand, rock or gravel sites or at least hard bottom. Again, there are exceptions. But don't worry about them. The so-called "mud flats" of Mille Lacs are famed walleye hang-outs in mid-summer. But the flats are actually humps and they are quite hard. At times during the summer, the Mille Lacs walleyes will go off the humps into truly pure, unadulterated soft mucky bottom. But their forays over mud are the exception not the rule.

Just as the sun always rises in the east, Minnesota's walleye season always opens on the Saturday nearest May 15. Let's open the season and follow it through until winter once again caps the state's waters in ice.

The first two or three weeks of walleye fishing are a shoreline affair. Having completed spawning in the shallows, the walleyes tend to hang around the rock, sand or gravelly shores in water seldom deeper than 15-feet. Usually less.

Sometimes the walleye concentrations found at this time of year are spectacular, particularly where rivers or creeks enter a lake. Still, some walleye fishermen are disgruntled. Most of the walleyes will run to the smaller side, lots of 1-pounders, some two's and a few threes. The real lunkers, 6-pounders or better, are rare. That's because most of the walleye concentration is made of up small male fish. Meanwhile, the larger females already have begun to disperse to their summer haunts. Hence, they are not where most of the fishermen are. But the lunkers are scattered and difficult to find.

But as the days roll by in June, the walleye becomes more predictable. And, if you're a lunker hunter, more promising. It is then the walleye can be found rather consistently in its usual hangouts — deep shoreline points, sunken islands, sandbars, rockbars. The fish producing depths range from about 15 to 30 feet. Not that all of the fish have moved. The shoreline, particularly with sharp drop-offs will continue to be productive.

At that time of year — about mid-June — a practical depth to start fishing is about 20 feet. If that fails, move up or down in increments of 5-foot depths in trial and error fashion. Sooner or later, if you're fishing typical walleye hangouts, you should make contact.

Today those hangouts are popularly called "structure." Your grandaddy called them "hotspots." Structure is an irregularity in a lake or river bottom, such as a sunken island, a sandbar and so forth. A boulder or hole in a river would be structure. Fish usually hang around such structure. More specifically, fish tend to congregate near the "breaks" on the structure. A break is a sudden change of depth. (See Illustration) For example, suppose a sandbar gradually deepens to 10 feet, then sharply drops down to 15 feet and then drops off again at 20 feet. There would then be two breaks on the sandbar, so to speak. One at 10 feet and another at 15 feet. A walleye fisherman in early June would undoubtedly start fishing at the point where the sandbar in 15-feet of water drops off to 20 or more feet. In May, you'd probably try the 10-foot "break" first.

EDGE OF SUNKEN ISLAND

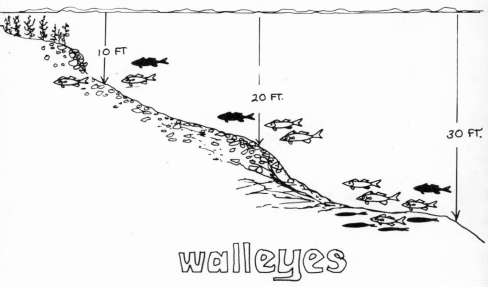

Starting in mid- to late June, most of the walleyes have gathered in their summer haunts where they'll stay through much of the fishing season.

But some of the walleye haunts are better than others. Sunken islands or humps in a lake are renowned walleye magnets. But as summer progresses into July, some of these hotspots turn cold. The only way to discover that fact is to fish those spots. Then, you'll probably conclude that sunken islands or humps no longer hold walleyes or "they just weren't biting."

For reasons known mostly by the walleye, you'll find there's a difference in sunken islands, particularly their cover and depth. In mid-summer, walleyes tend to frequent the underwater humps with weedy tops, those that peak less than 20 feet under the surface. Those weed-free humps or islands, which are devoid of weed or rock cover often are abandoned by walleyes. Or nearly so.

And then comes August.

August is a fine vacation month in Minnesota, unless you're expecting to taste some of that famous walleye fishing you've heard about. Time and again, Joe Blow, the visiting fisherman, brings his family to Minnesota in August, thinking he'll slip out and nab a few walleyes, too. And time and again, he's usually disappointed.

Oh, there are walleyes to be caught, for sure. And they're still hanging around the typical walleye places. And they're active, probably gorging themselves every day.

But in August, the lakes are choked with the bite-sized tidbits that walleyes love. Young-of-the-year perch, primarily. Plus there are jillions of other minnow species swimming around just waiting to be inhaled. In other words, the August walleye fisherman has got some tough competition. In other cases, the walleyes may have dropped to deeper structure within a lake. Maybe 40 to 50-feet or more. Finding them then becomes more time consuming and difficult.

The walleye fishing hum-drums usually continues into September. By then, most of the visiting anglers have returned home. Minnesotans, themselves, turn to the hunting seasons or the Super Bowl quest by the Vikings football team.

The walleye addicts keep at it, however. And they often find almost "opening day" fishing action once the nights turn cool and fall takes over. The walleyes become a shoreline fish again, hanging along the deep drops and making forays into the shallows. Often the fishing conditions are miserable by summer's standards. Anglers wear snowmobile suits, not T-shirts; felt-pac boots, not tennis shoes.

But catching 8 to 10-pound walleyes has a way of keeping you warm. A few years ago, Al Lindner, Lee Rudsenske and several other top-notch Minnesota walleye hunters found a bonanza of giant-sized walleyes under the gray November skies on Cass Lake. They fished with large minnows in 20 to 25 feet of water along sharp shoreline drop-offs. The action wasn't fast, but it was steady. More importantly, nearly every walleye taken was a "hawg." A "hawg" is a mighty big fish, my friends.

The lesson here is timing. If you really want to experience walleye fishing in Minnesota, come before August. Go to a reputable walleye lake. And pick your fishing spots based on the time of the year, remembering that the walleyes move into deeper water as the summer progresses. If you don't find them there, move back toward shore where there are drop-offs alongside weedbeds. On certain lakes (these are determined largely by trial and error), the resident walleyes spend a considerable amount of time along the outside or inside edges of the underwater weedbeds. Sometimes they'll be cruising within the aquatic jungle, itself. They are difficult to catch because it's difficult to present a clean, weed-free bait. But when it's the only game in town, you have no choice.

A few summers ago, I motored out to the "mud flats" of Mille Lacs in late July for perhaps one last fling at walleye fishing before the August slump. Other fishermen already had the same idea. There were boats by the dozens drifting or trolling on the edge or top of the flats, which generally peak between 20 and 25 feet and drop off to 35 to 40 feet.

After an hour or so I hadn't had a strike. And as far as I could see, no one else had either. Why fight the system, I thought. The northern pike ought to be active along the bulrush bays, which have patches of pond weed on the outside edges. So I motored back toward shore, switched tackle, and began casting a black and orange spinner bait amid the weed beds. The water was only about 10-feet deep.

I had caught a couple of small northerns, 3-4 pounders, when suddenly, my lure was stopped by a vicious strike. A good northern, I thought. The fight was good but much unlike a northern pike. Finally, the fish surfaced, flashing its golden sides in the summer sun. I couldn't believe it. A 6-pound walleye. On a lure. In the weeds. In shallow water.

So I guess you never know. Still, the majority of walleyes are caught in their traditional underwater haunts. So always start in those places first. Then begin to use your imagination. Like I said, walleye fishing consists of a lot of hunting.

Live Bait For Walleyes

When a fish hits an artificial lure — something made out of lead and feathers or molded in plastic or carved from wood — there's something special about the occasion. And fishermen of any age can feel it.

Walleyes are quite catchable on artificial lures, particularly in shallow water. But once the fish move deeper, the purist fisherman, the one who won't touch live bait, is apt to starve to death.

Let there be no doubt, live bait is the walleye fisherman's No. 1 weapon. Minnesota bait dealers annually sell thousands of minnows and millions of nightcrawlers and leeches. The minnows are raised from domestic ponds or gathered from the wild. The leeches are trapped from certain lakes and bogs. And most of the nightcrawlers, except those sold at roadside stands, are imported from the golf courses in Canada.

So that's the torrid trio — minnows, nightcrawlers and leeches. Some days one bait will outfish the other two. And sometimes you'll hear about some lunker nabbed by an angler who was using frogs, salamanders, crayfish or a gob of chicken liver.

But from a practical viewpoint, if you're going to be successful with walleyes, you must master the techniques to fish the torrid trio.

Using Minnows Once the only walleye bait in Minnesota, the minnow gradually is becoming the third choice,

Walleye fooled on a weighted hook or ice-fly.

after leeches and nightcrawlers. Still, you'll find minnows in every walleye angler's boat for the first few weeks of the season and again in late fall. In those periods, early and late season, the minnow is probably the most consistent producer.

Most Minnesota bait dealers carry at least three different minnow species and a number of different sizes. Fatheads, shiners and sucker minnows are the most common. Of the three, fatheads and shiners are the favorites. And of the two, fatheads are more practical, since shiners can be extremely difficult to keep alive. For that reason, fatheads probably catch more walleyes. But I think the shiner is more effective on big walleyes.

The typical walleye minnow is from 2 to 3½-inches long. Larger minnows sometimes work better for fall fishing but they're seldom used any other time.

As a bait, minnows are used in several different ways. Most commonly, the minnow is fished alone, that is just attached to a hook. Some anglers prefer to use a spinner and minnow combination, with the spinner rotating just ahead of the minnow. And a jig fisherman often will place a minnow on the jig hook to give his feathered lead-headed jig a touch of realism.

The proper way to hook a minnow depends on how it is being used:

For still-fishing with a bobber, lightly hook the minnow under the dorsal or back fin or through the lips.

For drifting and trolling, hook the minnow through the lips so that it follows naturally.

For jigs, hook the minnow through the lips or through both eyes so the minnow gives the appearance of being injured, swimming on its side. (See Illustration).

Using Nightcrawlers Called "garden hackle" by trout fishermen, the nightcrawler has become a walleye fooler supreme. Don't ask me why a walleye — miles from shore — would be interested in a nightcrawler. But I'll guarantee you that they are interested.

Chose plump, healthy nightcrawlers. Skinny, half-dead 'crawlers are less effective as are the regular earthworm, the smaller relative of the nightcrawler.

hooking live bait for walleyes
minnows

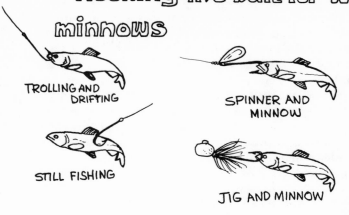

TROLLING AND DRIFTING

SPINNER AND MINNOW

STILL FISHING

JIG AND MINNOW

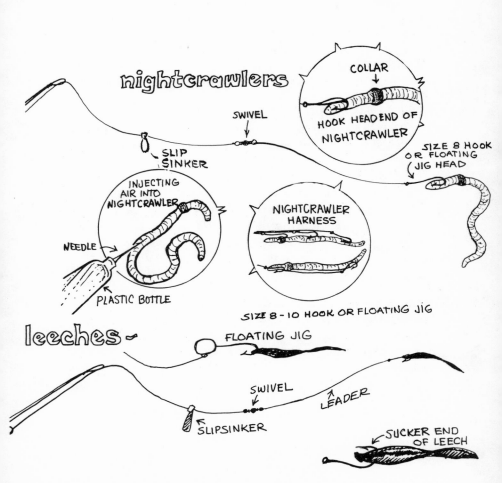

nightcrawlers

COLLAR

SWIVEL

HOOK HEAD END OF NIGHTCRAWLER

SLIP SINKER

SIZE 8 HOOK OR FLOATING JIG HEAD

INJECTING AIR INTO NIGHTCRAWLER

NIGHTCRAWLER HARNESS

NEEDLE

PLASTIC BOTTLE

SIZE 8-10 HOOK OR FLOATING JIG

leeches

FLOATING JIG

SWIVEL

LEADER

SLIPSINKER

SUCKER END OF LEECH

Nightcrawlers once were considered only a mid-summer walleye bait. But in recent years, fishermen have discovered that nightcrawlers will work from opening day until late in the season.

The nightcrawler may be fished in the same manner as the minnow, except still-fishing is probably less productive because the nightcrawler will not move much on its own. Slow trolling or drifting are the best nightcrawler fishing methods, although a "piece" of nightcrawler added to a lead-headed jig often works well.

Something else also has been discovered about nightcrawlers. They seem to be more effective on walleyes if the nightcrawler is "pumped" full of air first. Yeah, you heard me right. The air is injected with a hypodermic needle and plastic bottle. Slip the needle gently into the 'crawler and squeeze the bottle firmly. If done properly, the nightcrawler will puff up slightly, giving it extraordinary bouyancy. The air does not kill or appear to harm the 'crawler, but it does keep the bait floating higher off the bottom.

Yes, but aren't walleyes a bottom fish? Well, yes and no. Walleyes are known to suspend off the bottom at times. Sometimes as much as 10 feet. When suspended, the walleye will seldom move "down" to pick up your bait. That's why it's often important to keep the bait floating high. How do you know when? Simply by trial and error.

The suspending nature of walleyes recently caused the development of "floating jigs" or "floating rigs." A floating jig looks like a regular lead-headed jig, except the "head" is made of cork or some other floating material. The floating rig is similar except the cork slips onto the line and against the hook, thereby floating the bait off the bottom. You can regulate the floating height by changing the length of your leader between the swivel and hook.

No matter how you fish a nightcrawler, don't be afraid to switch to a new 'crawler when the old one seems to be "waterlogged." A change to fresh bait not only helps psychologically when the action's slow. It may, in fact, change your luck.

(Photo courtesy of Lindy-Little Joe Co.)

Outfitted for walleyes, Gary Roach scoops out a dandy 4-pounder. Note the "backtrolling flaps" on the boat's stern, which allows the boat to troll in reverse without taking water over the transom.

Using Leeches The name of the fisherman who discovered that leeches were a deadly walleye bait has been lost to the waves of time. But he must have been a gutsy sort, the kind that wouldn't faint while reading his own obituary. Because leeches are like squirmy chunks of slippery liver with a suction-cup mouth.

Some fishermen probably will never get used to handling them, although they are not the bloodsucker we know.

But lordy can leeches catch walleyes.

The leeches may be hooked at either end, although most fishermen slip the hook through the sucker-end. However, Dick Sternberg, a Minnesota fisheries biologist who also is an accomplished fisherman, pointed out to me one time that the leech does not swim sucker-end first. Most of us drag our leeches around backwards when we

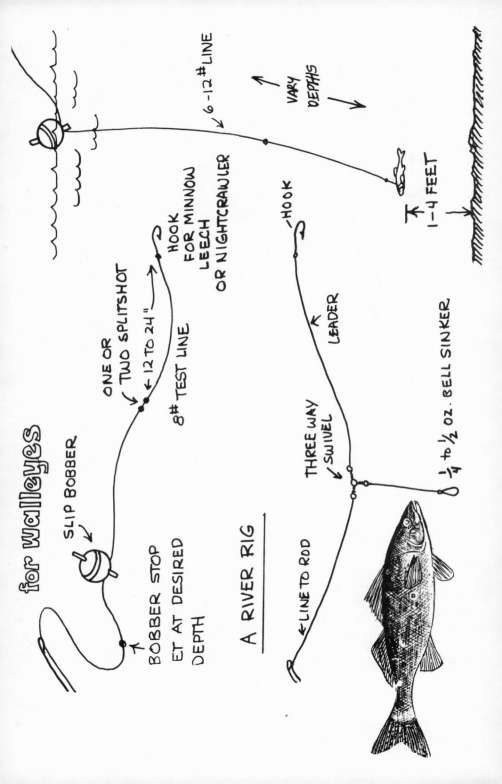

for Walleyes

SLIP BOBBER

BOBBER STOP
ET AT DESIRED
DEPTH

ONE OR
TWO SPLITSHOT

←12 TO 24"

8# TEST LINE

HOOK
FOR MINNOW
LEECH
OR NIGHTCRAWLER

6-12 # LINE

VARY
DEPTHS

1-4 FEET

A RIVER RIG

HOOK

LEADER

THREE WAY
SWIVEL

LINE TO ROD

¼ to ½ OZ. BELL SINKER

hook the sucker-end. The walleye doesn't seem to care, however.

Again, leeches may be used much like minnows and nightcrawlers are used, trolled, drifted or still-fished. In addition, leeches are effective any time during the walleye season, although they appear to be most effective in mid-season.

The discovery of leeches gave rise to a growing phenomenon called the "bobber brigade." These are anglers who fish for walleyes with a slip-bobber, a splitshot, small hook and a lively leech. It's a deadly combination.

The use of the slip-bobber allows an angler to fish extremely deep water without using a fishing rod 100 yards long. The bobber slips freely on the fishing line until it hits a "bobber stop," a small wire or bead pinched on the line, which stops the bobber at a desired depth. Since the bobber stop passes through the rod guides, you can cast or land a fish with a short line as the bobber slips toward the hook. (See Illustration).

You'll find that leeches come in varying sizes — from less than an inch to 3 inches or more. Generally the larger or "jumbo" leeches work best.

You'll also find that the walleye's preference for nightcrawlers or leeches will vary. Not only from day to day but from hour to hour. Many times I've started the day with nightcrawlers, for instance. Caught two or three walleyes and then . . . nothing. Until I switched to leeches. Then the action resumed. Once it slowed, I'd switch back to nightcrawlers or even minnows until some combination inspired another strike.

Choosing Hook, Line and Sinker This is the business end of walleye fishing and very important. Almost any combination of good line (no more than 12-pound test), an adequate sinker to reach the bottom and a hook of proper size will suffice to catch a walleye.

River walleye fishermen do better with a "river rig", consisting of a 3-way swivel, a bell sinker and a hook. (See Illustration). Believe me, there's a difference. I was using the conventional live bait rig on the Mississippi River one spring while fishing buddy, Bob Nybo, a Red Wing river rat, went with the time-worn river rig. While we were fishing in the same boat, Nybo's better luck convinced me there was more than luck involved. I soon put together a river rig and started catching walleyes. Obviously the river's current was holding my bait too tight to the bottom. The river rig allows the bait to rise up where the walleyes are looking.

But undoubtedly the most popular and versatile terminal tackle used today is known as a live bait rig — a slip-sinker, a swivel and hook. (See Illustration).

Most of the other live bait terminal tackle in use involves minor changes. Some fishermen don't like to use a slip-sinker, prefering a non-slip weight such as a rubber-core sinker or chain sinkers.

The type of sinker may not be as important as the weight, however. You'll do better if you maintain a "feel" with the bottom. It's best to use enough sinker to achieve that bottom contact. Generally, a ¼-ounce sinker will be adequate in water up to about 25 feet. Then, switch to a ½-ounce weight. On windy days, when your boat will be drifting faster, you may find you'll also have to go to a heavier sinker. In shallow waters or calm days, an ⅛-ounce weight will work fine.

But stay in contact with the bottom. Know where you're at and you'll be a better walleye fisherman.

Speed and the Strike These are the two most common mistakes made by novice walleye-seekers. They troll or drift too fast and cannot recognize the walleye's soft "non-strike."

Generally I don't think you can hurt your success by trolling too slowly. The need to move slow and still control the boat has led to the popular technique called "back-trolling." It looks just like it sounds. The outboard is placed in reverse and the boat moves stern first instead of bow first. Fishermen who practice backtrolling are easy to spot: their boats have large customized mudflaps affixed above the transom on each side of the outboard engine.

walleye live bait rigs

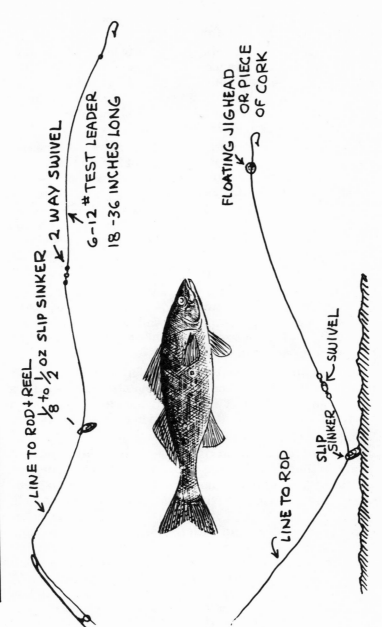

LINDY OR LIVE BAIT RIG

LINE TO ROD + REEL →

⅛ to ½ OZ SLIP SINKER

← 2 WAY SWIVEL

6-12 # TEST LEADER

18-36 INCHES LONG

FLOATING JIGHEAD OR PIECE OF CORK

SLIP SINKER

SWIVEL

LINE TO ROD

FLOATING RIG

These "flaps" serve one purpose: to keep waves from breaking over the low transom.

A backtroller's boat may look gaudy but the technique is very efficient. It's much easier to control the path of a boat that is being "pulled" and not "pushed" by the outboard. What's more, it's much easier to achieve slower trolling speeds since the boat is "pushing" more water ahead of the square stern compared to a pointed bow.

It is not necessary to backtroll, if there's a pleasant wind for drifting. Then, it's a matter of letting the breezes move the boat on, over or alongside walleye haunts. Use the outboard to control your path or slow your drift.

In strong winds and heavy waves, it is almost impossible to backtroll (without swamping the boat) and your drifting speed likely will be too fast to suit a walleye. In that situation, it's usually best to set anchor, holding your boat on the edge of a drop-off.

When bobber fishing, the walleye strike is easily detected. Yesireee, the bobber goes down. But with the conventional live bait rigs, the walleye's soft attack on minnows, nightcrawlers and leeches are often missed by novices and veterans alike.

It's a non-strike really. You'll seldom feel a "jerk" so don't wait for one. Instead, the walleye strike is more like a light snag. You'll detect a gradually increasing tension on the line as if the bait had hooked on a boulder. Sometimes it is a boulder. Sometimes it isn't.

For that reason, most fishermen fish walleyes with an open reel that is ready to give line instantly. Your line then should be held by one finger or two fingers, which helps detect the growing tension. Once the tension is felt, quickly drop the line off of your fingers, giving slack in the line. Let the walleye run with the bait, if it wants to. Then how long should you wait? That's a tough question. When you've had a strike, seconds seem like minutes. But you'll have to decide that question by trial and error. Count to 10 slowly and set the hook firmly. If you miss the fish, you might wait longer next time. If you counted to 10 and the walleye is landed with the hook already buried in its stomach, you know you can probably set the hook sooner on the next fish.

Not every strike ends with a walleye, of course. Sometimes they'll almost smack the bait, take line convincingly and then drop the hook. If that happens often in a day, some anglers will add a "stinger" hook, a hook that trails at the rear of the bait. Otherwise, there's not much you can do, except hope the walleyes quit teasing.

There are times when you can't backtroll, drift or anchor for walleyes. You must cast.

One opening day on Minnesota-South Dakota border waters, Babe Winkelman and I headed for Big Stone Lake near Ortonville. Babe had fished the lake many times before and knew of potential hotspots. We fished those places for several hours but they all proved to be "cold."

Finally, we happened to backtroll along the edge of a wind-swept point, which had waves breaking into the shallows and muddying the waters. That meant the water wasn't much more than 3 to 4 feet deep. For no reason except a hunch, I reeled in and flipped a nightcrawler into the shallows along the edge of the muddy water. Boom, I had a strike and landed a 1½-pounder.

"That's the best news we've had all day," said Babe.

Immediately we quit backtrolling. Instead, Babe used the outboard to hold the boat against the wind within casting distance of the extreme shallows. Two hours later we had a dozen plump walleyes, a two-man limit, dangling on the stringer.

If we had tried to backtroll or drift over the shallows our luck probably would have suffered. Walleyes in 6 feet of water or less are easily spooked even by a boat quietly drifting overhead. In those cases, it's best to cast the bait, reeling it slowing back to the boat in hopes of a strike.

Walleyes On Jigs and Things

The walleye has absolutely no qualms about smashing imitations, feathered hooks or painted plugs.

Jigs, plugs, spoons, spinners — all have been known to take walleyes, sometimes more effectively than live bait.

But perhaps the most famous artificial offering for walleyes is the lead-headed jig. Black, yellow, perch and white colors are best. Two of the best jig fishermen I know, Ray Ostrom and Dick Sternberg, use jigs very effectively in waters of 20 feet or more. But most fishermen have their best luck in water less than 15-feet deep, simply because the jig is much easier to fish.

The jig is used to imitate a minnow or a crayfish. That is, the jig is fished in such a way that it darts on the bottom, raising and falling, raising and falling.

The walleye, like the bass, tends to hit the jig when it is falling or immediately after it settles to the bottom. Knowing that, the trick then is to detect the strike. And the key to detecting the strike is to make sure the jig falls while you maintain some tension on the line. Of course, you must also impart the action to the jig. A straight retrieve seldom is effective on walleyes, thus you must lift and drop the jig.

With tension on the line, the strike will come in the form of a "thunk" felt through the line or the line will twitch slightly. Set the hook. The best jig fishermen are line watchers.

The jig's effectiveness is often improved by "tipping" the jig with a minnow, leech or piece of nightcrawler. Although good jig fishermen seldom need such aids.

While live bait fishermen may be in the majority, the plug casters for walleyes undoubtedly have more fun. The walleye is no coward when faced with a tasty-looking plug.

The two most popular plug-type lures are the Rapala and Flatfish. Both may be cast in shallow waters, particularly for evening fishing, or both may be trolled. (See Illustration). Speed is somewhat less important, although troll only as fast as necessary to give action to the lure.

The strike, of course, is easily detected and the walleye is on immediately. Or off immediately.

Night fishermen, armed with floating or sinking Rapalas, often gather on the rocky shoals on Mille Lacs in May and June. As the sun sets, they anchor in water of 6 feet or less and cast into the boulder-strewn shallows.

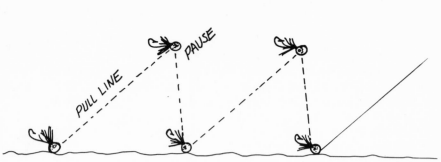

PULL LINE PAUSE

proper walleye jig action

trolling walleye lures

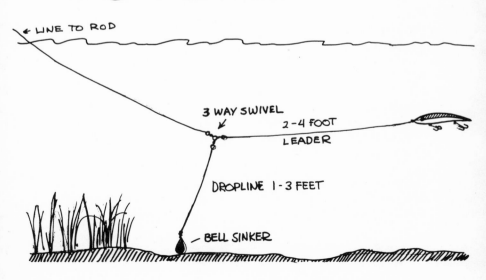

← LINE TO ROD

3 WAY SWIVEL

2 - 4 FOOT
LEADER

DROPLINE 1 - 3 FEET

— BELL SINKER

Under the cover of darkness, the walleyes will move into the boulder fields in search of prey. That's when the action can exceed your highest expectations.

Any time you land enough walleyes to fill a frying pan is cause for celebration. Day or night. Veteran walleye hunters often look for gray, overcast skies with westerly winds. Typically, that's walleye catching weather. But don't be discouraged by bright, sunny days with calm waters. Walleyes are catchable then, too.

If you've ever tasted fresh walleye filet, that's all you need to know.

Ice Fishing For Walleyes

Take what you know about summer walleye fishing, add a healthy scoop of patience, and you'll catch walleyes through the ice, too.

Basically, the walleys will be found in similar haunts, ranging from a depth of about 20 to 35 feet deep. Trial and error is the only way to find them. Only now it's more work, since you'll have to drill 6-inch holes through the ice that may be 12-inches or more in thickness. Usually more.

Also dress warmly, if you plan to fish outside. On many lakes in Minnesota, ice fishing houses can be rented by the hour or day. These houses usually are heated and quite comfy. Shirt-sleeve fishing in the dead of winter.

Winter also neutralizes most of the elements. You have no wind or waves. You can't cast or troll, so there's not much need for fancy fishing gear. Most ice fishermen use small ice fishing "sticks" and land their fish by hand-lining. In other words, you can own the most expensive ice fishing rod in the world for $2.98. And fishing, itself, is boiled down to a pure hook, line and sinker . . . and a small one at that.

Minnows — shiners and fatheads — are used almost exclusively by live bait anglers. A spinner or ice-fly hook may be used with the minnow.

While the ice fisherman is limited to fishing "vertically" through the ice, there are a few artificial lures available to the purist. The most popular are the Swedish

Pimple, and Rapala's Balanced Jigging lure or Pilkki lure. Each may be fished alone or with a small minnow. The lures are designed to be pumped up and down, giving the action of an injured minnow. The action need not be vigorous. All fish in ice cold water tend to be somewhat sluggish. They have no desire to chase something that appears hard to catch. In fact, if you don't dress properly for the cold, you will also begin to feel a little sluggish.

A selection of ice fishing lures for walleyes.

panfish

for kids of any age

KEN HAAG

Panfish/

For Kids Of Any Age

Panfish make the angling world go-round.

Without them, some of the glamorous fishes of freshwater would be hard-pressed to survive. I mean if a muskie didn't have perch to feast on, can you see it chasing black gnats?

But the real losers would be the kids of angling. All of us kids. The kids of any age who never tire of watching a bobber dip or stalking the shallows for saucer-shaped bluegills or sunfish.

For the panfish are what fishing is all about. They provide action, yet they are not taken without some skills. They are small but their fighting hearts are big. They are abundant, plus the panfishes rank alongside the walleye out of the frying pan.

And they almost always can be caught. Well, almost always. I remember an ice fishing trip to a strange lake for bluegills. Picking a likely-looking spot 20 yards away from the bulrush shores, I took a hand-auger and began drilling through two feet of ice. The hole finished, I dropped down a heavy sinker to check the depth. I was in about 18 inches of water. Worthless.

I dug another hole further from shore. This time I hit 24. Inches, that is.

And I dug another. Three feet of water.

By then I was too exhausted to drill yet another ice fishing hole. I quit. It's one of the few times I've been skunked fishing for panfish.

Minnesota is blessed with an abundance of panfish water. My definition of panfish include the bluegills and other sunfishes, the crappie and the perch. And you'll find one or all of them in just about every fishing lake in the state, excepting some of the pine-shrouded waters in Minnesota's Boundary Waters Canoe Area.

If panfish mean something stunted to you, then you've also come to the wrong place. Minnesota is noted for its lunker-sized panfish, the 1 or 2 pound bluegills, crappies and "jumbo" perch. Not that you won't find populations of stunted panfishes. They exist. But if that's all you can find — bluegills no larger than a silver dollar — then you're fishing in the wrong places. For even lakes with a bad fish-stunting problem usually have lunker panfish lurking somewhere.

I'll never forget the reaction of Jack Ehresman, a friend and fellow outdoor writer from Illinois. Jack arrived in Minnesota to chase some romantic fish like smallmouth bass. We were fishing together on a scenic lake near Grand Rapids one day when he accidentally caught a nice-sized bluegill. Nothing spectacular but nice. Meanwhile, we hadn't done much with the romantic fish.

Suddenly Jack blurted, "To heck with this, I'm going after them big 'gills." And he did.

Surprised by his reaction to a bluegill that wasn't even a 1-pounder, I later asked Jack why he was so excited. After all, he was from Illinois where I thought big bluegills were as common as corn. It was then Jack informed me that Illinois has nice bluegills but Minnesota's ran larger on the average. And he was determined to catch them when he had the chance.

Catching Sunnies

The bare-footed boy with his pant cuffs rolled, sitting on the bank with a cane pole and a Folger's coffee can of worms, had the right idea.

You don't need much more than that — a cane pole, line, bobber, sinker and plain hook. Most of us have been weaned of cane poles, which may or may not be fortunate. Whatever, no matter what you use, it must be used in the right waters.

Early summer is the premium time for catching sunnies. The fish are spawning in the shallows and are easily located. Minnesota has five kinds of sunnies, the popular bluegill, the pumpkinseed, the green sunfish, the warmouth and the orangespotted sunfish. Most have similar habits and live in similar waters. Since the word sunfish means bluegill to most anglers, the following advice will be given in the same way.

Let's start with the earthworm. But do we really have a choice? The earthworm curled on a small hook undoubtedly catches more sunfish than any other baits combined.

I'd like to suggest a light line, maybe 6-pound test at the most, a small splitshot, a size 8 or 10 hook and a bobber about the size of a quarter. But it probably doesn't matter. I've seen fishermen use black casting line and bobbers the size of basketballs . . . and still catch sunfish.

Maybe that's the beauty of it all.

There is a little trick in baiting the hook, however. Bluegills are famed bait stealers. And when earthworms cost 50 cents a dozen, you can't afford to feed the thieves, just the biters. By the way, nightcrawlers also work on bluegills. But use only a small 1-inch piece of nightcrawler at a time or you'll go broke buying bait.

The baiting trick is to weave the worm on the hook as if you were darning a sock. (See Illustration). In that manner, the bluegill is almost forced to inhale the hook if it wants the worm.

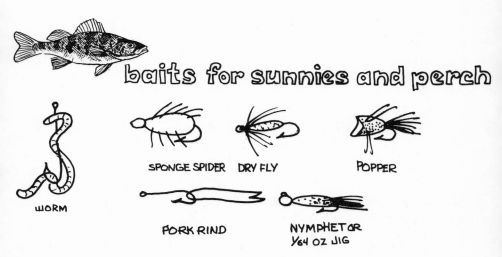

baits for sunnies and perch

SPONGE SPIDER   DRY FLY   POPPER

WORM

PORK RIND

NYMPHET OR
1⁄64 OZ JIG

There is no correct depth to fish bluegills with a bobber. That depth must be discovered by trial and error. When the sunnies are spawning, they usually are in less than 6 feet of water. Sometimes less than 2 feet. So the bobber must be set accordingly. Some people are content to sit and watch a motionless bobber, waiting for it to dive. But you'll often increase your sunfish action by jiggling the bobber occasionally. Jiggling the bobber, of course, also causes the hooked worm to vibrate, attracting the bluegill's attention.

Catching sunnies in the shallows is the easy part, however. When the fish have completed spawning, they move into deeper water and out of sight. They are still highly catchable; it just takes more hunting.

Like most other fish, sunnies like to be near something. Usually weedbeds where there's a good supply of insects, snails and tiny minnows — the bluegill's favorite foods.

Other famous haunts include boat docks, bridge pilings, sunken treetops, stump fields. Most people stand on a boat dock and cast out from it. Too bad. They'd have better luck if they quietly dropped a worm underneath the dock.

But if you're looking for lunker bluegills (and who isn't?), the underwater weedbeds located near 20 or 30 feet of water are prime spots. There are weedbeds and then there are weedbeds, however. The most productive aquatic vegetation consists of the various pondweeds, leafy plants that grow to just under the surface with small "seedy spikes" that peek above the water. But if you don't find pondweed, don't panic. There may not be any in the lake. So find whatever aquatic vegetation you can find that is closest to deep water. The bluegill may like pondweed but if there's none around the fish can hardly pack its grips and move to a different lake.

You'll likely find the plate-sized bluegills near the outer edge of the weedbed or suspended off the bottom nearby. There's no way to find out except by trial and error. But don't be afraid to fish deep. Maybe 15 feet or more. For that matter, I've caught bluegills in 25 feet of water. Nice ones, too.

To reach the deeper bluegills, you have to switch to a

slip-type bobber or no bobber at all. Instead, pinch on a small splitshot that sinks slowly. Cast it and the bait along the edge of the weeds. Allow time for the bait to sink and then retrieve slowly. You'll get a strike. I'd almost promise.

Now you can do all of this using a lowly earthworm for bait. The bluegill is more versatile than that, however. They may be fished on the surface with small poppers or floating spiders; they may be fished with sinking spinners or wet flies, like a weighted nymph or spider. Not to mention one of the all-time great bluegill foolers — a small 1-inch strip of white porkrind and a hook.

These artificials may be fished shallow or deep, depending on how much split-shot or sinker is added.

But all artificials should be fished slowly, either twitched or pulled steadily. Bluegills tend to be browsers, eating this, eating that. They feel no urgent need to chase any fast-moving morsel. That's why minnows seldom are an effective bluegill bait. They'll work, of course, but tidbits of worm meat or imitation insects are better.

fishing Bluegill flies and poppers

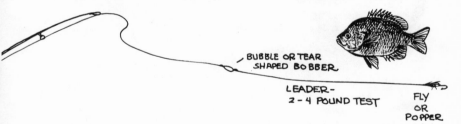

BUBBLE OR TEAR
SHAPED BOBBER

LEADER -
2 - 4 POUND TEST

FLY
OR
POPPER

You don't need a flyrod to throw artificial wet or dry flies or poppers to surface-feeding sunnies. And that's good. Because taking bluegills on the surface is a really fun way to fish. You can cast a fly or rubber spider with a conventional spinning or spin-casting rod and reel by using a small, clear-plastic "bubble" or "bobber" about 3 to 4 feet ahead of the fly. The bobber provides enough weight to make the cast. Then merely twitch or slowly

Minnesota is known for its "platter-sized" bluegills, if you can find them.

retrieve the bobber while the fly follows. Poppers may be fished in the same manner. Of course, if you have mastered a flyrod use it. On a flyrod, the gamey battle of a 1-pound bluegill will make a 1-pound trout seem like a water-logged hammer handle.

Early morning or late evening are prime times for topwater fishing for bluegills. Listen for the "slurping" noise of bluegills feeding on the surface. You'll find it's music to the ears.

Catching Perch

Only about 25 of Minnesota's 146 fish species are sought-after or caught regularly by fishermen. But of those 25, perhaps the least appreciated is the perch. It's considered a pest, a bait-stealer and a rather dull catch.

I must admit the perch is not the brightest thing with fins. It's abundant but highly populated with below-keeping sizes. Invariably, when fishing for something else, a perch will show up on the end of the line. Because it's there when you didn't want it, the perch is a disappointment.

My 5-year old daughter doesn't feel that way, however. She thinks perch are great. They bite, they fight. They're fun to catch.

Perch are also related closely to the tasty walleye and the flavor of perch filets proves it.

Minnesota's perch also are available in jumbo sizes, ranging from ½ to 1-pound or more. So they're worth fishing for. Call them, poor man's walleyes.

Perch are fished similarly to sunfish, except that big perch are more apt to take small minnows and leeches (although big bluegills will inhale leeches nicely). In addition, perch are apt to be found more widely spread than sunfish. While the sunfish hangs around weedbeds and sunken islands, perch will also frequent sandflats, sandbars, weeds, rocks, you name it. I've seen perch in 4 feet of water and caught them in 35 feet of water on the same lake on the same day.

Come to think about it, if you drag a worm around long

enough I can't think of why you wouldn't catch a perch. It may not be a jumbo but it'll be a perch. Finding the jumbos just takes more searching. On some lakes, such as Mille Lacs, the search usually isn't a long one.

About the only time perch may be difficult to catch is after the sun goes down. Like bluegills, perch feed almost solely by sight. When it gets dark the perch get closed mouths.

Just remember that the perch will take the same baits and lures as sunfish, with the exception of surface lures. You shouldn't ever get skunked. But you might get sick of catching.

Stan Nelson happily shows up a dandy bluegill and two hefty crappies.

Catching Crappies

To a Minnesota fisherman, crappies are the first sign of spring. They are the first fish to greet anglers weary of snow, solid water and Super Bowl defeats. Crappies are not only the first fish; they are the only fish. When the ice breaks up in mid-April, most of the other fishes are protected by closed seasons or difficult to find.

Not so with the crappie.

The crappie is one of the first fish to seek the shallow bays, warmed ever so slightly by the April sun. In doing so, they move into the shallows in huge concentrations. And they're hungry. While the crappie can be difficult to find in mid-summer, the opposite is true in the spring.

Check out lagoons, boat basins, channels, bays — any area of shallow water and you'll likely find concentrations of crappies. Also check the northerly shores of lakes. The northern shores usually have the warmest water first. Southerly winds push the warm water to the north end and the sun's rays hit a north shore longer in the day, particularly when the south shore is shaded by vegetation or high banks.

So what's the point? Armed with light spinning tackle, a bobber, splitshot, hook, and small "crappie" minnows, anybody can catch crappies in the spring.

Minnesota has two crappie species, the common "black" crappie and the not-so-common "white" crappie. Some lakes, such as Minnetonka, have both species. But generally the white crappie is found in more southerly waters in the state; the black in northern lakes.

The black crappie, as its name implies, is richly speckled with deep, dark markings. The white crappie is pale in comparison with faint markings.

Crappies spawn later in the spring when the water temperature hits 60 degrees or so. Again they are vulnerable to the fisherman who stalks amid their spawning grounds, usually on shallow, bulrush flats or other sandy bays. Small minnows, jigs or jig-minnow combinations are effective when used with or without a bobber.

If using jigs alone, light colors often work best, such as white, pink or yellow.

Since you're fishing shallow waters, depth is seldom a mystery. But it is better to set your bobber so that the jig or minnow floats higher than midway off the bottom. That is a general rule, however. The most effective depth again is found by trial and error.

The speed of retrieve also can make a difference. The slower the better. If there's a slight ripple on the water, let the small waves bounce the bobber and in turn bounce the minnow or jig.

Mid-summer crappie fishing is a whole new ball game. By then, the crappies have re-gathered into schools and have moved to deeper water, sometimes 30 feet or more.

The schools can be very difficult to find. And once located the school may move off, meaning your search must start all over again. Fishermen with depth sounders or fish locators often use the electronic devices to help spot crappies. Or fish at least. There's no accurate way of determining exact species on the locators without first catching "one of the signals."

Still, crappies, too, are structure fish. They like to be near drop-offs, sunken islands, deepwater shoreline drops and so forth. Deep water next to bulrush clumps, points or

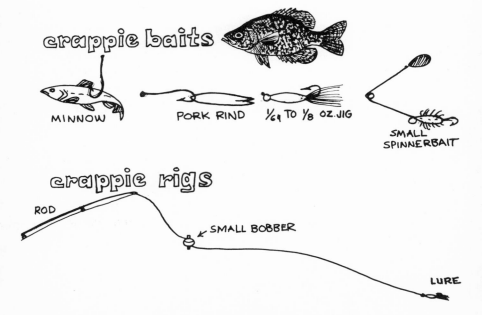

crappie baits

MINNOW   PORK RIND   1/64 TO 1/8 OZ. JIG

SMALL SPINNERBAIT

crappie rigs

ROD

SMALL BOBBER

LURE

flats are typical crappie hotspots. Concentrate your fishing in water 15 to 25 feet deep. Drop a lively minnow to the bottom and then slowly raise it a few feet at a time. If you don't make contact, repeat the process, working the edge of the drop-off until you find the crappies. Then, mark the spot. Anchor or drift over the area.

If you lose the school, keep drifting to cover as much water as possible, if the breezes are not too strong.

You'll find the crappie is a notorious morning and evening fish, becoming increasingly active during those two periods. Sometimes it's almost impossible to nab a summer crappie until the sun's rays begin to fade. Then, it can switch to gangbusters.

But don't count your crappies yet. Both white and black crappies are known as "paper mouths," that is their jaws appear to be held together with tissue paper. The fisherman who insists on setting a hook that would stop a Mack truck is likely to lose more crappies than he'll catch. The idea is to set the hook firmly but gently. Don't horse the crappie to shore or the boat. If you do, the hook will easily tear out, leaving the crappie perhaps somewhat shook but not seriously injured. Held steadily, the hook in a paper mouth will hold — still attached to a fine-eating, scrappy crappie.

Ice Fishing For Panfish

If it wasn't for panfish, ice fishing in Minnesota would be a notch below watching haircuts for pure excitement. Sure there are walleyes, northern pike and lake trout to keep the ice angler going. But these fish can be very elusive when the mobility of the fisherman is reduced to a small hole in the ice.

Fortunately, the abundant panfish take up the slack. By sheer numbers, they will be present under just about any ice fishing hole that was dug with a little judgment.

You'll rarely find bluegills and perch cruising in water deeper than 20 feet. So confine your fishing in shallower water in the vicinity of the weedbeds and drop-offs visited in the summer.

Crappies tend to be more elusive in the winter, that is they'll often suspend over deeper water. Nevertheless, stick near structure . . . drop-offs on underwater points, sunken islands and so forth.

Of course when a lake is covered by 18-inches of ice and equal amounts of snow, it can be a little difficult finding the right spots. Some anglers use their electronic depthfinders, the portable models. The sonar signal will go through ice, although the transducer must be in some kind of liquid to work.

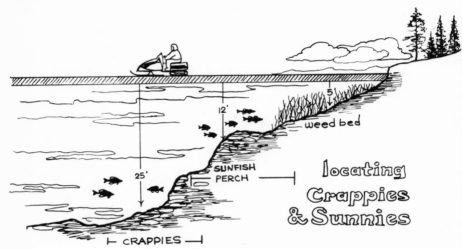

locating Crappies & Sunnies

I usually eyeball the shoreline, looking for hints that will indicate the existence of points. Then, it's guesswork. Drill a hole in the ice. Clip a heavy sinker on the end of your fishing line and drop it to the bottom to find the depth. By drilling several test holes you can find the dropoff or changes in depth. Such a trial and error method is hard work, particularly with thick ice and a hand auger, but there is no other way. Except to use a powered auger, gas engine or electric. Then, it's fun again.

The perfect spot is where bluegills and perch roam during the day and crappies move in at evening. Fishing friend, Gary Roach, of Lindy-Little Joe Co., and I found such a place a couple of winters ago. We were fishing in about 20 feet of water on the side of a long slope, which dropped quickly from shallow to deep water.

The afternoon action was perfect. A nice bluegill here, a nice perch there. Occasionally a small northern pike would cruise by, dispersing the panfish schools but they'd eventually return. And the action would start again.

But as the western sun faded, the action gradually slowed until . . . boom, the first crappie showed up. Then another. And another. When we quit we were one crappie short of a limit to add to a fine mess of bluegills and eating-size perch.

Clearly the key to winter panfish success is the ice hole that you choose to use. Your chosen bait seldom is critical. Fortunately, ice fishermen are a congenial bunch and rather gregarious. An ice fisherman with a hotspot seldom objects if other anglers stop to fish in the same vicinity. Panfish are abundant and prolific. You'll not fish them into extinction.

Winter sunfish and perch often may be caught with the same baits and lures used in the summer. With the exception of poppers or other topwater lures. Instead of earthworms, however, most ice fishermen use various grubs for live bait — wax worms, goldenrod grubs, mousies, meal worms, red worms and so forth. Most are available at bait shops. Or some anglers collect or raise their own. Golden rod grubs are found in the galls (round bulges of the golden rod plant). Carefully cut open the gall and you'll find a small white grub.

The grubs or worms may be fished on small, plain hooks (size 8 or 10) or with special hooks, called ice flies. These are hooks with a dab of lead molded around the hook shank and painted. The painted lead acts as an attractor. Some ice flies have a small spinner blade for an attractor.

One of the best bluegill lures — winter or summer — is a weighted rubber or sponge spider, tipped with a grub. Remember that bluegills and perch prefer hor d'oeuvres not full course helpings.

ice flies, baits and lures

GOLDEN GRUB (LARVAL FORM OF YELLOW MEALWORM)

HELLGRAMMITES (LARVAL FORM OF DOBSONFLY)

MAYFLY LARVA (NYMPH STAGE)

CADDIS FLY LARVA (WITH SAND CASING)

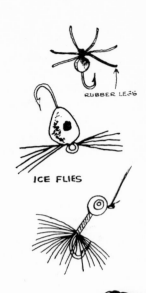

RUBBER LEGS

ICE FLIES

WAX WORM
(LARVAL FORM OF BEE MOTH)

MOUSIE (IMMATURE FORM OF SYRPHUS FLY)

SMALL SHINER (HOOKED BEHIND DORSAL FIN)

The typical panfishing rig consists of an ice fishing jig stick, light monofilament line (2 to 4-pound test), a split-shot or two, the hook or ice fly and a small bobber. Very small. About the size of a dime. Larger bobbers not only are unnecessary, they're a sure way of reducing your luck on panfish.

Be sure to give the grub or ice fly a little "action" once in awhile. Jiggle it lightly, then pause. Repeat a couple of times a minute. You'll find the jigging action of the grub will entice more bites. Or at least keep your mind occupied.

As in summer, crappies under the ice tend to be morning and evening fish. There are exceptions, of course. But the serious winter crappie fisherman seldom bothers to chase crappies until an hour or so before sundown.

The tools of the crappie chaser are similar to the bluegill addict, except minnows are the bread and butter bait. Minnows fished on a bare hook, minnows fished with small 1/64 or 1/32-ounce jigs or minnows attached to ice flies.

When the crappies are really turned on, it's fun to forget the live bait and base your luck strictly on artificials, small maribou jigs or crappie queen jigs or small lures such as the Rapala Pilkki or Swedish Pimple.

With artificials, there's no fussing with grubs or minnows. Catch a fish, land it and sink the lure again. An

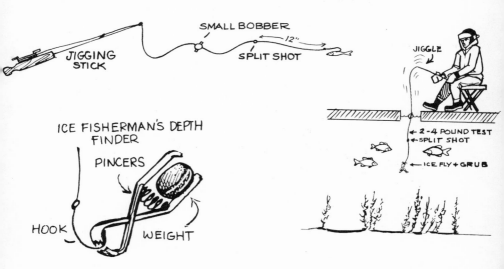

ice fishing for panfish

know your ice

NO!

OKAY
MAYBE

FINE

1"   2"-3"   4"   5" or more

artificial lure is severely limited in winter, of course. All you can really do with it is jig up and down. A minnow in comparison swims under its own power and is much deadlier. Still, a crappie caught on a fake bait under the ice is much more gratifying. And every angler should experience the feeling.

In Minnesota, you are permitted to fish with two lines in the winter. But the ice angler's handiest tool is a 5-gal. pail. It serves as a tackle box, a fish box and a seat.

I once wandered up to a lone ice fisherman, perched on his pail.

"How they bitin'?" I asked to be friendly.

"Oh, they kinda quit," the man replied, elusively.

I looked around him and there wasn't a fish on the ice, the usual sign of good fishing.

"Well, have you caught anything?" I continued.

"Yeah," he replied, "got a few nice ones, too."

At that, he raised up off his pail. It was brimming with dandy bluegills up to a pound or more. He said I could join him. But he was right. They, the bluegills, had kinda quit. For me, not for him. His fish were already in the bucket.

Winter fishing in comfort is the only way to go.

northerns-muskies

the toothy critters

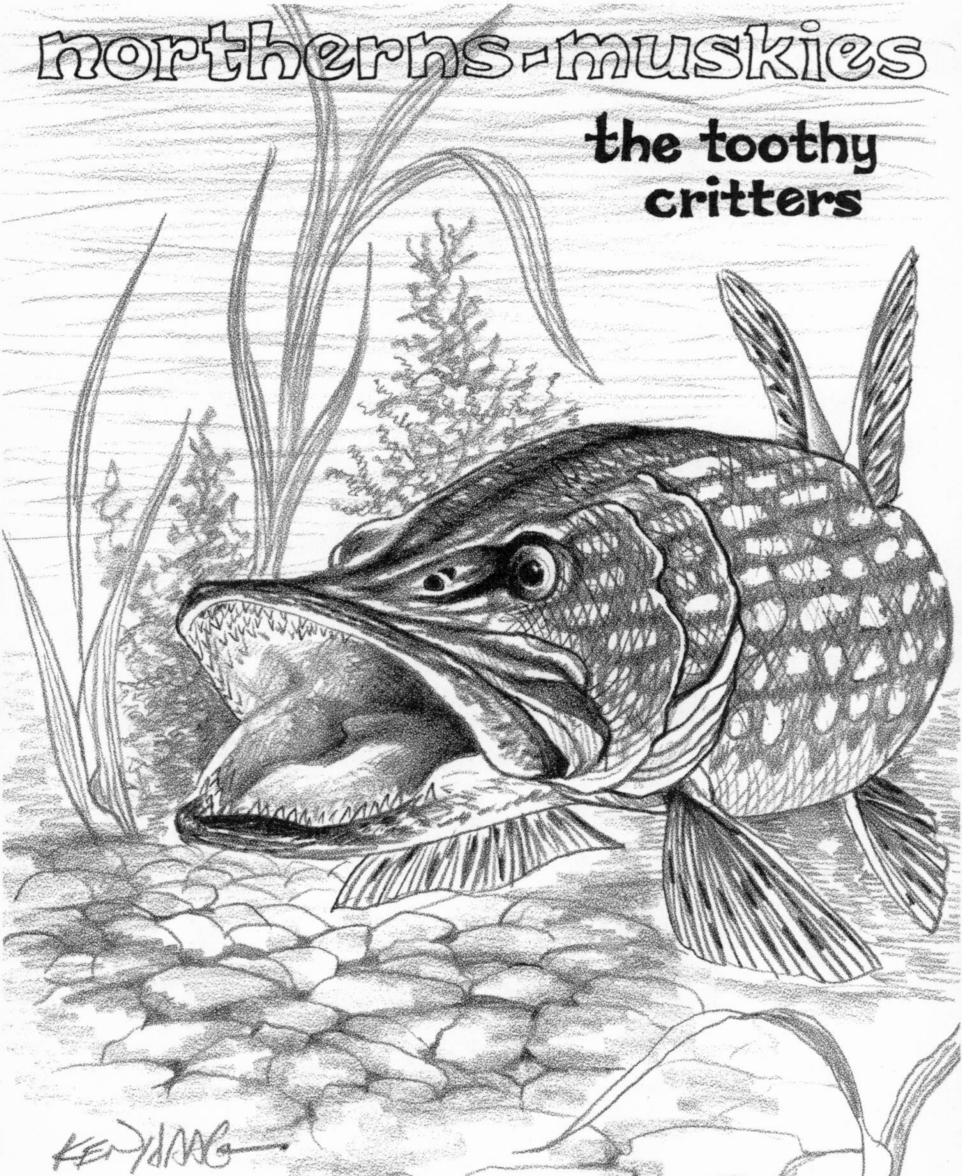

Muskies and Northerns/
The Toothy Critters

Minnesota's muskies and northern pike are eating machines.

Each species is shaped like a camouflaged torpedo with gaping jaws and more teeth than a buzz saw. They are a predator's predator, swift, deadly and, in their young life, cannibalistic.

And they are opportunists. They attack not necessarily out of hunger but by instinct. A crippled-looking victim is one muskies and northern find hard to pass up. For that is how they survive. The muskies' food must always be alive first. The northern pike has similar tendencies, although it will act as a scavenger and inhale whatever looks eatable even if it is not alive.

But it is this willingness to attack, and to do it with gusto, that makes the northern pike and muskie such a worthy adversary for the hook and line fraternity.

Of the two, the northern is the most popular. It is widely distributed in the state's lakes and rivers and it is easier to catch. The muskie, on the other hand, is found only in a limited number of lakes and rivers. And as everyone knows, the muskie is stubborn, suspicious, moody and plain damned hard to catch.

Yet the muskie and northern are often confused in the hands of fishermen. It is important to know the difference, since muskies under 30 inches in length are illegal to catch and keep.

Muskies and northerns are both members of the Pike family and, as such, closely related. Yet they are distinctive. The northern has a more pointed snout and its body is dark with light markings. The muskie has a flat nose with a silvery body and dark bar-like markings. Remember, northern, light marks; muskie, dark marks. The northern is "lighter" in another way. It never grows to the sizes reached by muskies. In Minnesota, 10-pound northerns are fairly common and a trophy is considered to be a

20 or 25 pounder. Whereas a muskie is not really considered a fish "for the wall" unless it is over 30 pounds. Of course, no one sneezes at 20-pound muskies, either.

The abundance of small northern pike also makes them rather unpopular in some waters. These 1 to 3 pounders are famed bait stealers and line cutters. That's why they're called "snakes" or "hammerhandles," rather uncomplimentary names. The fisherman who catches a small muskie, praises it, handles it like gold and sends it back to the waters to grow up — we'll leave that paradox to the psychiatrists.

Finding Muskies and Northerns

While both fish are equipped to be freshwater versions of *Jaws*, they are not man-eaters. They will not find you. Muskies have been known to grab a fallen waterskier or two but such incidents are rare. And any fisherman who jabs his fingers into the mouth of a hooked muskie or northern deserves whatever bloody appendages he gets back.

Otherwise, you must be the aggressor.

Muskies and northern pike are both fish of the aquatic jungles. They live, hide and eat around, by or in vegetation.

Both fish also are known to frequent deep water haunts away from weedy shallows or sunken islands. But they are difficult to find and probably not worth the effort. If you roam the weedbeds, the weedy bays, the bulrush points, the jungles of the lake, you'll find muskies and northern pike sooner or later.

It helps to know key weed species, however. Muskies and northern pike have a penchant for an aquatic plant known generally as "cabbage" or "pondweed". It is a member of the family Potamogeton, if that helps. But do learn to identify it. (See Illustration).

Thick beds of cabbage, ideally located on points or drop-offs, are excellent places to fish. Not only for muskies and northern pike. But also for largemouth bass, bluegills, perch and sometimes walleyes.

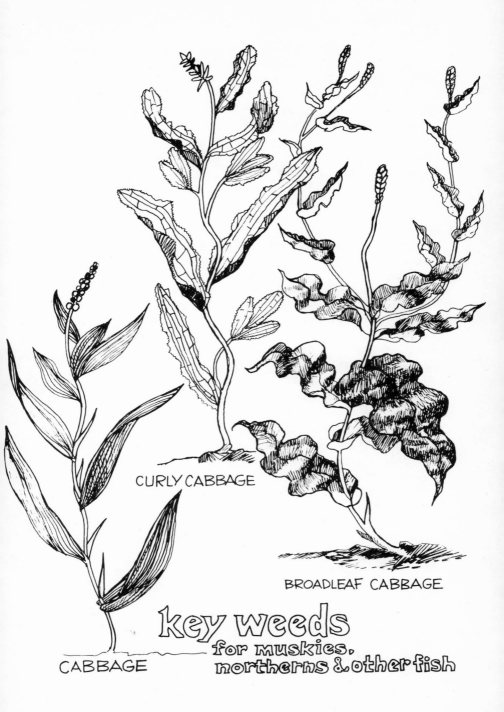

CURLY CABBAGE

BROADLEAF CABBAGE

CABBAGE

key weeds
for muskies,
northerns & other fish

That should give you an idea of why the muskies and northerns are there. That's where the food is. Where you find food, you'll find the two eating machines.

Now that you know that muskies and northerns are aggressive fish, that they relate to a lake's vegetation, let's get to the nitty-gritty.

Catching Northern Pike

In Minnesota, the statewide catch of northern pike ranks second only to the walleye. And that's a bunch. So — obviously the northern is no phantom. Your chances of hauling in 15 to 20-pound northerns may not represent great odds but there are times to try and times not to try in Minnesota.

Generally, the northern pike fishing gets better as the summer season wears on. The very best action comes in the fall, however, starting in September. The northerns then tend to go on a feeding binge. Big pike move into the shallows and become recklessly hungry. This normally happens after the first cold snap or when the nights turn cool and the days are Indian summer.

That doesn't mean that lunker northerns can't be taken other times. They are. On live bait. On spoons, plugs, spinnerbaits and other artificials. Or combinations of both, such as jigs and minnows.

By far the most common method of taking northern pike in Minnesota is with live bait. (See Illustration).

A medium or medium-heavy action rod will serve you well — spinning, spin-cast or casting types. Monofilament of 10 or 12 pound test will be sufficient, providing you know how to handle an ornery fish. Northerns are tremendously strong and powerful swimmers. They'll leap, roll or flop on the end of the line like a wild puppet.

If you don't feel comfortable with 12-pound line, by all means go to heavier monofilament. In most cases, it will not hurt your success. Northerns generally are not line shy. In fact, they fear nothing in their world, except each other.

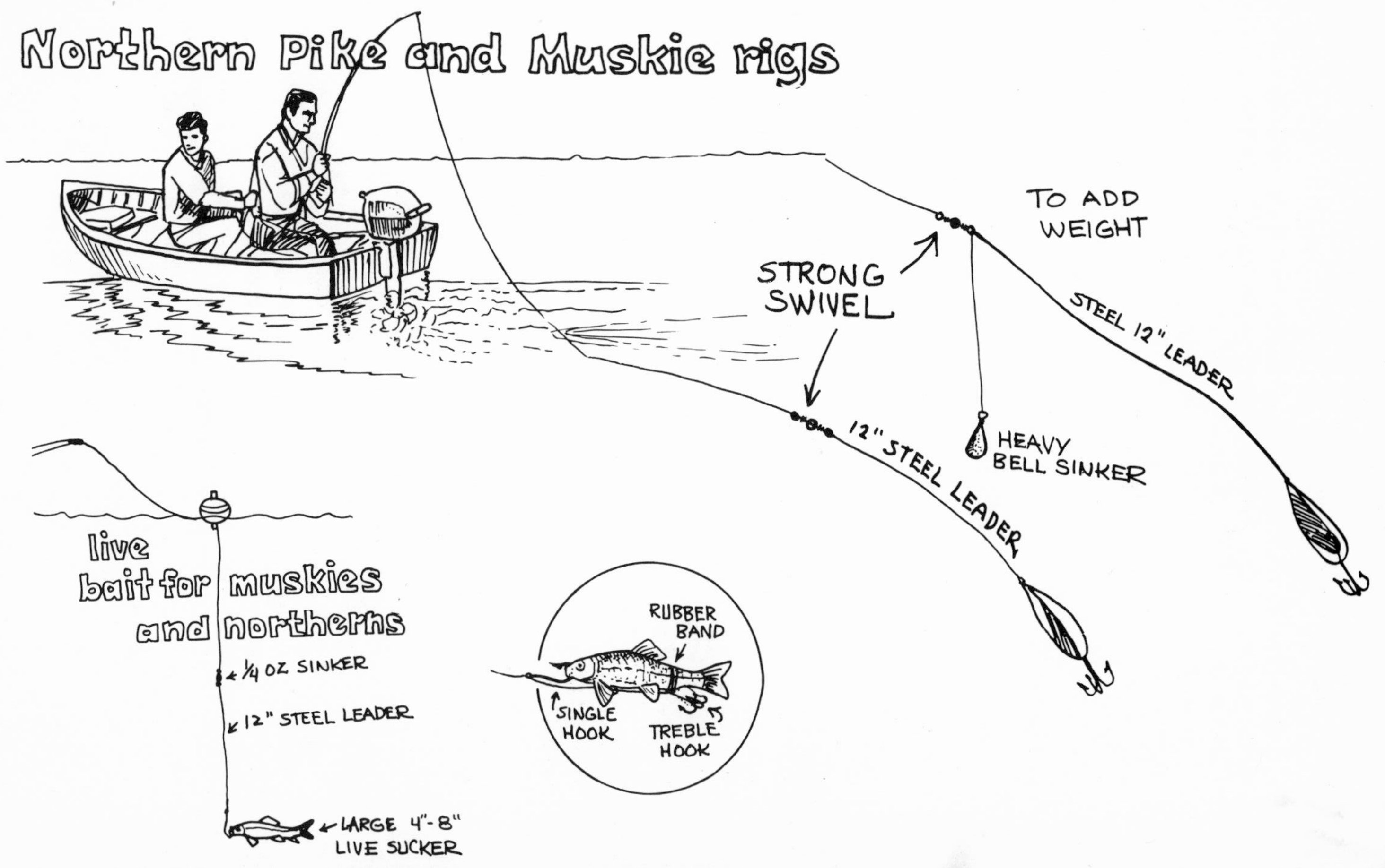

Northern Pike and Muskie rigs

TO ADD WEIGHT

STEEL 12" LEADER

HEAVY BELL SINKER

STRONG SWIVEL

12" STEEL LEADER

RUBBER BAND

TREBLE HOOK

SINGLE HOOK

live bait for muskies and northerns

¼ OZ SINKER

12" STEEL LEADER

LARGE 4"- 8" LIVE SUCKER

Steel leaders are important, however. The famous dentures of northerns and muskies are quite capable of slicing the toughest monofilament without losing a stroke. A 6 or 12-inch steel leader — single or woven wire — will help put your mind at ease. However, there are times when you should take your chances. The action of some lures, such as the Rapala, are badly impaired by the weight or stiffness of a wire leader.

Speaking of special leaders, the only time they are really necessary is when northern pike or muskies are the objective. Time and again, I see beginning fishermen use a steel leader for all of their fishing. The practice is . . . well, stupid. The idea is to present any bait or lure as natural as possible. Rarely can that be accomplished with a thick leader ahead of the hooks. Besides, a steel or wire leader is simply not necessary, except for the toothy critters.

The usual live bait for northern pike consists of one kind of minnow — large suckers from 4 to 8 inches long. Generally, the larger the bait, the larger the fish. The live suckers may be fished in several ways: hooked through the lips to be casted and retrieved or still-fished on the bottom. Or, it may be hooked lightly under the dorsal or back fin and still-fished with a bobber. For those anglers who insist on using jumbo bobbers, the size of softballs, now's your chance. You'll need a fairly large bobber to keep the sucker from swimming away.

Again, you can use a conventional bobber or a slip-bobber depending on the depth fished. But since you'll be fishing in or along the edge of weedbeds, you'll seldom be fishing in water deeper than 10 feet. Then, it's a waiting game. Waiting for the bobber to suddenly plunge under the surface. When it does, you'll have to wait some more. Northern pike tend to act like cats, preferring to play with their victims before gorging. Often, a northern will hit and run considerable distances with the large minnow still within its jaws. Then the pike will pause and resume swimming. That pause usually means the minnow is headed for the pike's stomach. Then strike. Take up the slack in your line and set the hook with a mighty force. And hang on.

Robert Schara, the author's brother, beams proudly at his trophy northern pike.

Dunking sucker minnows is a lunker pike technique. But you need the patience of a young oak tree. And some of us don't have it.

Trolling is the next best thing. Effective yet a shade more active than watching bobbers float. For northern pike, there's not much to it. Flip a lure out behind the boat, start the outboard and cruise back and forth along the outer edges of the weedy shores.

That simplicity probably says more for the Daredevle spoon — red and white, what else? — than anything else. For decades, the Daredevle has meant northern pike fishing. For good reason. The spoon was danged effective and still is. What's more, the fisherman need not do much of anything, except keep the spoon moving in the water.

Not even the trolling speed is important. In fact, the faster the speed the better the fishing. A northern is capable of darting about 30 miles per hour for short bursts. If it wants your spoon bad enough, the pike will catch it.

In fact, many anglers practice "speed trolling", using

Lures that work for both muskies and northern pike.

special diving plugs and opening a small outboard to half throttle. When the northern — any size northern — hits the speeding plug the collision is something to behold.

Almost any lure can be trolled, including jigs, although the speed should be considerably slower. In fact, the large sucker minnows also can be trolled if hooked within a sucker harness, a series of hooks which hold the sucker in a swimming position.

However, the troller's world for northern pike is made up mostly of spoons, Red-Eye, Doctor, Blue Fox (Nebco), Daredevle and many others.

Let there be no doubt, northerns are attracted to flashy things, more so than any other freshwater fish I can think of. And that leads to the subject of casting for northerns.

While casting represents more work and perhaps less efficiency, the caster has a much greater arsenal of shiny objects to attract the pike. And, in my opinion, the casting angler has more fun when he does connect.

The caster also can move in among the weedbeds, casting to open areas where pike will lurk when they're seriously hunting. Accuracy counts, of course. But if you like action you'll get it, pike or hooks full of weeds.

The caster's choice includes spoons and plugs, spinners and spinnerbaits. All are effective. Weedless spoons, such as the Johnson silver minnow, and the spinnerbaits, particularly white, orange and black colors, are extremely effective in the weedy jungles. The spinnerbaits (See Illustration) also are weedless in nature and can be cast into the thicket weeds and bulrushes.

And what about lily pads? Lily pads are not the first choice of discriminating anglers. Don't get me wrong. Fields of lily pads do hold fish, but other aquatic vegetation does better. For one thing, the pads are associated with soft, mucky bottom, the kind that few fish seek out.

If lily pads are the only vegetation available, fish them. Since the northern has no choice, it won't be far away. The one time the lotus or lily pad fields may produce excellent fishing is in the late fall. Then, the mud bottom, absorbing the sun's last faint rays of heat, may maintain slightly higher water temperatures. Enough to attract prey fish.

Northerns readily hit big artificial lures. When it happens, hang on.

Remember, where you find food, you find northern pike.

One of the top lures discovered by northern pike addicts is a combination of artificial and live bait — the jig and minnow.

As mentioned, the jig and minnow can be trolled slowly. But the combination also can be used in casting. The jig is pitched along the weedline edges, sunken islands, weedy points and allowed to sink. The retrieve is made with a pumping action of the rod. In that way the jig and minnow hops back to the boat or shore. The speed can vary. Sometimes you want the jig to bounce on the bottom. Other times, if the bottom is moss or weed covered, the jig is best fished rapidly so that it bounces above the bottom cover. In summer angling, you simply cannot move a lure too fast for a northern to nab. However, early spring or late fall — the cold water conditions — require a slower retrieve.

Northern pike have no qualms about smacking surface lures, yet many fishermen seldom try. That in itself is unfortunate. Topwater fishing for any fish is pure, un-adulterated angling excitement. Northerns absolutely smash a surface lure. Sometimes they hit with such velocity that they'll actually miss their target. On Rainy Lake, the huge and picturesque lake shared by Minnesota and Ontario, I was fishing topwater plugs for muskies on a warm, sleepy August afternoon when a northern pike made a believer out of me.

As the plug twitched noisily across the silent surface, the water suddenly exploded. An 11-pound northern shot skyward like a missile. Only it hadn't missed. The plug, a Mud Puppy, was stuck in the jaw and the fight was on.

I finally landed the pike but I didn't really care. The fish already had provided a day's worth of thrills.

Flyrod enthusiasts also have discovered that north-erns will happily take large streamer flies, too. A flyrod and a northern pike is a great matchup, particularly since you can't use a steel leader on a flyline.

Northern pike, once caught, are difficult to handle. Some anglers grab the pike by the eye sockets. This works but I don't recommend it. For one thing, I think such a hold is degrading to a great fish. For another, if you plan to release the northern, holding it by the eyes is likely to damage its eyesight.

The proper way to hold a northern is to squeeze gently but firmly around the back of the head and gill covers. Use a long-nosed pliers to remove the hooks. Never stick your fingers under the gill covers and into the gills. The gill rakers on a northern are like sharp teeth.

What else would you expect of an eating machine?

The king of freshwater fishes in Minnesota is the mighty muskellunge.

Catching Muskies

"In all of freshwater, there is no other fish like it. Muskie!

Even the sound of its name has an urgency, a sense of excitement. To experienced muskie hunters, the name symbolizes boldness, strength, jaws of needle-like teeth, obstinance, giantism. And — to many of the same veterans — the name also means ultimate frustration.

To others the muskie is a secretive fantasy, a torpedo-shaped cross between a slinky alligator and a cunning woman, a fish that lurks in watery depths, seldom to be seen."

That was an excerpt from my book, *Muskie Mania*, published in 1977. I used those words again to introduce the muskie because the fish hasn't changed a bit.

It remains Minnesota's most cherished trophy fish. Not only because of its size but because few muskies are caught with cheap shots. You usually have to pay your dues, particularly if you're seriously trophy fishing.

The good news is that Minnesota is becoming a better muskie fishing state. The fish has been introduced into more waters. Stocking efforts have been expanded. And the fish has attracted a collection of serious addicts called *Minnesota's Muskies, Incorporated*, an organization that has promoted and financed muskie conservation and propagation practices.

Muskies are found in about 80 lakes and rivers in the state. Of those, about 18 lakes have been designated as "official" muskie waters, meaning that winter spearing is prohibited. Minnesota allows residents only to winter spear northern pike, a practice highly criticized by many "hook and line" advocates. Attempts to restrict or outlaw spearing have failed so far, however. Muskie fans particularly dislike spearing because muskies often are accidentally harpooned when mistaken for northern pike. Therefore, spearing is not allowed on some of the state's prime muskie waters.

Like the northern pike, the muskie is a fish of the aquatic jungles. And it is found in the same areas normally thought of as northern pike haunts.

The two fish will, in fact, share the same waters, although muskies often will not fare well in lakes with high northern populations. The muskie is one of the last fish to spawn. Hence, its young get a late start in life and are vulnerable targets of young northerns hatched earlier. That may be nature's version of fair play, however. For muskies are voracious meat-eaters. According to nature's plan, the avid meat-eaters must have population controls one way or the other. As a result, muskie populations seldom are "dense." A population of 1 or 2 muskies per acre of water is considered enough.

That's also the reason that muskie fishing is tough. It takes a lot of searching when you're looking for a couple of needles in the proverbial haystack. Once located, the muskie — if presented with the right bait in the right way — will open its mouth just like any other mortal fish. So — don't think they're impossible to catch. They're not. They're just harder.

The key to muskie success is hard work and patience.

Most of Minnesota's muskies are the "true" muskie as compared to the hybrid muskie, which is a cross between a northern pike and a true muskie.

The hybrid has been stocked in some waters. And if you catch one, you'll probably think its a true muskie because its fight and size are similar. The hybrid often is referred to as a "tiger" muskie because of its brilliant side stripes. When fishing in the Park Rapids region, you may also catch a "silver muskie" or "silver pike". It is a rare species and considered to be a mutant of the northern pike. The silver pike has bright silvery-sides and a plain dark back.

Muskies, themselves, will vary in coloration. Some will have dark vertical stripes, some light. Some will be almost silvery. And fishermen have names for every shade. Needless to say, the name game became confusing. Many fisheries scientists now believe a muskie is a muskie. And the color variations are simply due to the environmental changes, which occur from one lake to another. So much for academics.

When you hook a muskie you'll know it. They are

spectacular fighters, striking viciously and leaping like a crazed tarpon. Big northern pike may fight longer but a muskie's battle is more intense. They've been known to leap into boats . . . and out again.

So go prepared.

The muskie is one of the few Minnesota sportfish that requires special gear if you're going to fish seriously. You're in the heavyweight division now. A muskie rod is about as limber as a pool cue. For good reasons: muskie anglers use big lures and it's important to set the hook. You need a stout rod to handle both.

A typical muskie rod has a stout butt and stiff tip action with a length of about 5½ feet. Longer rods are fine, too. While you can fish muskies with open-face spinning or spin-cast (closed face) reels, the only practical reel is the free-spool casting reel.

For line, monofilament or braided Dacron work equally well. Use 20 to 30 pound test line and a 12-inch minimum length woven steel or wire leader with husky swivels and snaps. The leaders, snaps and swivels — the business end of your line — is very important. Don't look for bargains. Buy the best. Some muskie addicts, for example, use snaps rated at 100-pound test. Don't underestimate the power of an ornery muskie. For if there's a weak link in your knots, swivels, leaders — a 15 or 20-pound muskie will find it.

Okay, so now you're loaded for bear.

Some fishermen get their kicks out of tossing giant sucker minnows into muskie haunts. It's effective. The sucker usually is floated by a fat bobber or trolled in a harness of hooks.

But in one man's opinion, chasing muskies with suckers is like getting married without a honeymoon. You're missing all the fun.

Muskies will gladly smash an artificial lure when they're in the right mood. You can troll that lure or cast it. Either way, you're in for a good time.

Trolling is considered the most efficient method of taking a muskie. Since muskies are usually widely scattered, trolling enables you to cover more water in less time. The world record, 69 pounds, 15 ounces, was taken by Art

Lawton as he trolled the St. Lawrence River in 1957.

Trolling has its disadvantages, too. Muskies often lurk close to the weedbed edges where it's almost impossible for a troller to roam without constantly getting snagged. And while the troller can cover more water, he cannot fish as precisely as the caster.

But most of all, the troller misses one of the most exciting moments in freshwater angling — the muskie's follow. Afraid of little or nothing in their watery world, the curious muskie often will cruise a short distance behind a lure being retrieved. Muskie fishermen watch for it. Sooner or later, it'll happen. The big fish will follow the lure like a puppy being led on a leash. One of two things will happen. The muskie will hit right at the boat or it'll stare at the fake meal and sink out of sight. Meanwhile, the angler will babble nonsense while his knees quiver like aspen leaves. And he'll thrash his lure around in Figure 8 patterns hoping the muskie will reconsider. The muskie seldom does.

(Photo courtesy of the In-Fisherman)

Proof that the muskie is an eating machine.

That alone is why I prefer casting. You can't eat muskie follows or mount them on the den wall, but they make fond memories.

Of course, there's no rule that says you can't do both. Most muskie fishermen do.

Speed and depth control are the two key ingredients to successful trolling. Assuming, that is, you've picked the right waters. Again weedbeds on points, bays, sunken islands with access to deep water are the places to start.

Speed is not particularly critical, except it should match the design of the lure being used so that the lure works properly. Depth control is achieved with the lure and speed. Most muskie trollers use a variety of diving plugs, such as the Cisco Kid, Swim Whiz, Rapala, Bombers, Hellbenders and others. The famed muskie bucktails also can be trolled. Many of these lures are designed to reach depths of 15 feet or so. Others are made to travel slightly under the surface or dive to 10 feet. The optimum depth is unknown until a muskie hits. And that hit will only come by trial and error trolling, varying the speed, depth, lure type and color. But it's interesting to note that spoons — the reliable takers of northern pike — do not rank high as catchers of muskies. Why I do not know. Spoons will take muskies, yet most muskie veterans go with other lure types.

In Minnesota, the muskie fisherman who likes to punish his arms, tire his shoulders and sweat and swear is a casting fanatic. Boy, is it fun. You've got to keep telling yourself that. Otherwise you'll quit too soon.

It only takes one cast to hook a muskie, etch a memory and land the most exciting fish in your life. It may be the first cast. Or, it could be the last of 10,000 casts. That's why you've got to be persistent to improve your muskie fishing odds.

Consider Chan "Doc" Cotton, the "Muskie Man" of Minnesota's Leech Lake, famous for its muskies. Doc Cotton once landed 108 legal-sized muskies in one summer of fishing. But lordly did he pay his dues. If Doc had any real secret, that was it. He never gave up.

A beginning muskie fisherman need only acquire

three, maybe four, different muskie lures for his casting debut. They are: a bucktail, a diving plug, a jerk bait and a topwater lure (optional).

The bucktail is the muskie fisherman's workhorse. If you can only afford one, make it black. The going quip among muskie veterans is that any color is good as long as it's black.

If you want a variety of bucktails, add the colors of yellow, red, and purple. White might be the next choice.

While you provide the casting and retrieving power, the bucktail does the rest of the work. They provide their own action, whether you crank them fast or slow. Doc Cotton retrieves his bucktails about as fast as the reel will take in line; other anglers prefer a slow, tantalizing action. Regardless, the bucktail is one of the greatest muskie-takers of all time.

The diving plug is the caster's tool for fishing at greater depths. But again, the plug provides its own action. Popular colors include perch-green, silver and yellow-black.

The diving plug is used most often along the deepwater edges of weedbeds, casted parallel and retrieved rapidly. Although the muskie usually hits the plug from the side the collision is impressive. But it's important to set the hooks hard. The muskie's strong jaws may otherwise grip the lure without being hooked.

The jerk bait perhaps symbolizes muskie fishing more than any other lure. Basically, a jerk bait looks like a small baseball bat with treble hooks. It is considered a lunker muskie lure and is most effective starting in late summer.

The jerk bait is fished as the lure's name implies. It's cast and then jerked slowly but rhythmically back to the boat. Imagine the antics of a very sick sucker that wanted to dive but was too weak to make it. That's just the kind of defenseless victim the muskie is looking for.

When the attack comes, you'll often see it with a jerk bait since the lure runs shallow. It's then time to set the hook hard. Not only once but twice or more.

As you might expect, the best jerk bait color includes black, either black back and white belly or all-black.

A selection of popular bucktail lures for muskies.

Sometimes cream colored or perch-colored jerk baits also are effective. But you can't really go wrong throwing black.

No doubt the epitome of muskie fishing is taking one of the giants on a topwater plug. All of the drama takes place before your eyes. You'll not only witness the strike. Sometimes you can see the charge as a wake builds on the surface and the muskie's huge forked tail surges toward the bait.

The color of a topwater bait probably isn't critical. Best that you stick with . . . you guessed it . . . black.

A topwater can be fished in various ways, whatever your imagination concocts in the forms of jerks and pauses. But the best topwater fishing I've ever witnessed was performed by Lloyd Bolter. Bolter tied on a black Globe and landed three muskies, the largest going about 26 pounds. His technique was to cast the Globe and then retrieve it full tilt, no pausing, no stopping. He didn't want to give the muskie time to think. Three of them didn't. They charged for the kill. When the third one was landed, Bolter, a Minneapolis fisherman, also was done. The lure was wrecked beyond immediate repair.

Now that you're well-armed with the basic weapons for facing the muskie challenge, what happens when you catch one? How do you handle such a good-sized fish?

Very carefully, my friends, very carefully. A muskie with a mouthful of hooks can be very dangerous. I know. I have two scars on a finger, one where the hook went in; one where it came out. Muskies should only be netted with a muskie-size net. Better yet, if you plan to keep the fish, knock it on the head before it comes into the boat.

Larry Bollig, a bewhiskered angler from Anoka, and I still have mutual nightmares about a dandy muskie he hooked one sunny afternoon. The fish had no sooner hit when Bollig, a big bear of a man, had the fish at boatside. We had no club. The landing net was built for crappies.

After some exciting, "What shall we do?" exchanges, we made the decision. Use the net. I scooped, the muskie stiffened out like a board and flopped neatly out of the net. Leaving the hooks behind. Two grown men started to cry. Originally, we figured the fish was about 20 pounds or so. But that's been awhile. Bollig and I both now agree the fish was at least a 30-pounder.

Of such are muskie dreams and mystiques made.

And therein is why the muskie is such a valuable member of Minnesota's fishing characters. Its trophy characteristics are unmatched. And as such, the muskie should be treated as a trophy, not as another meal in the frying pan.

That's why muskie enthusiasts preach the gospel of releasing muskies that are caught as under trophy size. A muskie carefully handled and unhooked will survive to grow and fight again.

Unfortunately, many well-meaning fishermen catch and kill muskies of 10 or 12 pounds. That's a nice fish, granted. But by muskie standards that's not a keeper.

If you choose to fish for muskies, set a goal. Once that's reached set another goal. And so forth. Those muskies that don't measure up should be released. Don't kill it just to impress your friends. If you tell a muskie addict you caught but released a legal muskie, he'll believe you.

He'll also know that you know what the "sport" in

sport fisherman is all about.

But be careful in removing the hooks. Carry a pliers and a sidecutters. If necessary, cut the hooks loose instead of tearing the muskie's jaw tissue. If the fish bleeds much, it's probably doomed.

If not, contribute something to the welfare and future of your own fishing. Release a muskie. Be a sport.

(Photo by Glen Lau)

When it's action you're after, muskies will oblige.

largemouth bass

ol' bucket mouth

Largemouth Bass/
Bucket Mouth

The largemouth bass has become the national super-star in freshwater angling.

In recent years, mature, responsible fishermen have gone dingy over the fish. They ride in $5,000 Bass boats; they wear Bass fishing clothes; they use Bass rods, reels, lures and they buy any gadget as long as it promises more Bass.

If you're good, you're called a Bassin' Man and you're a celebrity, of sorts, entering national fishing tournaments that pay thousands of dollars to the fella that catches the most Bass.

Much of the bass fanaticism has passed Minnesota by. The state's residents are mostly meat and potatoes fisher-men — walleyes and panfish.

Down south where the bass is king, the good ol' boys think of Minnesota in bass terms like they view Texans. They wear big cowboy hats but they got no cows. Minne-sota has water but no good ol' bass would dare live where it freezes.

Well, the good ol' boys are wrong.

Minnesota has super bass fishing, lots of bucket mouths. Except most Minnesotans don't know it. Nor would they give up their meat and potatoes if they found out. H. F. "Doc" Wellman, a deluxe tackle peddler, once pointed out that most of the lunker bucket mouths caught in Minnesota are caught by out-of-state visitors — southern fishermen.

That's changing. Slowly. Lordy, Minnesota even has bass clubs now and a few pot-money bass tournaments. A fishing buddy, Lynn Schultz, of Fergus Falls, might be called the "Father of Minnesota Bassin'." Lynn discovered the joys of the fish and Minnesota's bounty years ago. He preached about it in Jim Peterson's weekly *Outdoor News;* he placed an ad in his hometown paper to announce the formation of a bass fishing club.

Most folks probably thought he was nuts.

But, by golly, a few bass fishermen came out of the woodwork and Lynn founded the state's first bass fishing club, the Northstar Bassmasters.

Since then, Minnesota's largemouth bass has steadily gained admirers. And no wonder. There are bucket mouths, hawgs, anvil jaws, big mouths, popcorns, blacks, and Mr. Bass — all names for the largemouth bass.

You'll find bass widely distributed in the waters of Minnesota, except in some northeast lakes where the smallmouth bass roams. Despite their many differences, some anglers still confuse the two basses. The largemouth is most readily identified by the rather distinct lateral line along its sides. That and its big mouth. The corners of a largemouth's jaw extend past the eye whereas the smallmouth's jaws do not. The smallmouth also tends to be more golden in color and its eyes have a reddish hue.

And they inhabit different habitats. The largemouth fares best in lakes or the back channels of rivers. The smallmouth is more at home in the pools and riffles of Minnesota's rivers, although it does thrive in the rockstrewn waters of the northeast and in some central Minnesota lakes.

The largemouth bass is much more versatile, however. It can tolerate waters that are murky, warm, cold, clear, unpolluted or polluted. It will live in farm ponds, giant reservoirs or den room aquariums.

It will roam in 3-foot shallows or 20-foot drop-offs. It'll smack a hundred different lures or baits in a day. Or none at all. Or it'll nail one lure of one color and refuse all the rest.

Therein lies the key to the popularity of the largemouth bass. Every fishing trip is a new ball game. You can chase walleyes with leeches day in and day out and probably have success. Not so with Mr. Bass.

So — if you want to discover the magnetism of bass fishing, prepare yourself for an adventure. Bass anglers call it "finding the pattern."

The "pattern" is that unknown combination of a habitat, lure, color, speed, timing that will produce the bass on any given day. And it's that search for the pattern that makes bass fishing so interesting.

This facet of bass fishing is never more vivid than in a bass fishing tournament. Tournaments have been praised and criticized in debates over the propriety of competitive fishing. But fishing for money has proven one thing: the bass is the toughest competitor of all. I've watched some of the best bass fishermen in the country gather on the same waters. You'd think they would all take limits with the winner determined by who lucked into the largest fish. But that's not the way it works. In the same day, some of the "pros" will fill the boat; others will take a few and still others will be skunked outright. The next day, the results may be the opposite.

Why? It's the pattern. The pattern changes. The bass may move. They may want something flashy or something dull. They may want something fast or something slow. They might be energetic, they might be lazy. And on and on. Who knows? But the fisherman who unlocks the pattern is the only one who beats the largemouth bass.

In Minnesota the key to bass success is no different.

Everybody already knows one pattern. That bass tend to be sunrise and sunset fish, that they are feeding and therefore catachable. Who hasn't heard about the lone angler who paddled quietly into the silent lily pads on an early morn, armed with live frogs and lots of hope. Like some solitary watchman, he waits for the tell-tale gurgling sound of a lunker bass, slurping some meal near the grassy banks. Ever so gently, in slow-motion form, he pitches the wiggly frog in the fading ripples. And ... boom. In a flash, the gaping jaws of a largemouth sweep in the defenseless frog and the fight is on.

Yes, that's the classic picture of bass fishing. Go early or go late or otherwise forget it.

There is some truth to that. But bass fishermen these days don't suck their thumbs waiting for the sun to rise or set. Bass can be caught at any time of the day. Or night for that matter. It's just a matter of ... you guessed it ... finding the pattern.

Minnesota's bass fishing season — when the fish become legal catches — usually does not start until the last days of May. By then, the bulk of the bass spawning is well underway. You may also find some lakes areas marked with signs, indicating that certain places are off-limits to bass fishing until a later date. These areas are prime spawning grounds, protected to ensure that the bass spawning activities go on undisturbed.

The male bass during spawning is protective of the nest and will attack almost anything that comes near. Thus, the male is vulnerable to the hook. Without the paternal protection, the young bass or the eggs would be quickly eaten by marauding bluegills or perch. Fortunately, the bass is quite prolific. It is not necessary and no one expects every bass nest to be successful. If a few are protected as much as possible, the lake's bass supply will be plentiful.

In Minnesota, the bass spends spring, summer and fall in water less than 15-feet deep. There are exceptions, of course. Generalizing is dangerous, I know.

But as a rule of thumb, concentrate your search for bass in water less than 15-feet. I can only think of one instance where I caught bass deeper. And that was in 20-feet of water in a lake that was as clear as gin. Because of the water's clarity, the aquatic vegetation had enough sunlight to grow at that depth. (See Illustration)

Remember also that the bass is a cover freak. Cover meaning places to hide, stalk, lurk, rest or lollygag.

So already, on any given lake we've eliminated water deeper than 15 feet and water without cover. That leaves the shoreline weedbeds, reedy points, sunken islands with weedy tops.

If a bass has cover, the water depth is almost imimaterial. Remember that, too. For the following reason. A contented bass in Minnesota has no qualms about living in extremely shallow water. Like 3-feet deep or less. I know that's hard to imagine on bright, sunshiny days when your brows sweat just thinking about being outside. You'll want to believe that every fish in the lake is down in the cool, dark depths, hiding from the sun and the fishermen.

Not so folks. You might fish the shallows on just such a day and not get a strike. But those bass are not gone.

Where to find L.M. Bass

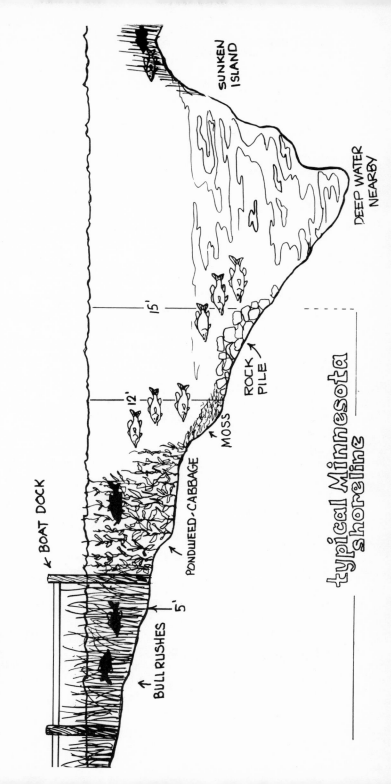

SUNKEN ISLAND

DEEP WATER NEARBY

15'

12'

ROCK PILE

MOSS

PONDWEED-CABBAGE

← BOAT DOCK

5'

BULL RUSHES

typical Minnesota shoreline

They're present. And if you hit the spot at the right time of the day ... with the right bait ... in the right way ... if you discover the pattern, you'll catch bass.

So let's have a closer look at bass cover. On a typical bass lake in Minnesota, you'll run into one of two types of cover designs. You'll find lakes with emergent bulrushes, cattails or other above water vegetation on the shallow flats or bays up to depths of about 5 feet. Beyond five feet, you're apt to find no weed growth or very sparse bunches. Think about that. If the bass seeks out cover, what choice does the fish have but to live within those 5 foot depths or less where the cover exists.

In other bass lakes, you find the usual shallow water emergent vegetation along with a band of underwater or submergent vegetation growing out into depths of 10 to 15 feet of water, depending on the water's clarity.

The bass then have a wider choice of locations. They may at times move up into the shallow flats to feed. Then, they'll retreat, moving back to the safety of deeper water and dense vegetation, often lingering on the outside edges.

At first glance, you might deduce that fishing lakes with less cover might be more productive since the bass has fewer places to hide. That's not necessarily so. Those lakes also may have much lower bass populations and they'll be concentrated in a small area or in many small areas. In that situation, they also can be hard to find. The best bass lakes are those with an abundance and variety of cover. You'll have more area to fish but there'll be more fish to find, too.

So you can see that bass fishing in Minnesota is a shallow water game. The aquatic weeds or the weedline (where vegetation stops growing) is structure to bass as drop-offs are to walleyes. Does that mean you can forget about such things as drop-offs or underwater points?

Granted a bass fisherman probably uses a depth map or depthfinder less than other fishermen. Still these fishing aids are helpful. It is not always possible to tell where the weeds stop (or start) by looking at a lake's surface. A depth finder will show such things clearly. If you still have trouble visualizing the weedline, drop floating buoy markers along the edge. Then cast or troll along those markers.

Of course, when the weeds stop growing, that means something in the underwater environment has changed. Usually, it's the depth. That means, there's a drop-off or a change in bottom. In other words, structure. The bass also is a fish whose behavior and haunts are regulated by structure.

But for bass, there's still another form of structure on almost every Minnesota lake. Man-made structure — boat docks, channels, marinas, bridge pilings, you name it. Some bass fishermen on Lake Minnetonka — a lake in the Twin Cities suburb surrounded by residential homes — fish nothing but the boat docks, boat basins and marinas. But no matter what they're called, to the bass they're cover.

Now that we know where the bass are apt to be, let's start fishing.

(Photo courtesy of Minnesota Department of Natural Resources)

Eight-year old Ginny Wettschreck holds "old bucketmouth," the superstar of sport fishing.

Bass On Live Bait

Allow me to reveal a prejudice: I think it's a shame to take bass with live bait. It wouldn't bother me if they outlawed the use of frogs, minnows, nightcrawlers, leeches, salamanders for bass fishing. You could still catch bass. The challenge would be greater but so would the fun. The very nature of the bass forces any serious bass fisherman to sharpen his skills, if he's limited to artificials. He must acquire casting marksmanship. He must know how to work each lure. He must develop a sense of touch to master plastic worm fishing, for example.

Live bait compromises these skills.

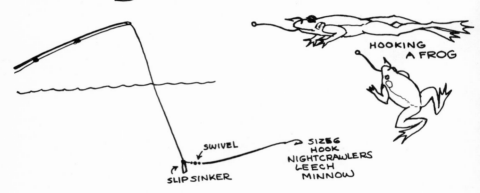

Not that you can't become a skilled live bait bass fisherman. Of course you can. But in the spirit of sport fishing, I'd encourage any bass angler to strive toward the exclusive use of artificials. Sure, there are times when the ONLY way to catch a bass is with live bait, particularly in cold water periods and following cold fronts. So what? So what if you get skunked sticking with artificials. Isn't it more important how you caught your bass, rather than how many? I think the fishing fraternity often forgets that.

I'm not saying that using live bait means you're some kind of a nitwit or a meathog. The tradition of pitching live frogs to unsuspecting bass is an old and respectable method of bass fishing. I've done plenty of it and I can't remember when I ever had a lousy time.

Live bait rigs (See Illustration), baited with nightcrawlers, leeches, crayfish, frogs and slowly trolled along the weedlines, around points and sunken islands and other bassy haunts are effective techniques.

Minnow and jig combinations or plain jigs also work well, trolled or casted into the same areas.

But you will soon find there are weedbeds and there are weedbeds. From a distance they look similar, particularly the stands of bulrushes or fields of lily pads. But to the bass, they are not the same.

You will note: some bulrush stands are thicker than others. Some grow in deeper water. Some have clean bottoms; others have a mixture of "junk" weeds entangled amid the bulrush stems. Basically look for the thickest stands in the deepest or shallowest water with the most "junk" weed intermixed. Same with lily pads. A nice pure field of lily pads with no other vegetation growing interspersed generally is poor bassin' water.

By now it should be obvious that weedless hooks are important, regardless of what bait is used. The weeds become less of a problem if you're trolling or casting on the outside edges, the deepwater edges, of a weedbed. But sooner or later, you'll find it necessary to pitch your bait smack dab into the jungle. So carry weedless hooks or lures.

Bass on Artificials

This is where the fun starts. Your choice of bass lures is infinite. No fish has stretched the imagination of lure inventors like the bass. You can fill three tackle boxes and still find enough "new" to warrant another tackle box.

Same with rods and reels. You could carry five rods and still not have enough variety in action to cover all possible needs. But you can make it with one rod.

The average bassin' man's rod has a rather stout butt and medium flexible tip. Most of his lures weight a ¼-ounce or more. To adequately cast lighter lures, you'll have to add another rod with a more flexible tip.

The most popular choice in reels is a free-spool casting reel. But if you can't handle that, you can do quite well with a medium-sized spinning or spin-cast outfit.

The choice of line for Minnesota bass fishing includes rather subjective judgments. Ten-pound test line is a good compromise choice. I know Harlow Ellsworth, the park Rapids "hawg" hunter, won't like that decision. Harlow fishes strictly for big bass. He uses big lures attached to heavy line, 20-pound test or more, and fishes in the thickest of the jungle. His one style of bass fishing lends itself to heavy line, however. For a variety of styles, 10-pound line should be adequate.

If we dumped all the bass lures into a pile and sorted them all into general categories, we'd end up with five piles: plastic worms, crank baits, spinnerbaits, spoons and topwater lures.

If you could choose but one, make it the plastic worm. This chunk of plastic is the greatest bass catching invention since the live frog. The fisherman who cannot fish a plastic worm is like a bird without wings. You won't get very far.

Properly rigged, the plastic worm is the most weedless lure available. Properly fished, it will take bass when most everything else fails.

The worm itself comes in a variety of shapes and colors. Some have straight tails, some curly. Some have legs, some don't. And so forth. Pick what you like. They'll all work.

Color is more important, however. Any assortment of worms should include the colors: black, blue, purple, grape and green.

You'll probably discover that black, purple and grape work best in most situations. In murky water, however, green often is effective. And in clear waters, blue may be best. That's why an assortment of colors are important. Later, you might want to add red, blue-white and other

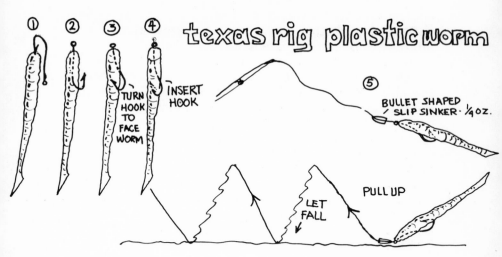

combinations.

The usual way of hooking a plastic worm is called a "Texas rig," (See illustration) which includes a ¼-ounce slip sinker and worm hook. There are variations, such as the jig-worm, which features a bare lead-headed jig with a worm threaded on the jig hook. No sinker is required with the jig-worm.

A plastic worm tossed into the water is rather useless unless it is given the correct action. Most lures provide their own bass-fooling gyrations. The plastic worm needs your help.

This is how it's done:

With the worm properly rigged, cast it toward the waters of your choice and let it sink. Hold the rod at a 10 o'clock position (straight up is noon) and reel in the slack. Now slowly raise the rod to 11 o'clock and pause. By raising the rod, you've lifted the worm slightly off the bottom. By pausing, you're letting the worm settle back to the bottom. Drop the rod again, reel in the slack and repeat. Basically, you're "pumping" the worm back to the boat, letting it rise and fall, rise and fall over the bottom, through the weeds, brushpiles or whatever. You can literally cast the plastic worm into any kind of garbage you can find and it won't "snag."

The bass almost always inhales the worm while it's falling. At the strike, you'll not hear bells, parades or snapping rods. You won't hear anything. And you won't feel anything unless you're alert. I can only describe the feel of a bass strike on a plastic worm as a "deadening thunk" or "tic" telegraphed up the monofilament. Also watch the line where it enters the water. On the strike you may see it jump or twitch. At that moment, drop the rod forward, reel in the slack and slam the rod back to set the hook. All of that should take a whole second. Some fishermen like to let the bass run with the worm for a second or two. That's okay. But underwater filming has proven that the bass inhales the entire worm on the initial strike. Bass don't have big mouths for nothing.

That's really all there is to worm fishing. You can vary the retrieve pattern, if you want. Change worm colors, shapes or whatever. But the basics remain the same. But don't give up. It takes practice to master plastic worm fishing. But it is well worth the price.

Crank baits are so named because you cast them out and crank 'em in. That's bassin' slang. If you saw a crank bait, you'd call it a lure or plug. And you'd be correct, too.

CRANK BAITS

But the hottest bass lures going are designed for fast retrieves and they are indeed cranked in. Most of the crank baits look like fat, pregnant plugs. They come in wild colors and in various designs. Some run shallow, 1 to 3-feet. Others go slightly deeper, 3 to 5, 5 to 7, 7 to 10, 10 to 12 and 12-feet and deeper. You'll want to have an assortment. Sometimes you'll be fishing the deep outside edge of a weedbed, so you'll need a lure that dives quickly and stays deep. Other times, you may want to crank a bait that runs shallow over top of sunken weedbeds. Get the picture?

I'm not convinced there is any standout color among the crank baits. But for starters, go with perch, yellow-green, and fluorescent orange or red.

When do you use crank baits? There is no one perfect time. Often the type of water you're fishing will determine if the use of crank baits is even possible. Most bassin' boys first pitch a worm and then follow with a crank bait or whatever.

Consider the crank bait as part of the arsenal you'll want ready in your search for the bass catching pattern of the day. And that goes for every lure in the box. Plastic worm fishing is "slow" — since the worm is bounced slowly — so you will not cover much water very fast with a worm. A crank bait, on the other hand, lends itself to covering a weedbed quickly to make contact with fish.

The spinnerbait is the shallow water version of a crank bait, so to speak. They don't look or act alike but the spinnerbait also can be used to fish spots quickly. Basically, you throw it and retrieve it. The spinning blade or blades and the pulsating plastic or rubber "skirt" on the spinnerbait does the rest. You can give a spinnerbait some action by letting it swim and sink, swim and sink. But a straight retrieve also will work, slow or fast.

The spinnerbait primarily is a shallow water lure, less than 10 feet. It seldom is used deeper because it sinks slowly (wasting time) and it generally is less effective than crank baits in deep water.

But lordy can the spinnerbait nail bass in the shallows. Although it doesn't look weedless, the spinnerbait can be cast into the thickest bulrushes or pulled through the cabbage weed tops with few hangups. Properly weighted, the spinnerbait — when pulled through the water — should ride vertically. A poorly-designed model will turn or roll. Get your money back.

Spinnerbaits are made with single, up-turned hook, dressed usually in colored skirt. Popular colors are: chartreuse, black, white, yellow or combinations thereof. I've had good luck with purple skirts, too. Or you can customize a spinnerbait by adding a pork rind, twister tail or plastic

SPINNER BAIT
ADD PORK RIND, OR
PLASTIC WORM
TO HOOK

SILVER SPOON   PORK RIND

worm to trail behind the hook. (See Illustration.)

In Minnesota, there is probably only one bass-catchin' spoon worth carrying. That's the old reliable Johnson Silver Minnow, which is weedless and versatile. You can fish the spoon like a lure, retrieving steadily. Or fish it like a plastic worm, letting it hop and fall through the jungle. And you can add plastic skirts, pork rinds or pieces of plastic worm.

Despite all the hoopla over "new" bass hook disguises, which hit the market every year, I watched Bill Dance, one of the nation's top professional bass fishermen, fish in the Bass Masters Classic with nothing but an old Johnson silver spoon. He finished as one of the leaders, too. Goes to show, some lures get old but never outdated.

Aside from its big mouth and fighting ways, the largemouth bass is most famous for its willingness to take things off the surface or in the air. Frogs, dragonflies, topwater plugs, you name it. Harlow Ellsworth swears he saw a big mama bass snatch a red-winged blackbird right off a lily pad one morning. I believe him. Bass have been known to inhale baby muskrats and ducks and possibly floating beer cans.

No doubt the first surface lure ever invented by a bass fisherman looked like a frog. For the floating frog, built in weedless fashion, remains as one of the favorites today. Twitch it or retrieve steadily. If the bass is looking up, he'll go.

Other surface baits were designed to imitate injured minnows, such as the Injured Minnow. Many have blades or scoops that gurgle or flutter making noises across the surface.

Still others, such as the floating Rapala, weren't particularly designed as a topwater bait. Yet, it works well. The floating Rapala, for example, dives when it's retrieved normally. But if it's merely twitched or popped, the life-like shape and action of the Rapala does the rest.

You'll hear about "buzz baits", which are modified spinnerbaits designed to sputter on the surface as it's retrieved rapidly.

All will work effectively if the bass is in the mood.

Bon Posz shows off a pair of dandy Minnesota largemouth bass.

Generally topwater fishing is best in early morning and late evening or on windless days when the water's surface is calm. Your popping, gurgling or sputtering topwater lure then may get the attention it deserves from Mr. Bass.

Topwater fishing produces the most dramatic action. And if I had my druthers, I'd take every bass on the top. No such luck, of course. Ranked against other bass fishing methods, topwater fishing is the poorest producer. It is the most exciting, however. In fishing, that's probably a fair trade.

No matter what lure is thrown (even the great plastic worm), there are two elements that can neutralize the most ambitious bassin' man.

Cold fronts and strong winds. Bass seem to be more sensitive to these elements than most other fish. A cold front is a weather phenomenon usually associated with high blue, cloudless skies and chilly breezes. Whatever, it can turn bass off almost completely. They won't chase nothing. Under those conditions, your best bet is to go with about 4-inch plastic worms (most are 6 to 8 inches long) or use live bait. And fish both extremely slow. During cold front conditions, you've got to beg a bass to bite.

Wind becomes a factor when it's blowing in on the shore you intended to fish. The wind, of course, stirs up waves. And both batter the downwind weedbed. I don't know the reasons but the bass in those wind and wave-struck shorelines get a case of lock jaw. Wind and waves sweeping across a point of underwater weedbeds may have the opposite effect, turning the bass on.

Wind also is a nemesis to the plastic worm fisherman. Since line watching and feel are important, the wind — billowing your monofilament — disrupts such communication and concentration. Whenever possible, cast downwind when you have no choice but to fish plastic worms in strong winds. Or better yet, throw a spinnerbait or crank bait, lures that make their own action and basically hook their own fish.

Pure, cold water also slows the bass down considerably. That's why few are caught through the ice. And most of them are taken accidentally.

But the largemouth is a great summer fish. When the walleye blahs start in August, the bass is still quite catachable and just as much fun. Some folks sneer at a bass filet. True, the bass cannot match the walleye in the frying pan.

So why fight the system. I release most of my uninjured bass to fight again ... or grow up. Big mama will go on the wall. In Minnesota, any bass over 5 pounds is bragging size.

A couple of final thoughts. You could pick any clear water bass lake and snoop in the shallows and not see a bass. You could then conclude that I'm crazy and no bass is going to be found in less than 3-feet of water. But if you checked out the shallows for 24 hours, you wouldn't say that. I've seen fishless shallows in one hour come alive with keeper-sized bass during the next hour. Bass have definite movement patterns. Sometimes they don't move, they just start feeling or get active.

I know of no way to forecast these movements. Some fishermen swear by the Solunar tables, fishing calendars or what-have-you. But in my book, the best method is to identify bass hangouts. Visit them and re-visit them. You'll pick up some fish. Or you'll hit a movement somewhere on the lake. And your fishing woes will be long forgotten.

And master that plastic worm. Once you do, the craze over bass fishing will be understood. And probably joined.

bronze beauty
smallmouth bass

Smallmouth Bass/
Bronze Beauty

The smallmouth bass is good for the angling soul.

Fiesty, muscular, trim, sporting, the fish is a picture of perfection.

And its chosen haunts in Minnesota encompass some of the most scenic, restful, wild, natural hideaways in the state. And some not so wild. For you can catch smallmouth in the heart of downtown Minneapolis under the traffic-laden bridges of the Mississippi River, an almost hidden asset in the Twin Cities.

I remember wading the river's edge for smallmouth bass just downstream from the Lake Street bridge while the morning rush hour traffic hummed overhead. It was kind of nifty ... pulling in scrappy smallmouth that were hidden among the urban masses.

The smallmouth bass is native to Minnesota, but its range has been expanded through highly successful stocking programs. It thrives in both lakes and rivers, although it is normally throught of as a fish of running water.

Not that that matters. The smallmouth simply is a fun fish to have on the end of a fishing line, regardless of where it's caught.

Or when. In Minnesota, smallmouth bass are catchable at all times during the angling season. If lakes don't produce, rivers will. Or vice-versa. A few hardy souls have discovered excellent smallmouth action just prior to the annual Ice Age. Fishing guide Rick James of Willmar, even looks forward to the chilly days of October and November when he takes live bait to the "smallies" on Green Lake in exchange for 3 to 5 pounders.

On Lake Minnetonka, famed for its largemouth bass and swamped by panfishermen, there's an avid minority of anglers who've discovered that smallmouth bass also lurk in the suburban waters. They seldom pursue any other fish.

Smallmouth fishing includes its own addictive

qualities. The fish is a renowned battler, almost always crashing to the surface to free its hooked jaws. And it will take live bait or artificials with almost equal vigor, including topwater lures.

On light tackle or ultra-light outfits, a 1 pound smallie will challenge your fish landing talents to the limit. However, there are other reasons for using lighter tackle for smallmouth than largemouth. The effective bait and lures for smallmouth are generally small and light, compared to the gluttonous-sized plugs used to fool the largemouth bass.

I'd recommend a 6 foot, medium-light action rod with a whippy tip. Or go to an ultra-light outfit. It'll come in handy for panfish as well. Six pound line is a good choice. Heavier line will shorten your casting distance with light lures. In addition, smallmouth usually are associated with relatively clear water, requiring the use of line of 6 pound test or less. Despite their fighting ability, smallmouth can be handled on light line since they are not usually caught within the jungles and brushpiles of a lake.

Smallmouth are to rocks what leaves are to trees. They'll always be together. Or almost always. I've caught smallmouth in bulrushes and cabbage (pondweed) patches also. But these two aquatic plant species normally grow in hard sand bottoms and rock often is present in the form of boulders or stones about the size of a lumberjack's fist.

Owing to the smallmouth's rocky environment, its natural food diet consists almost totally of crayfish and insects. Some minnows and leeches are inhaled for good measure.

That explains why the most successful live bait fishermen go with small minnows (preferably shiners) and leeches. Nightcrawlers also work well, however. All three baits may be fished on the usual live bait rig, featuring a splitshot or 1/8 to 1/4 ounce slip-sinker, swivel and size 8 hook. You can vary the length of your monofilament leader but 2 to 4 foot lengths are adequate. No steel leader, please.

Cast or slowly troll the live bait right along underwater

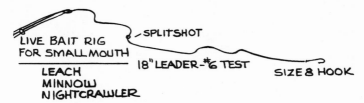

LIVE BAIT RIG
FOR SMALLMOUTH
SPLITSHOT
18" LEADER-#6 TEST
SIZE 8 HOOK
LEACH
MINNOW
NIGHTCRAWLER

points, through boulder fields or around sunken islands. You'll soon discover that the smallmouth's haunts also are a snag heaven as the rocks reach out and put a death grip on your slip-sinker. When you start losing enough tackle to threaten bankruptcy, try going to a single splitshot just big enough to take the bait down. Then troll extremely slow or anchor and cast from deep water to shallow. Or you can put on an extra heavy slip-sinker, say 1/2-ounce, and fish straight below the boat, slowly bouncing the sinker over the boulder tops. Going extra-light or extra-heavy will minimize your snagging headaches among the rocks. (See Illustration).

No matter. Do not present a live bait with much speed. Smallmouth are like bluegills. They like slow moving tidbits. I recall the time Bill Vint, a college buddy, and I were fishing smallies on Deer Lake by Grand Rapids. I was backtrolling along a rocky drop-off slowly but hurriedly. Bill and I had to quit fishing shortly.

"Well, let's get out of here," Bill said, quickly reeling in a nightcrawler. By chance, he happened to be watching as the nightcrawler rushed to the surface. Following but not striking were two or three smallmouth bass. Quickly, Bill dropped the nightcrawler back down into the watery depths. This time one of the smallies hit, a dandy 3-pounder. It wouldn't take the nightcrawler when it was moving fast, however.

Often the ideal technique is to cast the leech or minnow into the smallie's shallow haunts and let it lay. The smallmouth, which tend to roam amid the rocks, will usually find a still-fished bait within a short time.

Gary Roach, the Lindy-Little Joe fishing expert, won a bass tournament by simply flipping a leech into the shallows, then not moving it. Soon, the smallies became curious and moved in close to the leech. Finally, one of the bass would grab the bait. Gary was watching the whole thing with the aid of Polarized sunglasses. (Every angler should wear them. They cut the surface glare and allow clear vision for several feet underwater.) Gary's luck only ran out when another fisherman moved in and started casting repeatedly, spooking the smallmouth out of the shallow water.

Since the smallmouth feeds heavily on crayfish, it's reasonable to assume that a crayfish on a hook might be deadly bait. Crayfish will take smallmouth but the bait is not as effective as one might expect. Maybe we're using them in the wrong manner. Of course, crayfish are not carried by many bait shops and they're hard to gather on your own. That's another reason why they may be ineffective. They're not handy.

Personally, I don't worry about using crayfish. The artificial lures that resemble crayfish are deadly enough. Small 1/8th ounce jigs of brown, black, brown-orange or yellow are excellent choices.

Granted, it's risky pitching jigs into rock-strewn bottoms. You'll hook snags but you'll also hook smallmouth. The jig should be bounced easily over the rocks.

It's often best to add a small spinner to the jig, such as the Fuzz-E Grub Spin or the Ugly Bug Plus. The spinner tends to give the small jig more flotation so it may be retrieved slowly yet slightly above the snag-happy rocks.

You can make the jig and spinner almost suspend by keeping line pressure on the lure as soon as it hits the water. Then crank the reel slowly, never giving slack in the line. Let the spinner work, holding the lure in place like a helicopter.

Smallmouth bass seem to depend heavily on their eyesight to find food. So don't speed your lure through the smallie's hangouts. Give the smallmouth time to spot an easy meal. It won't take long.

A small jig tipped with a white piece of pork rind or short piece of plastic worm is also effective. Bob Cary, Ely's resident fisherman, guide, writer, canoe paddler and general philosopher, plays havoc on the smallmouth in the Boundary Waters Canoe Area with a small 1/16th or 1/8th ounce jig, tipped with 2-inch strip of yellow-colored plastic tubing. Or something like that. Cary never lets anybody memorize his secrets. He once led me to West Lake in the BWCA where we enjoyed nothing but the finest smallmouth action. There must be one hundred "West" Lakes in the BWCA-Quetico area.

While I didn't possess one of Bob's jig-worm concoctions, when the day ended I think we were even, fish for fish. (I must admit he did some paddling while I did more fishing.) My own "secret" lure was a non-secret. A Mepps spinner, probably the No. 1 selling lure in the world. Size 1 or 2 spinners are about perfect. Size 3 spinners start bordering on the size that smallmouth tend to refuse. At least that's been my experience.

A collection of top smallmouth bass lures, clockwise from the top: Mepps No. 2 spinner, small spoon, Vibrotail jig, Ugly Bug Plus, Rapala.

Spinners with plain or dressed hooks work fine. But if I had to choose from the dozens of spinner designs, it would come down to this: A No. 2 gold blade Mepps with a fox squirrel tail dressing on a single hook, not a treble hook. Why a single hook? Less snags from a practical viewpoint. The other reason sounds like bragging. But I've had such fantastic luck with the above-mentioned lure, the treble hook becomes a burden when catching and releasing dozens of bass in a day. Yes, I said dozens. And you don't have to go to some mysterious "West" lake to find such action. A couple of seasons ago, Cary and I simply fished in Basswood Lake, the most popular angling waters in the popular BWCA. We caught smallmouth by the dozens there, too. Right where thousands of canoeists would later paddle by.

Small crank baits or plugs also belong in any smallmouth bass angler's tacklebox. The floating models particularly work ideally over shallow, rocky reefs as a topwater or subsurface lure. One of the few times my favorite Mepps spinner failed to match any other lure occurred one day on Lake of the Woods with Ron Weber, the Rapala man. Ron was testing a new-colored Rapala that is best described as bathroom blue. The smallmouth bass absolutely would not leave the lure alone. I caught a few, but Ron took many. The color definitely was a factor because other Rapalas of the same size but different color did not work as well.

You'll find it's important to experiment with color when chasing the smallmouth. I've seen times, for example, when a copper colored spinner blade on a small jig and spinner vastly out-performed the usual silver or chrome spinner blade. The old adage: dark days, dark lures; bright days, bright lures often holds true for smallies.

Strangely, the conventional spinnerbaits — those used so effectively on largemouth bass — seldom impress the smallmouth bass. It's probably the size. There's no doubt that smallmouth bass go for smaller lures than their bucket mouth cousins.

I have, however, hooked nice smallmouth when fishing

for muskies with huge jerk baits, of all things. I wouldn't try to take a smallie limit that way. But it was interesting that the smallmouth would even consider such a mouthful. Keeps the suspense in fishing.

As you can see, smallmouth do not require a vast variety of lures or sizes. Small jigs, jig-spinners, spinners and a few miniature crank baits and plugs will take care of almost any smallmouth fishing situation. I have, at times, intentionally switched to all four lure types during a day of smallmouth fishing and enjoyed near-equal success.

Of course the key to any lure's success is where it is used.

In Minnesota's northeast region where the smallmouth bass abounds in the vast waterways, the lakes are surrounded by rocks and trees. There's rocks on the shores, rocks in the shallows and rocks in the depths. There's rock in one form or another everywhere. Since smallmouth like rocks, does that mean the smallmouth are everywhere?

You really didn't think the answer would be that simple, did you?

You could cast both arms off, fish in rocks every minute, and never catch a smallmouth. That's because the smallies like some rocks better than others.

In the northeast lakes, the smallmouth is not a deepwater fish. It will be found on or near shallow areas — bays, sunken islands, reefs, underwater points or shoreline flats. The more shallows, the more smallmouth. There are miles of rock-strewn shorelines in the northeast lakes that look good but aren't because shallows break too quickly into deep water. Or the nature of the rock, giant tilted slabs, car-sized boulders, do not offer the smallmouth food or cover.

When fishing small northeast lakes, I've often fished the entire circumference of the lake just because it seemed convenient. Such exercises gradually revealed clues as to what rocks held bass and what rocks didn't. After awhile, I could look ahead and predict what the results might be.

In early season smallmouth fishing, the key was to find shallows with small rounded rocks interspersed with

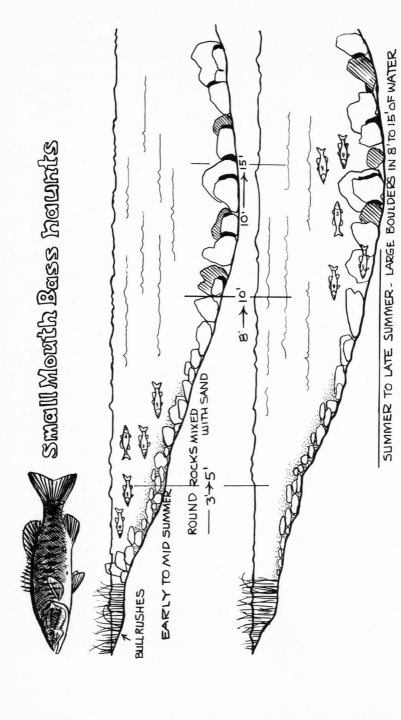

Small Mouth Bass haunts

BULLRUSHES

EARLY TO MID SUMMER

ROUND ROCKS MIXED WITH SAND — 3' → 5'

8' → 10'

10'

15'

SUMMER TO LATE SUMMER - LARGE BOULDERS IN 8' TO 15' OF WATER

sand. The rocks ranged from about fist-size to basketball-size. These were shoreline areas. But the farther such areas extended from shore the more fish it produced.

Shallow bays of sand, interspersed with a few boulders, with tree trunks and branches along the water's edge also are hotspots, particularly during the spawning time. Such bays can be checked out easily, since the bass often can be seen cruising against the light sand background. Active smallmouth nests, which show up as large, round white spots on the bottom, also are easily spotted.

Gene Groth, of Grand Marais, and I once hit a small-mouth lake on the Gunflint Trail on the 4th of July. To my surprise the smallies were still spawning, although the bulk of it appeared to be over. Moving quietly into sandy coves and bays, we could almost pick out the smallmouth we intended to catch. They were easily spooked, however, in the crystal clear waters. But with long casts and 4 pound test line, we managed to catch and release more than 75 bass in about five hours.

From mid-to late-summer in the northeast lakes, the smallmouth will utilize slightly deeper water, such as sunken islands, reefs and flats scattered with small boulders in about 10 to 12 feet of water. Small islands of boulders often give visual clues that the adjacent bottom is similar. Often the proper depth is where the bottom, itself, fades from view, although you still can faintly see the tops of the round boulders. Visual references are, of course, quite dependent on the clarity of the water.

Again, the important consideration is the amount of shallows available. One small rock island with 30, 40 feet of water on all sides will not be productive. Generally, pick the shallowest part of the lake where there's an abundance of small tree-covered or bare, rock-covered islands and humps. In fact, think in terms of what the crayfish and minnow life seek. Like other predator fish, where you find the food, you'll find the smallmouth.

The smallmouth's haunts are somewhat different further south in Minnesota, however. The abundance of rocks no longer are present, there's more vegetation and more sand. In some cases, water clarity is changed and the water temperatures are higher in the summer season. Still, where you do find rocks you'll probably find the small-mouth, preferably the deep sunken islands that may top out 15 to 20 feet below the surface. Generally, you'll have to fish deeper, 25 to 30 feet or more, and fish with live bait, such as leeches, for much success. Earlier in the season, shallow rock and sand humps, like those found on Lake Minnetonka, are worked effectively with live bait or artificials, such as jigs tipped with minnows or nightcrawlers.

Minnesota's rivers may represent the best smallmouth fishing opportunity in the state. On an average, the smallies may run slightly smaller in a river but not necessarily. The St. Croix and Upper Mississippi are quite capable of yielding 5-pounders or better. And those are trophies by any standard. The largest smallmouth I've known to come from a river went better than 7-pounds. That trophy was yanked out of the St. Croix River by a fisherman who couldn't bring a stuffed fish in the house. So the fella didn't have much choice. He butchered the best fish he'll probably ever catch.

Dan Gapen, the Big Lake tackle-maker and river man, was the first to show me the untapped smallmouth action in Minnesota's rivers. Gapen and I floated the upper stretches of the Mississippi, above the Twin Cities. We'd pause by the pools or deepwater banks and cast Ugly Bugs or Hairy Worms (jig-worm combination) into the slow moving current. Along the grassy banks, topwater lures, such as the Hula Popper, worked well. But the banks had to be grassy. Therein was a lesson. Smallmouth hanging by the grass banks had been conditioned to expect frogs or grasshoppers or other food on the surface. Bang, they'd hit. But along muddy or high banks, topwater lures were seldom touched.

But rivers offer more than just another opportunity to catch smallmouth. Finding smallmouth is greatly simplified in a river. Rivers normally aren't exceptionally deep so the bass don't have any choice but to be relatively shallow. Rivers reveal good fishing spots to the angler who knows how to "read" what the river is saying. For

(Photo courtesy of Dan Gapen)

Dan Gapen shows why he finds river fishing so exciting.

example, smallmouth may hang out in deep riffles, in pools or on the edge of river eddies. The bank of a river also may reveal what bottom lies below particularly in the slow moving stretches of river. I know of an area of the St. Croix that features mud banks and sandbars primarily. But on short stretches, the bank will be composed of rock outcrops. You'll find the smallmouth among the rocks. But as soon as the rock bank disappears so does the bass fishing.

Reading the river involves noting how the bottom features — rocks, boulders, deadheads (logs) — disrupt the surface. A smooth river surface may be deep water or shallow sand. Riffles and rapids are familiar and pools form below them.

But while rivers often reveal likely fishing spots, the constant current often spoils the anglers best catching plans. Somehow your lure never goes where you expected or wanted it to go. Or it won't go down, held on the surface by the rush of the current and the resistance of your line.

The trick is to always cast upstream or across the current and let the lure tumble or ride downstream. In other words make the current work in your favor. The only time I cast downstream is on small trout streams and then only when I'm using small spinners. River pools can be fished in about any direction unless there's a current or

In Minnesota, the smallmouth bass is typically found in the pine shrouded lakes of the northern forests.

eddy. In that case, make the casts against the current.

Smallmouth may be found at both the head or tail end of a pool.

About the only time rivers are not a wise choice is during high water or flood conditions. The high water makes reading a river quite difficult since the bottom obstructions are now further away from the surface. In addition, flooded rivers are usually quite murky, full of food and somewhat dangerous to the angler unfamiliar with powerful current.

The best river fishing usually is in mid through late summer when the snow melts and heavy rains of spring are long gone downstream. Then, the river is normal or below normal levels. The current is readable and friendly and the bass have moved into normal river haunts.

Jigs and jig-spinner combinations again are the river angler's best smallmouth weapons. The colors that work in lakes also work in rivers with a slight edge to black or brown. The current, not the angler, provides most of the action for the jig. As it should.

Again make the current work for you, leading the bait past the nose of smallmouth stationed within the deep cuts or behind boulders or in the pools and eddies.

Aside from heavy rains, other elements that affect smallmouth bass fishing in lakes are not as noticeable in rivers. Particularly cold fronts, wind and warming water temperatures. In rivers, the constant mixing of water ensures that the temperature of river water is pretty much the same from top to bottom.

It doesn't take much time to appreciate river smallmouth fishing. But it does take time to experience the best fishing that rivers can offer.

Clearly, Minnesota's smallmouth fishing in running water is vastly overlooked and possibly underrated. But it's never dull. Rivers constantly change, season to season, week to week. Fish often move a lot. Every float trip or wading exercise will be different. But there will be smallmouth to catch.

That never changes.

the beau brummells
trout

Trout/
The Beau Brummels

Minnesota's trout and salmon — sleek, trim and well-dressed — are the least publicized assets in a state that likes to boast of its fishing.

Must be a classic oversight. Surely, Minnesota has nothing to apologize about. With more than 1,500 miles of trout streams, dozens of trout lakes (including some 140 reclaimed trout lakes) and a healthy chunk of frigid Lake Superior, Minnesota has more than its share of cold water.

In fact, Minnesota possesses the most inland lake trout water outside of Canada and Alaska. And the state's potential for developing additional cold water lakes for rainbow trout is enough to give any fisherman visions of sugar plums dancing in his head.

While state fisheries experts often worry about the effects of pollution, habitat destruction, and fishing pressure on such fish as walleyes, the outlook for trout in Minnesota has steadily improved in past years.

The sea lamprey, which destroyed the lake trout fishing in Lake Superior, has been controlled. New fish toxicants and technical know-how have helped reclaim northern lakes for trout. Dedicated fish managers, like Mel Haugstad, have worked diligently in the limestone bluff country of Minnesota's southeast to stablize the stream banks, create trout habitat in the pasture streams and stimulate the return of natural trout spawning.

A new multi-million dollar trout and salmon hatchery on Minnesota's North Shore of Lake Superior promises to provide the necessary hatchery stock to ensure the steady improvement in the state's trout and salmon programs.

Minnesota's trout streams are roughly located in the southeast, central and northeast portions of the state.

The southeast, a land of hardwood timbers, limestone bluffs and pastoral, Little Switzerland valleys, provides strictly brown trout fishing. Most of the browns are sustained by stocking from the Lanesboro Trout Hatchery, although there are native browns in some streams.

Brown trout also are the main quarry in the central Minnesota trout rivers, which wind sleepily amid the alder thickets and popple forests.

Minnesota stocks few rainbows in streams (except rivers emptying into Lake Superior) because of the rainbow's penchant for migrating to waters where its chance of survival is nil. (The southeast streams, for example, eventually empty into the Mississippi River, which is not trout-supporting water.)

In the northeast, a land of spring-fed brooks, spruce swamps and timeless beaver dams, native brook trout abound in its forest-shrouded waters. Some rainbows also are present in the backroad streams but most have been stocked in deep, cold lakes.

Lake Superior adds two varieties of trout fishing: the lake, itself, where anglers troll or cast from shore; and steelhead fishing, the spring spawning run of rainbows up the many North Shore streams that empty into the big lake.

Last, but not least, is the lake trout fishing, which starts from the blue waters of the Grand Rapids region to the stained lakes of the Boundary Waters Canoe Area.

There are some scattered trout lakes or streams in the state's western regions and even one marginal trout stream near downtown Minneapolis.

So — if you've got a hankering to match wits with a trout, Minnesota has the intellectual fishing grounds.

My own angling teeth were cut on Mississippi River bluegills followed by Livingood Springs trout. That's like jumping from grade school to university post-graduate studies. I didn't catch many trout in those early attempts but I spooked the scales off a bunch of them.

Most novice fishermen don't give a trout enough credit. They stomp up to the bank and throw out a gob of worms big enough to choke a starved robin. They use monofilament line the size of baling twine tied to a shark hook.

Danged if some of them don't catch trout. I blame trout stocking for that insult to a trout's intelligence. Sometimes streams are intentionally stocked with more trout than the stream's food supply can support. So, the trout get hungry, careless and downright stupid.

Minnesota's trout managers try to avoid that. They're all for catching trout but they'd like to see a little skill and savvy required to do it. Hence, the stocking trips are carefully scheduled so all the trout don't get dumb at once.

Trout fishing is famous for an eternal quest called mastering the art of fly fishing. About 8 out of every 10 fishing books written are about fly fishing for trout. I don't know who's buying them all but somebody must be. I see no need to rehash all of the ins and outs of using a flyrod, matching the hatch or keeping the hackles dry.

Rather, let's cover the basics of trout fishing in streams and lakes with emphasis on live bait and artificials; information about lake trout and Lake Superior angling methods; and a diatribe about steelhead fishing in Minnesota's streams (which is a perverted version of fly fishing).

Fly fishing is, of course, the epitome of trout angling. And Minnesota's trout are just as willing to rise to a well-placed dry fly as their Montana brethren. If you have not tasted the challenge and thrill of fishing flies, then I urge you to give it a try. But to offer a short course within these pages is not practical.

Read what I'm about to divulge in the following pages.

Then, faster than you can say "Sparse Gray Hackle", you will be on your way to becoming a fly fishing snob.

Minnesota's trout are no different than anyplace else. They are suspicious, spooky and possess excellent eyesight. That means that any hooked offering sent to a trout must arrive naturally and well-camouflaged.

For most stream and lake fishing (except steelhead), monofilament line no heavier than 4-pound test is recommended. Go ahead, use 6-pound line if you want but I wouldn't. The need for light line means you want a light-action rod with a spinning or spin-cast reel. An ultra-light outfit, which works fine for panfish and smallmouth, will serve your trout fishing needs, too.

In trout fishing, everything else is small. Use small split-shot when you need weight and use small hooks, sizes 10, 12 or 14 for all live bait.

hooking live baits for stream trout

SALMON EGG HOOK

SALMON EGG

OR

NIGHTCRAWLER OR WORM

GRASSHOPPER

LIVE BAIT RIG

SMALL SPLITSHOT

2#4 TEST LINE

12" TO 18" LEADER

SIZE 10-14 HOOK

Once you accept light line, small hooks and small lures, you've got half the battle won. I realize it takes luck to land a 3 or 4-pound trout on 2-pound line. But if you go armed to "horse" trout, your chances of fooling that 4-pounder are nil to begin with.

Trout streams and lakes are notoriously clear. Except for the riffles, you can see just about everything on the bottom. And if you don't see any trout in one stretch of stream, you might as well walk up to the next pool. Right?

Wrong, thunderfoot.

Trout have imaginative hideaways. They can glide under banks, logs, rocks, moss, grass — places you'd swear weren't big enough to hide a dime.

Don't let your eyes deceive you. Besides that, whenever you can see a trout, chances are it can also see you. Unless you approach low and from the rear.

In Minnesota, the popular baits for trout include small live minnows, nightcrawlers, earthworms, salmon eggs, grasshoppers, miniature marshmallows and canned corn. (see illustration) Yes, corn. Some people buy their bait in a supermarket instead of a bait shop. Crayfish tails, slices of chub meat and other weirdo concoctions also work. Oh, how I know.

In boyhood days, while I toyed with spinners and flies — and began to think of myself as a trout fishing aristocrat — my father ventured to the local trout stream to fish the bridge hole. First, he caught a small chub with a piece of worm. Then, he sliced off a slab of white chub meat, slipped it on a hook and plunked the whole thing under the bridge.

He came back home with a 23 inch brown.

Thus, I sneer at no one's choice of live bait.

My Uncle Bob was an accomplished fly fisherman, however. He could handle a wet fly as good as I've ever seen. One gray, muggy morning, Uncle Bob and I were fishing trout. He went to one pool; I walked to another. Suddenly, I heard him yell for me. He had had a good-sized brown take a swipe at his fly. And he wanted me to watch the next time he sent the fly into the big brown's lair. On the very next cast, the brown was on, a dandy 18-incher. I noted what fly Uncle Bob was using and started rummaging through my own fly collection.

About then, it started to sprinkle. A few minutes later it was pouring. Uncle Bob shuffled upstream to the next pool. Shortly, he yelled for me again. This time the trout was already hooked. He just wanted me to watch the fight. It was another nice brown, 14 or 15 inches long.

But he didn't take the second fish on a fly. The downpour already had sent muddy trickles of water into the blue of the trout stream, an addition that didn't go unnoticed by Uncle Bob.

Seeing the muddy water pour into the pool, Uncle Bob quickly switched to live bait, a single, fat nightcrawler. On the first drift, his switch paid off.

A fly fishing purist might scoff at Uncle Bob's idea of how to fool trout but the reasoning remains sound. That's knowing how and when to present your hooked bait to a trout. Uncle Bob tied on a nightcrawler because he suspected the trout would be looking for such goodies amid the muddy run-off water.

A trout fisherman also must "read" a stream for clues as to where trout might be lurking and to use the current to deliver the bait. That is a learned skill and obtained only with experience and practice. Generally trout prefer the quiet pools, deep riffles, undercut banks and so forth.

Worms or nightcrawlers are the live bait angler's basic trade with minnows a close second. Live bait may be fished with a small bobber. But usually the idea is to drift the bait naturally, using a small splitshot about the size of a BB to keep the bait down. The hook should be hidden as much as possible.

The trout's strike often is not vicious. The bait, tumbling slowly in the current, will merely stop. Then, the trout may take line when returning to its lair to finish the meal. That's the time to set the hook.

In lake fishing, the rainbow trout is somewhat of a puzzle. It can be found almost any place, near shore, near islands, near drop-offs or near nothing. The trout's structure in a lake is based more on water temperature than anything else. That's why a trout — in a clear, cold lake — may indeed use all sides and all depths of its watery home.

The angler's best technique is to troll or drift, covering as much water as possible and experimenting with depths. With any luck at all, you'll soon discover that a particular shore or bay or point may produce more strikes than other areas.

Again many lake anglers use bobbers effectively in lakes to control the depth of their bait.

Otherwise, the presentation of the bait — utilizing light line and small tackle — remains the same in a lake or a stream.

Aside from flies and live bait, a trout fisherman in Minnesota may use a vast selection of "hardware," spinners, spoons and small, trout-designed plugs. Among the more popular selections are Mepps, Colorado and Hildebrandt spinners, Daredevle spoons and the tiny Flatfish. In most cases, the smallest sizes made by those manufacturers are best for trout.

Scenery, solitude and streams is what trout fishing is all about.

Lures work equally well in lakes or streams. In flowing waters, most artificials are cast downstream or across the current and reeled upstream ... imitating the swimming action of a minnow. Live baits, of course, are cast upstream or across the current and allowed to drift with the current.

Although trout water is normally clear, you'll seldom see the strike before it's actually over. The trout can move "as quick as a flash."

In lakes, artificials may be trolled or cast. To add weight to a lure for trolling, place an adequate sinker about 4-feet ahead of the lure. A habitual troller may go to lead-core line or purchase "downriggers" to keep the lure at extreme depths.

The speed of trolling generally isn't critical. In fact, trout tend to be gullible for fast-moving lures. If you give a trout too much time to examine your false meal, its sharp eyes may detect something ... well, fishy.

Minnesota's Brookies

Almost every stream in northern Minnesota with a steady supply of cold water is occupied by native brook trout, considered to be the most colorful of all the trout.

Brookies, measured by trout standards, also may be the dumbest in the family. Nor do they reach giant sizes. A 10-incher is a nice one.

Nevertheless, the brook trout has its own fraternity of addicts. The fish is a favorite of fly fishermen and anglers who enjoy creeks and streams away from the maddening crowds. In northeast Minnesota, many of the brookies haunts are guarded by clouds of mosquitoes and jungles of alder sufficient enough to discourage a bull moose.

The brook trout addict won't be denied, however. Armed with a short flyrod or ultra-light outfit, he'll charge through the boondocks with his trusty box of tied flies, spinners or can of worms.

I once joined a brookie zealot as the mosquitoes and black flies helped carry us over windfalls and spruce swamps to a small, grassy creek no bigger than a street gutter. While it was no place to swing a fishing rod using normal contortions of the body, one could with a bit of ingenuity get the fishing line close to the water.

The brookie addict soon wandered off to a thicker part of the creek bank. Suddenly, he began to whoop and holler. First I figured the mosquitoes had finally pushed him to the initial stage of insanity. But there was too much joy in his shouting. I crashed through the underbrush to find him on his knees in a praying position. He was holding aloft with two hands a 13 inch brook trout. A man nuts with joy.

Don't expect to get much help in finding brook trout hotspots. The brookie fraternity is a tight-lipped bunch. While many brook trout streams and creeks are marked on maps of the Superior National Forest, for example, the many beaver dams that may also hold trout are unknown except to the angler who finds them. Once located, brookies are the easiest trout to catch on live bait, primarily worms or nightcrawlers. Grasshoppers work well when available. And if you can thread mosquitoes on a hook, you'll have plenty of them, too.

Lakers of the Inland Waters

If it wasn't for ice fishing, Minnesota's lake trout might rank as the state's most underfished sport fish.

Except for early spring and late fall, the lake trout in Minnesota's inland lakes (excluding Lake Superior) are creatures of extreme depths. And few summer anglers go after them.

During the open water season, some lake trout are taken in May when the northern waters still are cold and the lake trout are lingering on the rocky reefs. Come fall, the trout will return to the reefs to spawn. However, Minnesota's lake trout fishing season on the inland lakes usually ends in late September prior to the spawning run.

Although lake trout are not as "line shy" as other trout, it's still a good idea to use light line, 4 to 6-pound test.

In early season, lakers often are caught on live minnows, such as shiners, trolled along the rocky reefs. Other live baits are less effective.

The best artificial lures may have different shapes or designs but they'll almost always be white or silver in color. White jigs, silver spoons and silver-blue plugs are good choices. Sometimes plugs and spoons of fluorescent red are worth trying.

As the lake surface temperatures rise, the lake trout descends to the cooler depths to feed on smelt, tullibees, whitefish, herring and other deep water fishes. You'll note the lake trout's eating preferences are composed of fish that are silvery in color. Hence, lures of the same color are effective for mid-summer fishing.

During the summer, the lake trout will roam in depths from 30 to more than 100 feet deep. The proper depth to fish can only be determined by trial and error, however.

There's also the problem of trying to troll with a lure at 50 or 75 feet. Sinkers weighing several ounces can be used but then depth control is difficult. And if you do catch a laker, reeling in the fish and the heavy sinkers is like fighting a bucket of water.

Some anglers use wire line or lead core line to reach the depths but those aids also take some of the sport out of landing a fish.

downriggers for trout

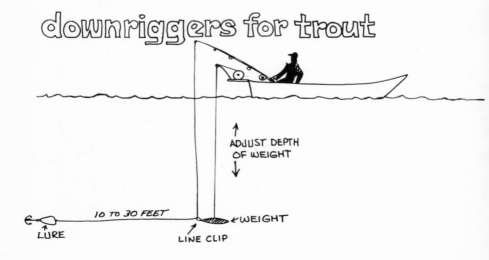

ADJUST DEPTH OF WEIGHT

10 TO 30 FEET

LURE

LINE CLIP

WEIGHT

Undoubtedly, the best way to go is with a downrigger. A downrigger is a giant reel of cable and a heavy lead ball. Your fishing line is snapped to the ball and lowered to whatever depth you want. (See Illustration.) The lure then trail behind the ball at whatever distance you want. When a laker strikes, the impact pulls your fishing line out of a clip on the ball. Then, your line is free and you can play the fish as if it was hooked in shallow water.

Downriggers — long familiar to saltwater anglers — are effective devices for finding deep-cruising lake trout in Minnesota.

Downriggers are not cheap toys, however. So — unless you plan to do a lot of deep water fishing, they are not a practical investment. Despite the costs, a couple of fishing buddies, Jay Anderson and Jim Cook, decided to explore downrigger fishing potential in Minnesota. So far they haven't been disappointed. They've used downriggers for lake trout in the northern lakes and Lake Superior. But most surprisingly, they've caught walleyes on Mille Lacs while trolling Rapalas with downriggers. The future of such fishing tools on inland waters may be just in the making.

More lake trout are taken through the ice in Minnesota than by any other method. The advent of the snowmobile has taken anglers back into lake trout lakes that once were isolated by the deep snows of winter. Nothing is isolated anymore.

Finding lake trout under the ice again is mostly a trial and error technique. Shoreline drops or deep water holes between islands are good places to start searching. Lake trout normally don't roam much. Hence, lake trout hotspots once found will be good season after season. A newcomer is then best-advised to follow the crowd.

Lake trout are scavengers as well as predators. As a result, many ice anglers used dead bait with good results. Smelt, ciscoes, lake herring — kept frozen until ready to use — are popular. In most cases, the dead bait is threaded on special hooks. (See Illustration) and fished on or near the bottom.

The lake trout is a slow eater. It will pick up a dead bait and run at a snail's pace. Patience is required of the angler. Often minutes will pass before the laker has consumed the bait. If you set the hook too soon, you'll get nothing.

The most effective artificial lures include airplane jibs, heavy spoons, and sonar jigs. (See Illustration) White, silver or fluorescent red colors usually work best. The airplane jig is so named because it has wings, designed to move the jig in a circular pattern when it's pumped up and down on the end of a fishing line. Sonar jigs flutter and

Ice fishing lake trout

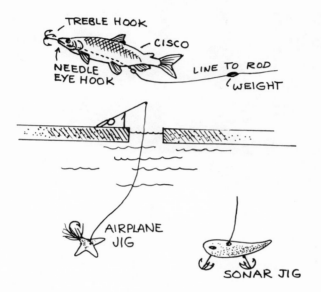

vibrate, imitating a minnow on its death bed. Both lures require your constant attention since their action is dependent on your pumping action at the other end of the line.

Sometimes it helps to add a piece of "cut bait" — a slice of cisco or chub meat — to whatever lure used.

Because of the depth lake trout may roam, the conventional ice fishing sticks are exchanged for a short rod and reel. You may need 100 to 200 feet of line to adequately fish for lakers. That much line is more easily handled on a reel. In addition, lakers are active battlers under the ice and you have to give line fast. That's difficult to do when your fishing line is wrapped on an ice fishing stick.

With expressed joy, Ron Peterson nets a dandy lake trout for Ted Burger. Lake trout are making a comeback on Minnesota's inland sea, Lake Superior.

Comeback of Lake Superior

Not many years ago, Lake Superior was a fishing desert, pretty to look at but lousy to fish.

It was Minnesota's version of a dead sea. Superior's once famed population of lake trout had been decimated by the greed of commercial fishermen and the stupidity of engineers who built the waterways to permit the invasion of the sea lamprey from the Atlantic Ocean. The lampreys killed the big spawning lakers and the fisherman's nets were uncontrolled. Steelhead (migratory rainbow trout) also fell victim to the blood-sucking lampreys as did other trout species.

Soon, the commercial lake trout fishermen were gone, An industry with nothing to sell must die.

However, the lamprey continued out of control as attempts to eradicate the pest failed. Fisheries scientists finally achieved a breakthrough when a chemical was developed that selectively killed the young lampreys in the streams where they hatch.

Gradually, the lamprey population was knocked back. Never eliminated but severely controlled.

Since then, Lake Superior has been the center of a massive trout stocking effort, led by the U.S. Fish and Wildlife Service, Minnesota, Michigan, Wisconsin and Canada.

By the millions, lake trout, rainbows, browns and several salmon species were dumped into the big lake in an effort to restore the sport and commercial fishing.

Today, Minnesota's share of Lake Superior harbors more lake trout than prior to the lamprey eel invasion. Coho and chinook salmon have been added and the lake's steelhead populations also are on the increase.

In short, the angling future on Lake Superior is now. And more anglers are beginning to discover the "new" hotspot, trolling out on the big lake or casting from shore.

Lake Superior is not your everyday fishing lake, however. It is a cold sea, capable of sinking ocean-sized vessels. Commonsense and boating know-how are important. Boating far from shore without a craft equipped with a compass, marine radio and other safety gear is not advised.

Fortunately, it isn't necessary to fish far out on the lake. Nor is it necessary to fish deep. Throughout most of the fishing season, most of the trout and salmon are catchable near the surface because of the lake's cold water temperatures.

Most trollers use spoons and plugs. Popular colors are silver, blue, flourescent red, white. The surface lures are trailed directly behind the boat or trolled with the aid of "outriggers" — balanced boards that carry the lure out to the side of the boat. Downriggers also are utilized to reach deeper waters.

It is not necessary to have a fortune in equipment to sample the fishing in Lake Superior. During calm seas, conventional small fishing boats may be used to troll the big lake, particularly around the mouths of incoming streams.

Shore fishermen often cast from the same spots as the trout are attracted to the stream mouths for food. Again, the casting fishermen use spoons and plugs of bright, flashy colors.

Minnesota attempted to develop its own coho salmon program along the North Shore but the project did not provide much returns in the form of fishing. Since then, the chinook salmon has been introduced into Minnesota waters of Lake Superior. Early signs indicate the chinook plantings will provide more fishing, although the program still is in its infancy.

Lake Superior fishing generally improves as the summer wears on. July and August are better months than May and June as the surface temperatures increase, attracting bait fish to the top. The trout and salmon will be near the bait fish.

The rebirth of Lake Superior is like a new fishing frontier in Minnesota. Much experimentation still needs to be done to develop more consistent angling techniques. In effect, the big lake represents a whole new ball game to state anglers.

And we're just beginning to know the rules.

North Shore Steelhead

Aside from muskies, no Minnesota fish stirs the emotions of fishermen like the steelhead in the North Shore streams.

The steelhead is a rainbow trout that lives most of the year in Lake Superior. Come spring, the fish migrates up the snow-swollen streams along the North Shore to spawn.

The steelhead's movements into the streams give anglers a chance to match wits with a fish of exceptional beauty, grace and strength. As such, the steelhead is considered a true fishing trophy, regardless of size. The average size steelhead taken is about 3 pounds but 6 pounds are common and fish exceeding 10 pounds are taken every spring.

Most of the steelhead action starts in early April and continues into early June. However, the best fishing normally goes from mid-April to mid-May.

There are 59 streams on the North Shore that attract steelhead. However, the amount of stream available to the fish depends on the location of natural barriers, such as waterfalls. And the steelhead fishing season depends on how long the snow run-off continues. For once the stream flow begins to fade the migration run of steelhead ends quickly.

A migrating steelhead spends an average of about 10 days in a stream before completing spawning and returning to Lake Superior. The young steelhead, after hatching, spend from 2 to 3 years in the stream before moving to the lake.

To the spring steelhead fisherman, the stream's water temperature holds the important key to success. For as the temperature reaches the 40 degree mark, the intensity of the spawning movement and the activity of the steelhead increases.

But no matter what the temperature, steelhead fishing will challenge all of your angling skills. About the time you think you're an "expert", you'll get skunked the next time out.

It's important to "read" the stream, looking for deep runs, places where the steelhead may pause on its tough travels upstream. Once you catch or locate a fish in a particular spot, chances are that particular stretch will always hold a steelhead. Many veteran steelheaders do nothing but fish from "spot" to "spot", ignoring the waters in-between.

Steelhead fishing requires much different equipment than conventional angling. To do it right, you need a stout 8½ to 9 foot flyrod with a single action or automatic fly reel. If you don't know how to cast a flyrod, don't worry. The flyrod is not used in that way. The bait or lure is not cast but "swung" much like you'd swing a bobber and worm with a cane pole.

Nor do you use flyline. Rather, fill the fly reel with 8 to 12-pound test line.

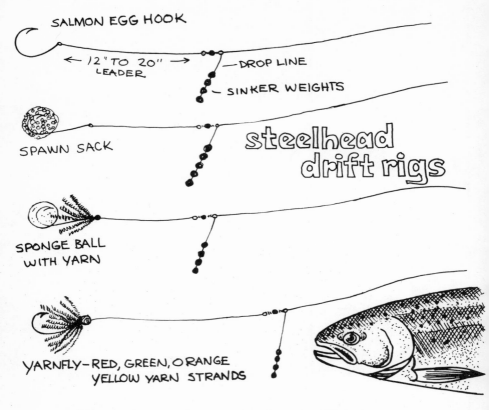

SALMON EGG HOOK

← 12" TO 20" → LEADER

DROP LINE

SINKER WEIGHTS

SPAWN SACK

steelhead drift rigs

SPONGE BALL WITH YARN

YARNFLY—RED, GREEN, ORANGE YELLOW YARN STRANDS

Now you've got the proper rod, reel and line. But don't forget chest waders or hipboots. Wading is very necessary in steelhead fishing and the water is too cold to use tennis shoes.

The steelhead fisherman's arsenal includes spawn bags (salmon eggs clustered in a net sack), single salmon eggs, steelie puffs or sponge balls (imitate a cluster of spawn and yarn flies). (See Illustration)

The basic drifting rig or terminal tackle includes a swivel, 12 to 20-inch leader and a No. 4 salmon-egg type hook with a turned up eye. A short 3 to 6 inch drop line, tied to the swivel, is used to attach split-shot weights. (See

Illustration.) The amount of weight depends on the strength of the current. It's best to add just enough split-shot to keep the bait "ticking" along the bottom rocks.

It's important to remember that the steelhead really is not in a feeding mood. They seldom will chase any bait for any distance. A strike is made more out of reflex action than hunger.

Thus, your bait must almost hit the trout on the nose before you'll get a strike. Then, the strike won't normally come as any jolt.

Rather, your bait will merely pause or stop. Then, set the hook immediately. It may be a rock, a snag or the current, but set the hook anyway. it also could be a steelhead.

Because the bait must pass so closely to a steelhead, one drift through a deep run or pool is not indication of steelhead's presence. Be sure to make many drifts through a likely-looking spot before moving on.

I remember one trip with Ray Lakso, a Minnesota conservation officer from Two harbors, which burned that lesson home. Ray was kind enough to send me to his favorite hotspot first, a wide run with a huge boulder in the center.

"The best spot is right in front of that boulder," Ray instructed.

While I fished the area, Ray waited patiently down-stream, fishing a different spot. I tried several drifts. No luck. Figuring that was enough, I voluntarily left the spot and walked upstream.

Ray moved into my footprints, made one drift in front of the boulder, and pulled out a steelhead that went over 10 pounds.

Early in the steelhead season, spawn bags are the most productive bait. The actual eggs give off a scent, of course, which travels ahead of the sack. This is beneficial when the steelhead streams are murky and high. As the streams clear, sponge balls or yarn flies become effective. Generally, the clearer the water, the smaller the bait.

Sponge balls and yarn are made up of red, red-orange and yellow colors, resembling actual spawn. Some yarn

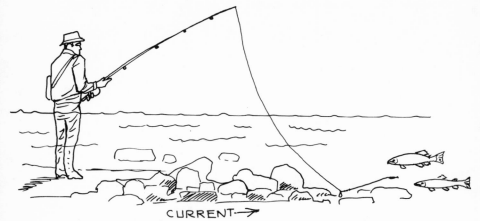

CURRENT →
WALK OR BOUNCE THE BAIT ON THE BOTTOM
USE SHORT CASTS WHENEVER POSSIBLE

fly tiers occasionally add green or white yarn to the fly. As the name indicates, the yarn fly is made up of actual yarn, ½ to 1 inch pieces tied in a bundle on a hook with a snell knot and trimmed to look like a cluster of trout eggs.

You can also add one strand of yarn to a spawn bag or sponge ball to serve as an attractor and help hide the hook shank.

Don't expect to master the art of steelhead fishing on your first attempt. Successful steelheading requires a sensitive touch and an understanding of stream fishing. And both only come through practice. The beginner should probably start with actual spawn bags, which are available at bait stores along the North Shore.

Once you hook a steelhead, hang on. The fish will likely leap, roll and streak downstream, using the powerful force of the current to its advantage. Rather than try to stop a surging trout, it's best to follow the fish downstream if possible. Chances are, the steelhead will stop once it reaches a pool where you can resume the battle with better odds for success.

The steelhead can be beached or netted. But don't try to scoop up a steelhead that still has some fight. I tried that once on a nice steelhead that fishing partner, Ron Weber, had on the line.

The moment I scooped with the net, the steelhead streaked. Right between my legs. A split-second later, it was gone. You wouldn't have liked the look on Ron's face. Or mine.

Lake Superior steelhead streams in Minnesota

Name	County	Miles of Steelhead Water	Name	County	Miles of Steelhead Water
Nemadji	Carlton	35.0	Cross	Cook	0.3
Chester	St. Louis	0.1	Temperance	Cook	0.1
Tischer	St. Louis	0.1	Onion	Cook	0.1
Lester	St. Louis	0.9	Rollins	Cook	0.1
Talmadge	St. Louis	1.1	Poplar	Cook	0.1
French	St. Louis	0.2	Lutsen	Cook	0.1
Schmidt	St. Louis	0.1	Jonvick	Cook	0.1
Sucker	St. Louis	2.0	Spruce	Cook	0.1
Knife	Lake	70.0	Indian Camp	Cook	0.7
Stewart	Lake	0.9	Cascade	Cook	0.1
Silver	Lake	0.2	Cutface	Cook	0.4
Encampment	Lake	0.5	Rosebush	Cook	0.1
Crow	Lake	1.9	Devils Track	Cook	1.3
Castle	Lake	0.8	Durfee	Cook	0.1
Gooseberry	Lake	0.8	Cliff	Cook	0.1
Twin Points	Lake	0.2	Kimball	Cook	1.6
Split Rock	Lake	0.7	Stone	Cook	0.1
Unnamed	Lake	0.1	Kadunce	Cook	0.3
Beaver	Lake	0.2	East Colville	Cook	0.5
Palisade	Lake	1.2	Brule	Cook	1.5
Baptism	Lake	0.9	Myhr's	Cook	0.1
Little Marais	Lake	0.1	Flute Reed	Cook	0.3
Dragon	Lake	0.3	Carlson	Cook	0.5
Manitou	Lake	0.1	Farquhar	Cook	0.2
Little Manitou	Lake	0.5	Reservation	Cook	3.6
Caribou	Lake	0.1	Unnamed	Cook	0.1
Sugar Loaf	Cook	0.1	Hollow Rock	Cook	0.1
Last	Cook	0.1	Unnamed	Cook	0.1
Unnamed	Cook	0.1	Grand Portage	Cook	0.1
Two Island	Cook	0.1			

A GUIDE TO LAKES MANAGED FOR TROUT AND SALMON

(Courtesy Minn. Dept. of Natural Resources)

LAKE	ACREAGE	SPECIES	NEAREST TOWN	ROUTE TO LAKE
Aitkin County				
Taylor	60.0	Rainbow	Hill City	5.2 mi. E. of Hill City on Hwy. 34
Townline (In Savanna Portage State Park)	32.7	Donaldson	McGregor	7 mi. N. of McGregor on Hwy. 65; 10 mi. N.E. on County Roads 14 & 36 to Savanna Portage State Park.
Turtle, Little	10.6	Rainbow	Aitkin	7 mi. S. of Aitkin on Hwy. 169, then 2.7 mi. E. on County Road 28, then 1.3 mi. N. on Twp. Rd.
Becker County				
Hanson	32.5	Rainbow	Detroit Lakes	7 mi. E. on State Hwy. 34; 3.5 mi. N. on County Road 29; 0.5 mi. E. on gravel road.
Long, Little (Long)	10.6	Rainbow	Park Rapids	4 mi. S. on State Hwy. 71; 4.5 mi. W. on Road 14; 2 mi. S. and 1 mi. W. on gravel road.
Beltrami County				
Benjamin	28.7	Brook & Rainbow	Blackduck	6 mi. S. on Pennington Road.
Spring	10.0	Brook & Rainbow	Bemidji	5.2 mi. W. on Hwy. 2; 5.6 mi. N. on Hwy. 89; 2 mi. W. on County Road 29; 0.9 mi. W. on State Fire Road.
Three Corner	10.0	Rainbow	Pinewood	1½ miles south on County Road 5 and 2 miles E. on Forest Trail.
Carlton County				
Corona	25.4	Rainbow	Sawyer	3.8 mi. W. on Hwy. 210; 0.6 mi. S. and E. on Long Lake Road; 0.2 mi. S. by trail.
Carver County				
Courthouse Lake	10.0	Rainbow	Chaska	East side of Courthouse on E. end of Chaska.
Cass County				
Cedar	15.4	Brook & Rainbow	Remer	6 mi. N. of Remer. Travel 1½ mi. N. on County Road 4, turn on County Rd. 52 and travel 4½ miles N. on County Rd. 52.
Diamond	73.38	Rainbow	Walker	8 mi. S. on Hwy. 371; 3.2 mi. on U.S.F.S. Road 2107; 1.3 mi. on access trail.
Hazel	11.4	Rainbow	Longville	4.5 mi. W. on Cass County Road 5; 0.5 mi. N. on access trail.

Margaret	12.5	Rainbow	Outing	2 mi. N. on Hwy. 6; 2 mi. W. on County Road 48.
Marion	8.2	Brook	Outing	2 mi. N. on Hwy. 6; 2 mi. W. on County Road 48.
Perch	12.8	Brook	Backus	5.5 mi. W. on Hwy. 87; 1 mi. N. on Pine Mountain Lookout Road; W. to Lake.
Snowshoe (Little Andrus)	23.6	Brook	Outing	2 mi. N. on Hwy. 6; 3 mi. W. on County Road 48, then ¾ mi. S.
Tepee	16.3	Brook & Rainbow	Whipholt	4.7 mi. So. on Lookout Tower Road; 0.8 mi. W. on Forest Trail.
Willard	7.1	Rainbow	Backus	3 mi. N. on Hwy. 371; 3 mi. E. on gravel road.
Clearwater County				
*Long	145.0	Rainbow	Zerkel	5 mi. N.W. of Lake Itasca on Hwy. 200.
Cook County				
Bath	36.0	Brook	Grand Marais	4 mi. N. on Gunflint Trail; 12 mi. N.W. on Devil Track Road (County Roads 8 & 27 & U.S.F.S. Road 323); 1 mi. S.W. on logging road — south side of road.
Bogus	17.1	Brook	Grand Marais	11 mi. N. on Gunflint Trail; 5 mi. E. on Trout Lake Road; 1 mi. N.
Boys	24.0	Brook	Grand Marais	11 mi. N. on Gunflint Trail; 2.2 mi. E. on Trout Lake Road; 0.2 mi. N. by trail.
Carrot	28.0	Brook	Grand Marais	20 mi. N. on Gunflint Trail; 4 mi. N.E. on old Greenwood Road; 2 mi. N. on U.S.F.S. Road 313 to Lake.
Chester	48.8	Brook & Rainbow	Hovland	10 mi. N. on Arrowhead Trail; 6 mi. W. on Forestry Road.
Dislocation	37.7	Brook	Grand Marais	21.5 mi. N. on Gunflint Trail; 5 mi. W. on Lima Mountain Road; trail W. to Lake.
Duke	11.0	Brook	Grand Marais	21.5 mi. N. on Gunflint Trail; 11 mi. S.W. on Lima Mountain Road; E. across E. Twin Lake; 0.5 mi. on trail to Lake.
Esther	87.0	Brook, Rainbow, Brown	Hovland	10 mi. N. on Arrowhead Trail; 7.5 mi. W. on Forestry Road.
Gadwall	20.0	Brook	Hovland	18 mi. N. on Arrowhead Trail to McFarland Lake; 2.5 mi. N.W. across McFarland Lake to Pine Lake (joined by short stream); 3 mi. W. across Pine Lake; 0.2 mi. S. on trail.
Gogebic	70.0	Brook	Grand Marais	28 mi. N. on Gunflint Trail; 4 mi. E. to Clearwater Lake; 7 mi. E. across Clearwater Lake; portage to West Pike Lake; 0.5 mi. E. across West Pike Lake; S. 0.25 mi.

LAKE	ACREAGE	SPECIES	NEAREST TOWN	ROUTE TO LAKE
Cook County cont.				
Jap	116.6	Rainbow	Grand Marais	53 mi. N.W. on Gunflint Trail to Sea Gull Lake; 3 mi. S.W. across Sea Gull Lake; 1 mi. S. by trail.
Jim	59.0	Brook & Lake Trout	Grand Marais	20 mi. N. on Gunflint Trail; 2.5 mi. N.E. on old Greenwood Road; 0.7 mi. N.W. on poor trail to Lake.
Junco	40.0	Brook	Grand Marais	4 mi. N. on Gunflint Trail; 5 mi. W. on Devil Track Road; 2 mi. N. on Ball Club Road.
*Kemo	184.0	Lake Trout	Grand Marais	4 mi. N. on Gunflint Trail; 10 mi. N.W. on Devil Track Road (County Roads 8 & 27); 1 mi. E. on old railroad grade; 0.2 mi. N. on trail; or by boat W. on Pine Lake & portage off E. end.
Kimball	79.4	Rainbow	Grand Marais	11 mi. N. on Gunflint Trail; 2 mi. E. on Trout Lake Road.
Leo	101.2	Rainbow	Grand Marais	30 mi. N.W. on Gunflint Trail; 1 mi. N. on Hungry Jack Road No. 65.
Manymoon	27.0	Brook	Lutsen	8.5 mi. N. on County Rd. 4 (Caribou Trail); 3.4 mi. N.W. on Forest Rd. 339; 1.2 mi. N.W. on logging road to Rice Lake.
Margaret	20.0	Brook	Hovland	11 mi. N. on Arrowhead Trail; 0.5 mi. S. on old logging road; 0.3 mi. N.W. by trail.
Mavis	10.5	Rainbow	Grand Marais	47 mi. N.W. on Gunflint Trail; 1 mi. S.W. to Round Lake; 0.5 mi. S.W. across Round Lake; 0.5 mi. S. on portage.
Mayhew, Little	41.0	Rainbow	Grand Marais	39 mi. N.W. on Gunflint Trail to Loon Lake; 2 mi. N.E. on Forest Road 132; 0.3 mi. S.E. on trail. Or, 44-rod portage from W. end of Mayhew Lake.
Meditation	32.0	Rainbow	Grand Marais	53 mi. N.W. on Gunflint Trail to Sea Gull Lake; 1½ mi. S.W. across Sea Gull Lake; South 0.1 mi. by trail.
Mink	57.0	Rainbow & Brook	Grand Marais	11 mi. N. on Gunflint Trail; 2 mi. E. on Trout Lake Road.
Missing Link	40.5	Rainbow & Brook	Grand Marais	47 mi. N.W. on Gunflint Trail; 1 mi. S.W. to Round Lake; 0.7 mi. S.W. across Round Lake; 0.5 mi. S. on portage.

Name	Value	Location	Type	Directions
Monkers	87.5	Grand Marais	Brook	4 mi. N. on Gunflint Trail; 2.5 mi. W. on County Road 17; 0.7 mi. N. on Old County Road 15; 0.2 mi. E. by trail.
Moosehorn	63	Hovland	Brook	2.5 mi. N. on Arrowhead Trail; 1 mi. W. on State Forest Road; 1 mi. N.W. on Tom Lake Road; 0.5 mi. N.E. on trail.
Muckwa	51.0	Grand Marais	Rainbow	16 mi. N. on Gunflint Trail; 1.5 mi. S. on Pine Mountain Road; 1.2 mi. on logging road; N.E. across Musquash Lake; 0.2 mi. on portage trail to Lake.
Mulligan	31.0	Lutsen	Rainbow	Lutsen to Brule Lake via Caribou Trail Road; N. across Brule Lake; portage to Lily Lake to Mulligan Lake.
Musquash	140.0	Grand Marais	Splake	16 mi. N. on Gunflint Trail; 1.5 mi. S. on Pine Mountain Road; 1.2 mi. W. on logging road.
Olson	34.4	Grand Marais	Brook	4 mi. up Gunflint Trail to Devil Track Road; 9.5 mi. N.W. on County Roads 8 & 27 to Two Island Lake Campground; 1.5 mi. S. out of Campground on logging road.
Pancore (Lost)	34.0	Tofte	Rainbow	12.2 mi. N. on Sawbill Trail; 4 mi. E. on logging road.
Pemmican	40.0	Grand Marais	Brook	28 mi. N.W. on Gunflint Trail; 4 mi. E. to Clearwater Lake; 5 mi. E. across Clearwater Lake; portage into Mountain Lake (portage marked); 7 mi. E. across Mountain Lake; 0.2 mi. S.
Pierz (Beaver)	88.4	Grand Marais	Splake	26.5 mi. on Gunflint Trail to East Bearskin Lake; cross E. Bearskin Lake; portage to Alder Lake; portage to Pierz (Beaver) Lake.
Pine	87.1	Splake, Brook & Rainbow		4 mi. N. on Gunflint Trail; 5.9 mi. W. on County Road 8; N. 4 mi. on County Road 27; 2 mi. E. on railroad grade.
Pine Mountain	102.5	Grand Marais	Brook & Rainbow	16 mi. on Gunflint Trail; 2 mi. W. on Pine Mountain Road (Forest Road 154)
Ram	67.0	Grand Marais	Rainbow & Lake Trout	21.5 mi. N. on Gunflint Trail; 6 mi. S.W. on Lima Mountain Road; trail W. to Lake.
Rog	55	Grand Marais	Brook	53 mi. N.W. on Gunflint Trail to Sea Gull Lake; 6 mi. S.W. across Sea Gull Lake; 0.1 mi. W. by trail.
Shady, North	32.0	Grand Marais	Brook	17 mi. N. on Gunflint Trail; 7 mi. N.E. on new Greenwood Lake Road; N. across Greenwood Lake; portage to North Shady Lake.

Cook County cont.

LAKE	ACREAGE	SPECIES	NEAREST TOWN	ROUTE TO LAKE
Shoe	25	Brook	Grand Marais	16.5 mi. N. on Gunflint Trail; 4 mi. E. on Forest Road 309; 3 mi. N. on Forest Rd. 1386; 0.6 mi. W. on Forest Rd. 144; 1.0 mi. N. on Forest Rd. 313.
Sock	20.0	Rainbow	Grand Marais	35 mi. N.W. on Gunflint Trail; 2 mi. N.E., past E. end of Mayhew Lake; 0.2 mi. W. by trail.
Squaw	13.0	Brook	Hovland	10 mi. N. on Arrowhead Trail; 7.5 mi. to Esther Lake; across Esther Lake; 0.5 mi. by trail S.W. to Lake.
Sunfish	80.4	Rainbow	Grand Marais	16.5 mi. N. on Gunflint Trail; 7 mi. E. on Forest Road 309; 1 mi. N. on Forest Road 141; 2 mi. E. on rough logging road.
Surber	7.2	Brook	Grand Marais	33.5 mi. N. on Gunflint Trail; 1 mi. W. on old Gunflint Trail; 0.2 mi. E. by trail.
Talus	18.7	Rainbow	Grand Marais	21.5 mi. N.W. on Gunflint Trail; 11 mi. S.W. on Lima Mountain Road; 0.5 mi. N.W. across West Twin Lake; 0.2 mi. W. by trail.
Thompson	16.2	Brook & Rainbow	Grand Marais	4 mi. N. on Gunflint Trail; 10 mi. W. on Devil Track Road (County Roads 8 & 57).
Thrasher	29.0	Rainbow	Grand Marais	4 mi. N. on Gunflint Trail; 12 mi. N.W. on Devil Track Road (County Roads 8 & 27, & U.S.F.S. Road 323); 1 mi. S.W. on logging road; north side of road.
Thrush	16	Lake Trout	Grand Marais	About 400 foot portage trail north from Thrasher Lake (see above).
Topper	51.0	Brook	Grand Marais	34 mi. N.W. on gunflint Trail; 0.6 mi. N. (passing E. end of Mayhew Lake); 0.3 mi. N. on trail.
*Trout	257.0	Rainbow & Lake Trout	Grand Marais	11 mi. N. on Gunflint Trail; 4 mi. E. on Forest Road 140.
Vale	20.0	Brook	Hovland	18 mi. on Arrowhead Trail to McFarland Lake; 2.5 mi. N.W. across McFarland Lake to Pine Lake (joined by short stream); 4 mi. W. across Pine Lake; 0.2 mi. S. on Trail.
Wee	13	Brook	Tofte	17 mi. N. on Sawbill trail; 6.9 mi. N.E. on Forest Rd. 165; 1 mi. N. on logging road (midway between Moore & Crescent Lake); on foot about 0.8 mi. N. on logging trails (BWCA).

The author shows why steelhead fishing in Minnesota is a trophy fisherman's dream.

LAKE	ACREAGE	SPECIES	NEAREST TOWN	ROUTE TO LAKE
Cook County cont.				
Wench	25.0	Brook	Lutsen	Lutsen to Brule Lake via Caribou Trail Road; 5 mi. W. down Brule Lake to N.W. Bay; portage trail N.W. to Lake.
Crow Wing County				
Allen	46.0	Rainbow	Emily	3.25 mi. N. of Emily; 2.5 mi. W. & N. around Roosevelt Lake; 0.3 mi. N.W. by trail.
Pleasant	21.9	Rainbow	Cross Lake	2 mi. N. on Hwy. 61; 1 mi. W. on County Road 8; 1 mi. S.
Portsmouth (Mine Pit)	130	Rainbow	Crosby	N.W. edge of Crosby on State Highway 6.
Strawberry	15.9	Rainbow	Jenkins	County Road 16 to Ideal Corners; 1.5 mi. S.E.; then 1 mi. W.
Hubbard County				
Blacksmith	35.9	Rainbow	Park Rapids	13.7 mi. N. on Hwy. 71; 2 mi. E. on County Road 89; 1 mi. N.E. on gravel road; 1.5 mi. S.E. on access trail.
Newman (Putnam)	39.4	Rainbow	Bemidji	5 mi. S. on Hwy. 71; 4 mi. W. on Road 54; 1 mi. S. and 1.25 mi. W. on forest trail; 0.4 mi. S. on forest trail.
Robertson (Coon)	18.5	Rainbow	Lake George Post Office	4 mi. E. on Hwy. 71; 2 mi. S.; 1.6 mi. E.; 1.5 mi. S. on County Gravel Road 2; 0.75 mi. W.
Itasca County				
Bear, Little	18.0	Rainbow	Marcell	14.1 mi. S. on Hwy. 38; 1 mi. W. on old Forest Trail.
Erskine	49.3	Brook & Rainbow	Effie	13.5 mi. E. on Hwy. 1; 0.3 mi. S. on old trail.
Greeley	15.8	Rainbow	Squaw Lake	6 mi. S.E. of Squaw Lake; 1.2 mi. W. on Third River Road.
Kremer	69.8	Brook & Rainbow	Marcell	10.3 mi. S. on Hwy. 38.
Larson	198.6	Rainbow	Effie	11.9 mi. E. on Hwy. 1; 2.7 mi. S. on Forest Road; 0.9 mi. S. on Forest Trail.
Lucky	13.0	Brook, Brown & Rainbow	Marcell	14.1 mi. S. on Hwy. 38; 1 mi. W. on old Forest Trail.
Moonshine (Little Moonshine)	24.5	Brook & Rainbow	Bovey	3 mi. E. on Hwy. 169; 12.2 mi. N. on Scenic Hwy.; 9 mi. W. on County Road; 0.8 mi. W. on Forest Trail.
Nickel (Nichols)	15.6	Rainbow	Bovey	3.1 mi. E. on Hwy. 169; 23.6 mi. N. on Scenic Hwy.; 1 mi. W. on County Road 45; 0.3 mi. S. on access trail.

Lake	Acres	Species	Access Town	Directions
Rainbow	10.2	Rainbow	Bigfork	10 mi. S.E. on Scenic Hwy.; 7 mi. E. on old Scenic Hwy.; 1.4 mi. N.E. on Forest Road; 0.6 mi. S.E. on access trail.
Surprise	11.0	Rainbow	Marcell	10.3 mi. S. on Hwy. 38.
Tioga (Mine Pit)	38.0	Rainbow	Cohasset	1.8 mi. S. on County Road 62; 0.2 mi. E. on County Road 63; 0.8 mi. S. on Township Road to public access on right side of road.

Lake County

Lake	Acres	Species	Access Town	Directions
Ahsub	62.1	Rainbow	Winton	Portage S.E. 162 rods from S.E. corner of Snowbank Lake to Disappointment Lake; N.E. to N. on Disappointment Lake; portage N. for 8 rods.
Beetle	23.0	Rainbow	Isabella	5 mi. N. on Forest Service Road 383, starting from State Hwy. 1 by Teamster Pond (9 mi. N.W. of Isabella).
Benson	20.0	Brook	Finland	9.7 mi. N.E. on Cramer Road; 9 mi. E. on State Park Road.
Bone	33.1	Splake, Lake Trout, Brook & Rainbow	Cramer	8 mi. N. on County Road 7; 3.5 mi. N.W. on Forest Road 172; 7 mi. N.E. on Forest Road 357 to Four Mile Lake; 3.5 mi. W. on Forest Road 170; 5 mi. N. on logging road.
*Camp 20	50.0	Brook	Winton	10 mi. E. on Fernberg Rd.
Divide (Towhey)	59.6	Rainbow	Isabella	5.5 mi. E. on Forest Road 172.
Echo	40.0	Rainbow	Cramer	6 mi. N. on County Road 7.
Eikela	13	Brook	Isabella	From junction of Hwy. 1 and Hwy. 2. 2 miles E. on Hwy. 1, then N. ¾ mi. on woods road, then N.W. on left fork for ½ mi. and right fork for ¼ mi. Walk ¼ mi. N.W. to Lake.
Found	57.8	Rainbow	Ely	17.5 mi. E. on Fernberg Road to Moose Lake Landing; by boat 7 mi. to portage on N. side of Newfound Lake; portage 30 rods.
Glacier Pond II	5.2	Brook	Winton	12 mi. E. on Fernberg Road; 0.5 mi. S. on trail.
Goldeneye (Duck)	9.0	Brook	Cramer	6.2 mi. N. on County Road 7; 0.2 mi. N.W. by trail.
*Hare	38.0	Coho Salmon	Cramer	8 mi. N. on County Road 7.
Hogback (Twin)	40.3	Rainbow	Isabella	12 mi. E. on U.S.F.S. Road locally known as "Dumbell Lake Road" or "600 Road"; 5 mi. E. on Wanless Road.
Jouppi	10	Brook	Isabella	2 mi. S. on Hwy. 1; ¾ mi. E. and N. on logging roads. Walk ¼ mi. E. to Lake.
Scarp (Cliff)	44.8	Rainbow	Isabella	12 mi. E. on U.S.F.S. Road known, locally as "Dumbell Lake Road" or "600 Road"; 5 mi. E. on Wanless Road; 2 mi. S.E. by trail; or portage from 1st Hogback Lake to 2nd; thence 400 feet E. by trail.

LAKE	ACREAGE	SPECIES	NEAREST TOWN	ROUTE TO LAKE
Lake County cont.				
Section 8	8.0	Brook	Isabella	5 mi. E. on Wanless Road.
Shoo-Fly	12	Brook	Isabella	4 mi. E. on Forest Road 172 to Dumbell Lake access; N.W. across Lake and across Beaver Pond out of N.W. corner. Walk ¼ mi. W. to Lake.
Skull (Section 14)	23.2	Brook	Winton	17.5 mi. E. on Fernberg Road to Moose Lake public landing. By boat 7 mi. to portage on S. side Newfound Lake. Portage 400 feet.
Steer	4.8	Brook	Isabella	14 mi. E. on Forest Road 172 to Beaver Lake; 0.2 mi. W. across Beaver Lake; 0.1 S. to Steer Lake.
Steamhaul	36	Brook	Isabella	6 mi. N.W. on Hwy. 1, 1½ mi. N. on Forest Road 177. Walk ½ mi. E. to Lake.
Tofte	111.63	Brook & Rainbow	Winton	12 mi. E. on Fernberg Road; 0.3 mi. N. on trail.
Trappers	18.9	Brook	Isabella	1 mi. E. on Forest Road 172; then 2.5 mi. N. on Forest Road to barrier on outlet stream; then portage E. 0.25 mi.
Twin, Upper (Bear)	18.4	Rainbow	Beaver Bay	5 mi. N.W. on old No. 1; 1.5 mi. E.
Wye	56.0	Coho Salmon	Finland	28 mi. N. on County Road 7.
Meeker County				
*Mud, Little	43.0	Rainbow	Watkins	3 mi. S.W. on County Hwy. 2.
Otter Tail County				
Bass	35.5	Rainbow	Pelican Rapids	9 mi. E. on State Hwy. 108; then 1.25 mi. S. on gravel road; 0.25 mi. W. on Beers Lake Trail; 1 mi. S.W. on trail.
Pine County				
*Grindstone	528.6	Brown, Rainbow, Kamloops, Splake, & Lake Trout	Sandstone	7.5 mi. W. on County Aid Road 17.
St. Louis County				
Alruss	28.0	Brook & Rainbow	Winton	1.3 mi. W. on St. Louis County Road 781; 9.7 mi. N. on Cloquet line; 3.3 mi. N.E. on Jackfish Spur; canoe W. across Sandpit Lake; 150-rod portage Portage from W. tip of Mica Bay on Namakan Lake for distance of 0.8 mi.
Beast (Wilson)	92.4	Rainbow	Ray	8 mi. N. on Jean Duluth Road; 1 mi. E. on Normanna Road; 7 mi. N. on fox Farm Road; 1 mi. E. on Briar Lake Road.
Briar	69.6	Rainbow	Duluth	

Lake		Trout	Town	Directions
Camp 4 (Wessman)	16.5	Rainbow	Buhl	2.3 mi. N. on County Road 125; 7.9 mi. N. on County Road 25; 0.3 mi. W. (private landing).
Cedar	24.5	Brook & Rainbow	Aurora	2 mi. S. on County Highway 100; W. 4 mi. on County Hwy. 6528.
Chant	19.0	Rainbow	Ely	1 mi. E. on Hwy. 169; 2 mi. N. on County Road 88; 9.5 mi. N. on Echo Trail; 3 mi. S.W. on Forest Road 644 to public access (across from Slim Lake portage) on N. Arm of Burntside Lake; 4 mi. S. by canoe to North Arm Narrows; portage E. 80 rods.
Clear	13.1	Rainbow & Brook	Duluth	4 mi. N. on Hwy. 53; 9.5 mi. N.W. on Lavaque Road.
Cub	10.0	Brook	Tower	9 mi. E. on State Hwy. 1; 2 mi. S. on Eagles Nest Road; 4 mi. E. and S. on Bearhead Lake Road (Lake located in State Park on N. side of Bearhead Lake 300 feet N. of Road).
Dollar	10.6	Brook & Rainbow	Chisholm	1.9 mi. N. on Hwy. 73; 3.0 mi. N. on Sturgeon Lake Road; 1.8 mi. N. on CAR 484.
Dry	75.1	Brook	Ely	6.5 mi.N. on Echo Trail; 1 mi. N.E. on access trail.
Dry, Little	9.4	Brook	Ely	6.5 mi. N. on Echo Trail; 1 mi. N.E. on Dry Lake access trail; S. across Dry Lake and portage 50 feet.
Elbow, Little	8.4	Rainbow	Eveleth	3 mi. S.W. to Iron Junction; 1.75 mi. W. on County Road 452; 1.25 mi. N. & E. on County Road 315; continue E. 0.5 mi. on rough trail; lake on N.W. side.
Gabrielson	14.95	Brook & Rainbow	Orr	1.3 mi. S. on Hwy. 53; 5.2 mi. W. on Nett Lake Road; 0.4 mi. S. on trail.
Hanson	21.6	Brook & Rainbow	Ely	1 mi. S. by boat from N. tip of N. arm of Burntside Lake into small bay; portage 0.5 mi. S. and E.
High	319.4	Rainbow	Ely	7.4 mi. N. on Echo Trail; 2 mi. W. on access trail.
Jammer	18.4	Brook & Rainbow	Virginia	10.6 mi.N. on Hwy. 53 from Junction of 53 and 169.
Loaine (Sand)	26.6	Rainbow	Duluth	8 mi. N. on Jean Duluth Road; 1 mi. E. on Normanna Road; 20 mi. N. on Fox Farm Road; 0.5 mi. E. on Rossini Trail; 0.5 mi. N. on trail.
Louis	22.6	Rainbow	Winton	1.3 mi. W. on St.Louis Co. Road No.781; 12.7 mi.N. on Cloquet line; canoe E. on Picket Lake outlet thru Mudro Lake to N. shoreline near outlet; portage N.W. 80 rods.
Norberg	8.0	Rainbow	Tower	9 mi. E. on Hwy. 1; 2 mi. E. on Eagles Nest and Bearhead Park Roads; 3.75 mi. S. on Bearhead Park Road; walk in 300 feet S. side of road.

LAKE	ACREAGE	SPECIES	NEAREST TOWN	ROUTE TO LAKE
St. Louis County cont.				
Normanna	2.0	Brook	Duluth	8 mi. N. on Jean Duluth Road; 1 mi. E. on Normanna Road; 0.5 mi. N. on Fox Farm Road; 0.7 mi. N. by trail.
Olson	10.0	Rainbow & Brook	Duluth	4 mi. N. on Hwy. 53; 9.5 mi. N. on Lavaque Road; 1 mi. E. on Fish Lake Road.
Pickerel	24.2	Brook & Rainbow	Side Lake	0.2 mi. N. on County Road 5; 2.2 mi. N. on McCarthy Beach Road; 0.2 mi. E. on Forest Trail; 0.1 mi. S. on trail.
Regenbogan	8.8	Brook & Rainbow	Ely	14.2 mi. N. on Echo Trail; 0.2 mi. E. on trail.
Silver	34.0	Rainbow	Biwabik	5.5 mi. S. on County Hwy. 4; 1.5 mi. E. on County Road 525.
Spring Hole	2.0	Brook	Duluth	County Road 4 to Ryan's Creek. About 1 mile in off of County Rd. 4.
Trygg (Twigg)	25.2	Rainbow	Orr	20-rod portage from Lac La Croix Lake S.E. from 41 Island; or, 40-rod portage W. from Takucmich Lake.
Twin Lakes	2.0	Brook, Brown & Rainbow	Duluth	Enger Golf Course.
Sherburne County				
Dodds Quarry No. 20	1.2	Rainbow	In St. Cloud	E. of Mississippi River.

*All lakes, except those marked with an asterisk, are designated trout waters wherein the possession and use of minnows, except in preserved condition, for bait is prohibited.

bullheads & cats
bewhiskered & becareful

Bullheads and Cats/
Bewhiskered and Becareful

On the angler's social ladder, Minnesota's bewhiskered fishes — the catfish and bullheads — are invariably near the bottom rung. If you're a trout fisherman, you're some kind of super angler with class, brains and piscatorial articulation.

But if you fish for catfish or bullheads, you're an unabashed nitwit.

Well, whoever decides such things must have hatched from an egg.

The only fishermen who are authorized to ridicule the sport of catfishin' or bullheadin' are the ones who've done it. And they're just kidding so the rest of you never really learn the truth.

Tell me, how could you improve on a night along a river bank with a lazy waters gurgling by to the melody of singing tree frogs and whippoorwills. At your side, is a trusty rod and reel or stout, fresh-cut willow stick. And down below the murky river water, you've got a gob of worms or a chunk of stink bait rippling gently in the ambling current.

Suddenly.

Lolapalooza! Your fishing line streaks for the far bank, threatening to take the fishing rod with it. You rear back and hang on, waiting for the next powerful lunge of a channel catfish hellbent to grab the river bottom.

Now tell me, does that sound like a sport only for nitwits?

Absolutely not. Some fish may fight with more pizzazz but none have any more determination than Minnesota's two catfish, the flathead or mudcat and the channel catfish.

What about the bullhead?

Well ... eerr ... to tell the truth, the bullhead fights slightly harder than a freshwater clam. It eats anything, including bare hooks, and it can live without water longer than a camel. And you might even wonder how anybody could call bullhead fishing a sport. Even with a loose definition.

You'll have to ask that question in Waterville, Minn., where thousands of normal fishermen spend their summers fishing for bullheads. Maybe they know something the skeptics haven't thought about yet.

The point is Minnesota has some great lakes and great rivers for catfishin' and bullheadin'. And you don't need any piscatorial degree to get in on the action.

Bullheads and catfish are members of the same fish family, noted for scaleless skin, chin whiskers and sharp needle-like spines on their pectoral and dorsal fins.

Lots of folks think the chin whiskers are poisonous filaments. But that's not true. The whiskers merely act like another set of senses to help locate food.

The fin spines do have mild poison glands, which make a puncture rather painful. That's why you should be careful when handling the bewhiskered fishes.

The catfishes and the bullheads will, indeed, eat just about anything. That leaves your choice of baits rather open. However, the flathead or mudcat is more persnickety. Whatever it eats must be alive first.

Channel cats and mudcats normally are considered a river fish. The two species often may be found in the same haunts, although the mudcat is much more difficult to catch. It is primarily active only at night. The channel cat can be taken almost any time of the day and night, although sunrise and sundown periods are probably best.

I don't think the bullhead knows what time it is. Or gives a dang. Bullheads probably are more commonly fished in lakes, although they survive nicely in rivers, ponds and possibly sewer lagoons.

The good folk of Waterville will probably chuckle about that ... all the way to the bank. The southern Minnesota town long has billed itself as the "Bullhead Capital of the World." And not one town has disputed the claim.

Many of the lakes in southern Minnesota are shallow and fertile, an ideal combination to raise tons of bullheads, simply and easily. And that's how the fish is caught, too.

Channel catfish may not be pretty to look at, but they're beauties to catch.

Almost any fishing outfit will do, any line, any hook, any bait. Worms, nightcrawlers, commercial stinkbaits are the favorites. Fish from a boat or the shore.

Bottom fishing — plunking the bait smack-dab on the bottom — is a typical ploy. Some anglers use bobbers to hold the bait only slightly off the bottom. Whatever turns you on.

By now, you must be wondering what all the fuss is about. If bullheads can't fight, if they're not big, if they hit anything, if they're tricky to hold without getting jabbed, why bother, huh?

'Cause bullheads are delicious to eat. And that's no bull. Skinned and entrails removed, a bullhead is nothing but pure, firm white meat with an easy-removed backbone.

A mug of cold beer, alongside a platter of deep-fried golden bullhead filets, is heavenly eating. Some folks will say better than a walleye.

Particularly the Waterville Chamber of Commerce.

Channel cats and flathead cats represent the sportier side of the bewhiskered fish family.

The channel cats have neater appearance with a bluish back, irregularly-spotted sides and a forked tail. Whereas, the flathead cat looks mean with permanent evil grin, brown-gray funky color and a fat, square-ended tail.

Both fish hang-out in the pools and sluggish waters or around sandy wingdams and spooky-looking log jams that quiver endlessly in the current.

The best time of the season to hit these spots is when the heat of summer has reached its peak in the lazy days of August. By then the rivers have pulled back to shallow riffles and deep holes, exposing handy sandbars to sit on while you ponder the next strike.

One of my favorite channel cat baits is rotten shrimp, sold in bait shops wherever good cat fishing exists. Nightcrawlers, cut bait (chopped up suckers or chubs) chicken livers, blood sausage ... anything with a lip curling odor will attract channel cats.

Don't know if it's true but I was once told about a farmer who lost a fine sow during the farrowing season. Rather than let it go to waste, he dragged it to a place just upstream from one of his favorite catfishing holes and let it ripen for a few weeks. They say when he finally returned there were so many catfish in that hole below the pig he could scoop 'em out with a dipnet.

I believe it.

Catfish bait can be still-fished or drifted with the current. For sure, you won't have any doubts about a strike. The channel catfish is one of the hardest striking fish in freshwater. It simply hits with a bang.

Channel cats also will smash artificial lures when they're in the mood. I've taken cats on crayfish-looking jigs, such as the Ugly Bug. But most cat fishermen don't want to get that sophisticated. After you've been handling stink bait for a long time, it's tough to switch to artificial lures.

By far the best way to fool flatheads is to fish at night with large chubs or suckers. Sometimes a super-gob of nightcrawlers, stuffed in a wad on a large 6/0 to 9/0 hook also works well. All baits are fished on the bottom with a heavy sinker.

Then, it's a matter of patience. Once the big cats make a move the evening could get downright exciting. If not, the only thing you've got to lose is a little sleep.

Channel cats and flatheads also are an excellent-eating fish, if you don't let their looks bother you.

Die-hard cat fishermen don't. Their nights or days on the mud-banked rivers are seldom dull and never boring. What excitement the big cats can't provide, a six-pack or two can.

miscellaneous bites

sturgeon

Carp and Others/
Miscellaneous Bites

In some Minnesota waters, fishing is like gambling.

You're never sure about what's on the other end of the line.

The Mississippi and St. Croix Rivers are famed pot luck fishing holes. Intending to catch bluegills, and using earthworms for bait, a friend and I once caught nine different species of fish in the Mississippi. As I recall the selection went like this: bluegills, crappies, redhorse sucker, largemouth bass, sheepshead, channel catfish, dogfish, sauger and walleye.

More than one walleye fisherman on Mille Lacs has hooked a "good fish" only to learn the anticipated trophy was a burbot, a freshwater member of the codfish family.

Bass fishermen, casting plastic worms exclusively for ol' bucket mouth, have set the hook into real "hawgs" only to find an eel-shaped bowfin or dogfish on the end of the line.

Of such are the agonies of surprise in the sport of fishing.

But not all are disappointments. Tackle maker, Dan Gapen, has a stuffed carp on the wall above his office desk. And not as a joke. The stuffed carp serves as a reminder that the fishing fraternity has some strange prejudices. The carp is considered a sport fish in some other countries. It can be caught on live baits and artificial lures. And if you're searching for a fighting fish, the carp will be a finalist in the contest.

Gapen's message is that sport fishing should rid itself of false prejudices and seek sport where it swims. In this case, the carp.

Carp are most easily caught with natural bait, if kernels of canned corn, boiled potatoes or gobs of bread dough can be called "natural." Nightcrawlers and earthworms also are effective.

Carp normally roam in shallows in mud bottom bays of

lakes or the backwaters, pools of rivers.

Fish the bait on the bottom, using a light slip-sinker or none at all and with or without a small bobber.

Bow and arrow fishing for carp also is popular in the spring when carp move into shallow creeks to spawn or otherwise root in the shallows. A fishing license is required.

That's another nice thing about carp fishing. There's no limit and the season is always open.

The Silvers Are Running

Among Minnesota's "second class" fishes, the one that gets the most respect is the white bass, also called the silver or striped bass. However, its popularity is not based on size or fighting skills.

Rather, the white bass has a penchant for committing suicide on a hook. Great schools of white bass roam the waters of Minnesota's St. Croix and Mississippi Rivers. And when they start "running" — moving in large schools near the surface — the white bass are catchable by the dozens.

To celebrate the occasion, the river town of Wabasha, declares its own holiday on the Mississippi.

The white bass become vulnerable and easy to catch at various times in the fishing season, starting early in May. August and September are the prime months.

The surest sign that the white bass are running is found in the air. In the form of gulls. When the gulls are seen in great bunches, circling over and diving into the water, you can bet that a school of white bass have gone into a feeding frenzy. The gulls hang around for the scraps, the prey fish crippled by the storming white bass.

When you can locate such a school, the catching of white bass is almost automatic. They'll hit minnows as well as spinners, small jigs and small plugs.

In other times, white bass will be found around the slack water in the St. Croix and Mississippi, most notably below the locks and dams.

White bass are quite eatable but are best smoked.

The Ugly Eelpout

The eyes beholding an eelpout or burbot will find no beauty. Compared to an eelpout, bullheads look like Prince Charming.

For those exact reasons, few Minnesotans realize the beauty of the eelpout is in the eating.

The fish is correctly known as a burbot. It's the only freshwater member of the codfish family from whence cod liver oil is extracted.

The burbot has scaleless skin like a bullhead, a long dorsal fin like a dogfish and a tail like a monkey. That is, it is capable of wrapping its tail around a fisherman's arm, momentarily raising the question of who caught whom.

Eelpout are most often mistakenly caught by walleye fishermen in the winter time, although summer anglers occasionally catch a few. The fish will hit minnows as readily as any other predator fish.

Unfortunately, anglers judge the eelpout strictly by its appearance. And ugly fish are usually wrapped on the head and tossed to the gulls. Hundreds of burbot are tossed on the ice and left or hauled to the garbage.

Too bad. The eelpout's flesh is white, firm and boneless. And quite good tasting. One winter, I convinced the late Swede Carlson, a Warroad fishing pilot, to add a few eelpout filets to a lunch of walleyes he was about to fry up on an ice shack stove.

Swede wasn't particularly enthusiastic over my suggestion but he relented. He wouldn't put the eelpout meat in his frying pan until every walleye was cooked. But he finally consented to take a bit of eelpout.

"Not bad," he grumbled.

"Tastes just as good as walleye, doesn't it?" I queried.

Swede wouldn't say yes and he wouldn't say no.

The Ancient Fishes

If you fish with minnows much for walleyes, northern pike, crappies, bass, you'll also catch a dogfish. It's an unwritten rule.

More properly called a bowfin, the fish is most easily identified by its rounded tail, a long continuous dorsal fin and large circular scales.

It's a voracious minnow eater and the only one of its kind, the sole survivor of an early primitive family of fishes.

Two other primitive fishes you might accidentally catch are the longnose and shortnose gars, which look similar except for the length of their long jaws heavily armed with teeth. The jaws are bony and narrow, and as such, are seldom taken by hook and line. But you never know. I caught two gars on the St. Croix River one afternoon, using a small spinner aimed at smallmouth bass.

From an angling standpoint, the gars and dogfish aren't really much to brag about. Their fighting style isn't spectacular and their flesh is not choice.

At most, the prehistoric fishes can give you a sense of history, possibly explaining why the cave men carried clubs not fishing rods.

(Courtesy of the Minnesota Department of Natural Resources)

The largest fish species in Minnesota's waters, the rock or river sturgeon.

Minnesota's Largest

You might know. The lake sturgeon, the largest fish that lives in Minnesota's waters, normally eats creatures too small to put on a hook. So they're seldom caught.

Probably a good thing. The lake sturgeon will grow to weights exceeding 200 pounds. With a lot of patience and a gob of nightcrawlers, the big fish are possible to catch. The two best known sturgeon waters include the Rainy River and the St. Croix River. I've heard horror stories from some of the St. Croix river rats who tell of hooking sturgeon longer than boats, of battling the huge beasts for hours.

Minnesota also has a smaller species, called the shovel-nose sturgeon, commonly found in the St. Croix, Mississippi and Minnesota Rivers. It seldom weighs more than 6 pounds, however. And is seldom caught on hook and line.

More Oddities

A hook really is nothing more than a customized spear. But, lordy, can it bring in a host of strange things. Like suckers and redhorse — fishes with mouths shaped like the end of a vacuum cleaner hose. Sheepshead, silvery fish with humpbacks; madtoms, miniature bullheads; buffalofish, quillback carpsuckers; gizzard shad; mooneyes; tullibee. And don't forget the whitefish, creatures of deep water that will take flies off the surface.

And that's just a few of the oddities that can show up on a hook. If you're not sure what you've caught, save it to show to one of Minnesota's fisheries managers or conservation officers. If they don't know, they'll find out.

There's only one oddity that you can't legally keep, the rare paddlefish. It's snagged more often than caught. The paddlefish has a nose that looks like the handle of a canoe paddle. What's more, the paddlefish looks a lot like a shark.

It's harmless, however. Minnesota's "sharks" have paddles, not "jaws."

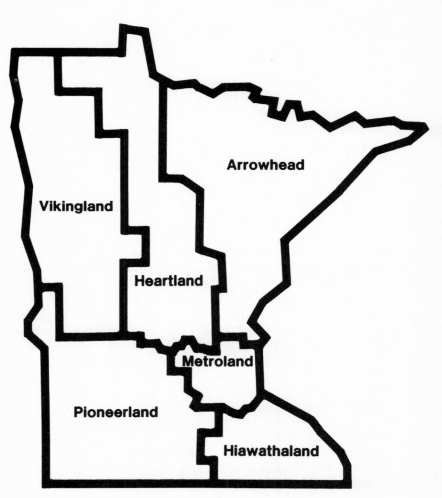

gone fishing

Arrowhead

Vikingland

Heartland

Metroland

Pioneerland

Hiawathaland

Part III
Gone Fishing

Picking a place to fish is like choosing a spouse. There are winners and losers.

It helps if you get to know each other first to see if you have anything in common. Super clear lakes are beautiful to look at but they're tough to fish on. A lake may be wonderful for bass but it's a disaster if you were expecting walleyes.

And all lakes or rivers can be temperamental. Generous one day, stingy the next. But that's a 50-50 proposition inherent in the fishing sport. A lake that's turned on is rarely kept secret. So ask around. Bait shops are great rumor mills. You can usually get an ear full of what's happening by simply asking.

Early in Minnesota's fishing season — mid-May to mid-June — the best lakes are usually shallow because the waters warm up slightly faster and the fish are more active. A difference of 3 to 10 degrees of water temperature at the start of the season is extremely important to your fishing success. Later in the summer, the opposite may be true. Deep walleye lakes, containing vast waters with depths of 40 feet or more, usually don't turn on until the first days of July. Then, the deep lakes may be more productive than shallow waters, if you're after walleyes.

Water temperature also determines the spawning times of many fish. On Minnesota's North Shore, for example, the steelhead first appear in good numbers in the rivers closer to Duluth. Later, however, the streams around Grand Marais may be at their peak for steelhead fishing.

As you can see, there are many variables that determine your angling success, not to mention the fish, itself.

However, the wise fisherman doesn't blindly choose a lake or river. Learn what you can before you launch the boat. A canoeist wouldn't think of floating a stream without first checking for waterfalls or dangerous whitewater rapids. A fisherman should do no less. Why fish the upper reaches of a steelhead stream when there's a barrier downstream that the steelhead cannot pass? Why fish a "walleye" lake if the fish were only stocked a year or two ago?

Again ask around or seek information from fisheries specialists or conservation officers with Minnesota's

(Photo courtesy of Minnesota Department of Natural Resources)

Picking the right lake at the right time is the key to fishing success.

Department of Natural Resources.

Your first stop is provided in the following pages.

With the aid and wisdom of Minnesota's Area Fisheries Managers, information from test netting fish surveys and the experience of fishing (my own and others), the top fishing lakes and rivers of Minnesota have been listed. Our intent was to give you the "best bets." For example, a particular lake may contain a number of gamefish. But the lake may provide the best fishing for only one or two fish species.

The listing of fish (see key) represents what each lake or river is best known for — fishing-wise. Of course, some of the decisions are subjective. Those of you with more intimate knowledge of particular waters may disagree with the listing. Perhaps you fished one of the lakes listed for walleyes and got skunked. That means you're a lousy fisherman. Or possibly you filled a stringer with walleyes on a lake listed here for largemouth bass. Good, you've got a hotspot of your very own.

To further simplify the list, we've divided the lakes and rivers into the tourism regions of the state. Thus, you can look at the region of the state you plan to fish and find all the lakes and rivers and species of gamefish.

The information on accesses to the lakes or rivers indicates "public", meaning an access or accesses are available. Boats may or may not be launched at some of the public accesses, however.

"Private" access means access is only available through privately-owned land or resorts. There may or may not be a charge at private accesses to launch a boat.

Because a number of lakes have the same name, the list indicates the lake's location from the nearest town. If that is not practical, the county is listed or a well-known area, such as the Boundary Waters Canoe Area (BWCA) or Voyageurs National Park.

Not every lake has been listed. Many have sporadic fishing records because of winterkills. Others have not been surveyed for fish populations.

But enough.

Let's Go Fishing . . .

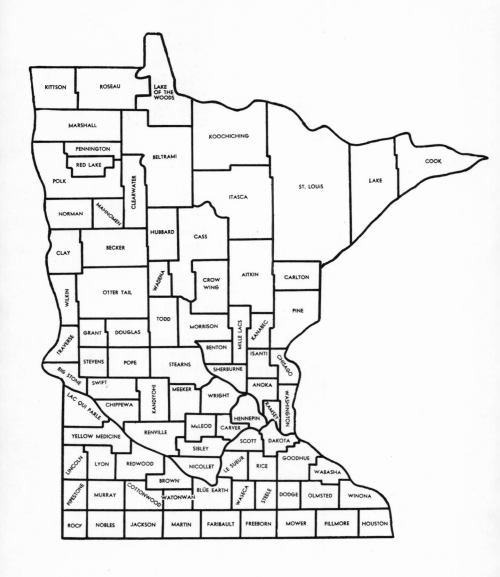

Arrowhead/
Wilderness Waters

Of all Minnesota's vast and varied fishing ground, the Arrowhead is the gem stone: wild and scenic, raw and untamed.

Its lakes are remote, its rivers roar.

It's a place for canoe fishermen with a sense of adventure and a strong back for portages.

Within the Arrowhead lies the Boundary Waters Canoe Area, the largest wilderness east of the Mississippi. On the east is the mighty, blue Lake Superior, an inland ocean. Further south the St. Croix River, one of the nation's first official Wild and Scenic rivers, carves a path between Minnesota and Wisconsin.

Elsewhere, there's a myriad of angling waters. Everything from walleyes to brook trout, lake trout to smallmouth bass.

To the west is the nation's newest national park, Voyageurs, encompassing primitive waters and packs of timber wolves.

Throughout the Arrowhead, the fishing grounds are consistent in one respect: they're good for the soul. Take a houseboat cruise on Rainy or Crane and seek the walleye and smallmouth. Assault the tea-colored rivers of the North Shore where the flashy steelhead lurks. Paddle the waterways of the BWCA where the fishing tradition is locked in time amidst a land unchanged. Or roam the forested banks of unspoiled brooks where native brook trout swim in the pristine current.

You will find some of the best smallmouth bass fishing in the country hidden among the pines. And there's enough walleyes to sooth the taste buds.

Muskie fishermen will find action in the Grand Rapids area and largemouth bass lurk in scattered waters, most notably in the southern reaches of the Arrowhead.

Much of the Arrowhead's fishing grounds are, by nature, infertile and delicate. As fish producers, the lakes generally rank quite low. That doesn't mean the fishing is poor. Quite the opposite, in fact. For once you find the fish you seek, they are usually quite catchable.

But even if they aren't, you'll find it hard to complain. Unless you talk to yourself.

KEY		
W=Walleyes	SMB=Smallmouth Bass	LKT=Lake Trout
NP=Northern Pike	LMB=Largemouth Bass	BKT=Brook Trout
C=Crappies	M=Muskies	RBT=Rainbow Trout
B=Bluegills	CTF=Catfish	BRT=Brown Trout
P=Perch	BLH=Bullhead	

Waters of Arrowhead

NAME	FISH SPECIES (listed by preference)	NEAREST TOWN	ACCESS
	Aitkin County		
Aitkin	BLH	McGregor	public
Cedar	NP, B, C, LMB	Aitkin	public
Clear	NP, LMB, B, C	Glen	public
Dam	W	Glen	public
Elm Island	BLH	Aitkin	public
Esquagamah	NP, C, B	Palisade	public
Farm Island	W, NP, LMB, C, B	Aitkin	public
Gun	NP, W, B, C, BLH	Palisade	public
Hanging Kettle	W, BLH	Aitkin	private
Hickory Pine	NP, B, C	Aitkin	public
Hill	W, NP, B, C	Hill City	public
Lone	NP, W, LMB, B, C	Aitkin	public
Long	NP	Glen	public
Mille Lacs	W, NP, P, SMB	Garrison	public
Minnewawa	W, NP, LMB, B, C	McGregor	public

NAME	FISH SPECIES (listed by preference)	NEAREST TOWN	ACCESS
Mississippi River	W, NP, M	Aitkin	public/private
Pine, Big	NP, LMB	Garrison	public
Pine, Big, South	NP, B, C, LMB	Finleyson	public
Rat	NP, B, C	Palisade	public
Remote	NP, B, C	Savanna State Park	public
Ripple	W, NP, B, C	Aitkin	public
Round	SMB	Garrison	public
Round	LMB, B, C	Tamarack	public
Sandy, Big	W, NP, BLH	McGregor	public
Sissabagamah	NP, B, C	Aitkin	public
Spirit	W, NP, B, C	Aitkin	public
Sugar	W, NP, B, C, LMB	Glen	public
Waukenabo	LMB, NP, B, C	Palisade	public

Carlton County

Bear	NP, B	Barnum	public
Blackhoof River	RBT, BKT	Wrenshall	public
Chub	W, NP, LMB	Carlton	public
Eagle	W, NP, B	Cromwell	public
Hanging Horn	NP, W, B	Barnum	public
Kettle River	W, SMB, NP	Kettle River	public/private
Moosehead	NP, B	Moose Lake	public
Nemadji River	RBT, NP, W	Wrenshall	public/private
Otter Creek	BRT, BKT	Carlton	public
Park	LMB, NP, B	Mahtowa	public
St. Louis River	W, NP	Cloquet	public/private
Sand	W, C, B	Barnum	public

Chisago County

Name	Fish Species (listed by preference)	Nearest Town	Access
Beaver Creek	BKT	North Branch	public/private
Center, North	LMB, NP, B, C	Center City	public
Center, South	NP, W, B, C, LMB	Center City	public
Chisago	LMB, NP, B, C	Chisago City	public
Comfort	LMB	Forest Lake	private
Fish	NP, B, C, LMB	Stark	public
Green	NP, W, B, C	Chisago City	public
Horseshoe	LMB	Stark	private
Kroon	NP, B, C	Chisago City	public
Linstrom, South	W, NP, B, C, LMB	Lindstrom	public
Little	NP, B, C	Center City	public
Rush	M, W, LMB, B, C	Rush City	public
St. Croix River	W, M, NP, SMB, CTF	Taylors Falls	public/private
Sunrise	BLH	Center City	private

Cook County

Alton	LKT, SMB, NP	Tofte	BWCA

NAME	FISH SPECIES (listed by preference)	NEAREST TOWN	ACCESS
Cook County cont.			
Bath	BKT	Grand Marais	public
Bearskin, East	SMB	Grand Marais	public
Bearskin, West	LKT, SMB	Grand Marais	public
Beth	NP	Tofte	BWCA
Birch	LKT	Grand Marais	public
Bogus	BKT	Grand Marais	public
Boys	BKT	Grand Marais	public
Brule	W, SMB, NP	Tofte	public
Brule River	RBT	Hovland	public/private
Caribou	W, P	Tofte	public
Carrot	BKT	Grand Marais	public
Cascade	W	Tofte	public
Cascade River	RBT	Grand Marais	public/private
Cedar	NP	Taconite Harbor	public
Chester	BKT	Hovland	public
Clara	W	Tofte	public
Clearwater	LKT, SMB	Grand Marais	public
Crescent	W	Tofte	public
Cross River	RBT	Schroeder	public/private
Daniels	NP, LKT	Grand Marais	public
Devil Track River	RBT	Grand Marais	public/private
Devilfish	LKT	Hovland	public
Dislocation	BKT	Grand Marais	public
Duck	NP	Grand Marais	BWCA
Duke	BKT	Grand Marais	public
Duncan	SMB	Grand Marais	public
Dyers	BKT	Taconite Harbor	public
Elbow	NP	Schroeder	public
Elbow	NP, P	Grand Marais	public
Ella	NP	Schroeder	public
Esther	BKT, BRT, RBT	Hovland	public
Finger	NP, W	Schroeder	public
Flour	SMB	Grand Marais	public
Flute Reed River	RBT	Hovland	public/private
Four Mile	W, NP	Schroeder	public
Fowl, North	W	Hovland	public
Fowl, South	W	Hovland	public
Frear	NP	Schroeder	public
Fredrick	NP	Tofte	BWCA
Gadwall	BKT	Hovland	public
Gogebic	BKT	Grand Marais	public
Grace	W, NP	Schroeder	BWCA
Greenwood	LKT	Grand Marais	public
Gunflint	W, LKT, SMB	Grand Marais	public
Hog	NP	Taconite Harbor	public
Holly	NP, P	Tofte	public
Hug	NP	Tofte	BWCA
Hungry Jack	SMB	Grand Marais	public
Indian Camp Creek	RBT	Grand Marais	public/private
Jap	RBT	Grand Marais	public
Jim	BKT, LKT	Grand Marais	public
John	P	Hovland	public
Junco	BKT	Grand Marais	public
Kadunce Creek	RBT	Grand Marais	public
Kelso	NP	Tofte	BWCA
Kemo	LKT	Grand Marais	public
Kimball	RBT	Grand Marais	public

NAME	FISH SPECIES (listed by preference)	NEAREST TOWN	ACCESS
Cook County cont.			
Kimball Creek	RBT	Grand Marais	public/private
Lake Superior	RBT, LKT	Grand Marais	public
Leo	RBT	Grand Marais	public
Lichen	W, NP	Tofte	public
Loon	LKT, SMB	Grand Marais	public
Manymoon	BKT	Lutsen	public
Margaret	BKT	Hovland	public
Mavis	RBT	Grand Marais	public
Mayhew	LKT	Grand Marais	public
Mayhew, Little	RBT	Grand Marais	public
Meditation	RBT	Grand Marais	public
Mesaba	LKT	Tofte	BWCA
Mink	BKT, RBT	Grand Marais	public
Missing Link	RBT, BKT	Grand Marais	public
Monkers	BKT	Grand Marais	public
Moosehorn	BKT	Hovland	public
Moss	LKT	Grand Marais	public
Mountain	LKT	Grand Marais	public
Muckwa	RBT	Grand Marais	public
Mulligan	RBT	Lutsen	public
Musquash	BKT	Grand Marais	public
Northern Light	NP, P	Grand Marais	public
Olson	BKT	Grand Marais	public
Onion River	RBT	Tofte	public/private
Pancore	RBT	Tofte	public
Pemmican	BKT	Grand Marais	public
Phoebe	W, NP	Tofte	BWCA
Pie	NP	Tofte	BWCA
Pierz	BKT	Grand Marais	public
Pike	SMB	Grand Marais	public
Pike, East	SMB	Grand Marais	public
Pike, West	LKT, SMB	Grand Marais	public/BWCA
Pine	BKT, RBT	Grand Marais	public
Pine	W, SMB	Grand Marais	public
Pine Mountain	BKT, RBT	Grand Marais	public
Poplar	RBT	Tofte	public/private
Ram	RBT, LKT	Grand Marais	public
Reservation	RBT	Grand Portage	public/private
Rog	BKT	Grand Marais	public
Rose	SMB	Grand Marais	public
Saganaga	W, SMB	Grand Marais	public
Sawbill	W, NP	Tofte	public
Sea Gull	W, LKT, SMB	Grand Marais	public/BWCA
Shady, North	BKT	Grand Marais	public
Shoe	BKT	Grand Marais	public
Sock	RBT	Grand Marais	public
Soda	NP	Schroeder	BWCA
South	LKT, SMB, NP	Grand Marais	public
Snow, Big	NP	Taconite Harbor	public
Squaw	BKT	Hovland	public
Sunfish	RBT	Grand Marais	public
Sun High	NP	Schroeder	BWCA
Surber	BKT	Grand Marais	public
Talus	RBT	Grand Marais	public
Thompson	BKT, RBT	Grand Marais	public
Thrasher	RBT	Grand Marais	public
Thrush	LKT	Grand Marais	public

NAME	FISH SPECIES (listed by preference)	NEAREST TOWN	ACCESS
Cook County cont.			
Timber	NP	Tofte	public
Toohey	W, NP	Schroeder	public
Topper	BKT	Grand Marais	public
Trout	LKT	Grand Marais	public
Tuscarora	LKT	Grand Marais	public
Two Islands	SMB	Grand Marais	public
Vale	BKT	Hovland	public
Wee	BKT	Tofte	public
Wench	BKT	Lutsen	public
White Pine	W, P	Tofte	public
Wine	LKT	Tofte	BWCA
Wonder	NP	Tofte	BWCA
Blue	LMB, B, BLH	Isanti	public
Fannie	NP, B, C, BLH	Cambridge	public
Green	W, NP	Cambridge	public
Long	B, NP, BLH	Isanti	public
Lory	C, NP	Braham	public
Skogman	LMB, B, C	Cambridge	public
Spectacle	LMB, B, NP	Cambridge	public

Itasca County

Amic	LMB, B, C	Squaw Lake	public
Ball Club	W, NP	Ball Club	public
Ball Club, Little	W, LMB, B, C	Ball Club	public
Balsam	W, LMB, B, C	Taconite	public
Balsam, Lower	W, LMB, C, B	Taconite	public
Bass	W, NP, B, C	Cohasset	public
Bass	SMB, B, C	Effie	public
Bass Brook	NP, W	Cohasset	public/private
Bass, Little	W, NP	Cohasset	public
Batson	W, B, C	Marcell	private
Battle	W, B, C	Big Fork	private
Bear	W, NP	Togo	public
Bear, Little	W, NP	Togo	public
Bear River	NP	Togo	public
Beatrice	W, LMB, B, C	Chisholm	public
Beauty	C, NP, B	Goodland	public
Bee Cee	RBT	Grand Rapids	public
Beeman Creek	BKT	Spring Lake	public/private
Bello	W, LMB, C, B	Marcell	public
Bevo	LMB, B, C	Big Fork	public
Blandin	LMB, B, C	Grand Rapids	public
Blackberry Creek	BKT	Grand Rapids	public/private
Bluewater	LKT, B, C	Grand Rapids	private
Bowstring	W, NP	Inger	public
Bowstring, Little	W, NP	Deer River	public
Bray	NP, W, B, C	Nashwauk	public
Bray	BKT	Nashwauk	public/private
Bruce	BKT	Swan River	public/private
Brush Shanty	NP, C, B	Big Fork	public
Buck	NP, W, B, C	Nashwauk	public
Buckman Creek	NP	Big Fork	public

NAME	FISH SPECIES (listed by preference)	NEAREST TOWN	ACCESS
Itasca County cont.			
Burnt Shanty	SMB, W, B, C	Marcell	public
Burrows	W, B, C	Marcell	public
Caribou	RBT	Marcell	public
Carpenter	LMB, B	Deer River	public
Cavenaugh	LMB, B, C	Cohasset	public
Chase	NP, B, C	Deer River	public
Clear	W, LMB, B, C	Coleraine	public
Clear	W, C, B	Wirt	public
Clubhouse	W, LMB, B, C	Marcell	public
Cole Brook	BKT	Grand Rapids	public/private
Cook Brook	BKT	Grand Rapids	public/private
Coon	W, LMB, B, C	Big Fork	public
Coon Creek	BKT	Togo	public/private
Cottonwood	B, LMB, C	Deer River	public
Cowhorn Creek	NP	Grand Rapids	public
Crooked	W, LMB, B, C	Marble	public
Crooked (Rock)	B, C	Big Fork	public
Crum	LMB	Effie	public
Cut Foot Sioux	W, NP	Squaw Lake	public
Cut Foot Sioux, Little	W, NP	Squaw Lake	public
Day	LMB, B, C	Grand Rapids	public
Deadhorse, Little	W, LMB, B, C	Marcell	public
Decker	NP, B, W	Squaw Lake	public
Deer	W, LMB	Effie	public
Deer	W, M, SMB	Deer River	public
Dick, Big	NP, B	Big Fork	public
Dinnerpail	NP, C, B	Grand Rapids	public
Dock	W, LMB, B, C	Marcell	public
Dixon	W, NP	Squaw Lake	private
Dora	W, NP	Dora Lake	public
Dunbar	W, LMB, B, C	Squaw Lake	public
Eagle	W, LMB, B, C	Marcell	public
Erskine	RBT	Effie	public
Five Island	LMB, B, C	Effie	public
Fletcher Creek	BKT	Wirt	public/private
Gale Brook	BKT	Big Fork	public/private
Grave	W, NP, B, C	Deer River	public
Greeley	RBT	Marcell	public
Gunderson	NP, LMB, B, C	Big Fork	public
Hale	LMB, B, C	Grand Rapids	public
Hanson, Middle	LMB, B, C	Coleraine	public
Harrigan Creek	BKT	Togo	private
Hart	W, LMB, B, C	Penguilly	public
Hart Creek	NP, SMB	Penguilly	public
Hatch	W, LMB, B, C	Marcell	private
Highland	NP, B, C	Marcell	public
Horn, Big	LMB, M, B	Deer River	public
Horseshoe	W, B, C	Marcell	public
Horseshoe	W, SMB, B, C	Marcell	public
Ice (Crystal)	LMB, B, C	Grand Rapids	public
Isaac	NP, LMB, B, C	Big Fork	private
Island	W, NP	Northome	public
Island	W, NP, C	Deer River	public
Island, Big	B, NP, C	Marcell	public
Island, Little	LMB, B, C	Grand Rapids	public
Jack The Horse	NP, LMB, B, C	Marcell	public
Jay Gould	W, NP, B	Grand Rapids	private

NAME	FISH SPECIES (listed by preference)	NEAREST TOWN	ACCESS
Itasca County cont.			
Jessie	W, NP, B, C	Talmoon	public
Jessie, Little	W, LMB, NP, B, C	Talmoon	public
Johnson	W, M, SMB, B	Marcell	private
Kelly	NP, C	Big Fork	public
King	NP, B	Big Fork	public
Kremer	RBT	Marcell	public
Lac La Bijou	NP, B, C	Togo	public
Lake of Isles	W, NP, B, C	Big Fork	public
Larson	RBT	Marcell	public
Lawrence	C, NP, B	Bovey	public
Leighton	LMB, B, C, W	Cohasset	private
Long	B, C, NP, W	Big Fork	public
Long	LMB, B, C	Effie	public
Long, Little	M, LMB, B, C	Marcell	public
Loon	LMB, B, C	Grand Rapids	public
Lost	LMB, W, B	Big Fork	public
Lost Moose	NP, B	Marcell	public
Lucky	BRT	Deer River	public
Maple	W, NP	Marcell	public
Matuska's Creek	BKT	Grand Rapids	public/private
Mink	NP, LMB, B, C	Marcell	public
Mississippi River	NP, M, SMB, LMB	Grand Rapids	public/private
Moonshine	RBT	Grand Rapids	public
Moore	LMB, B	Grand Rapids	public
Moose	W, M, NP	Deer River	public
Moose	W, NP	Northome	public
Moose, Little	W, NP, M, C	Deer River	public
Morrison Brook	BKT	Hill City	public/private
Murphy	NP, B	Grand Rapids	private
McAvity	W, LMB, B. C	Grand Rapids	private
McCarthy	NP, LMB, B	Nashwauk	private
McKinney	LMB, NP B, C	Grand Rapids	public
Napoleon	LMB, B, C, NP	Big Fork	private
Noma	NP, LMB, B, C	Squaw Lake	public
North Star	W, LMB, B, C	Marcell	public
No-Ta-She-Bun (Willow)	LMB, B, C	Remer	public
O'Brien	NP, W	Nashwauk	private
O'Leary	NP, W	Nashwauk	public
O'Reilly	W, NP, B, C	Taconite	public
Orange	B, M, LMB	Deer River	public
Owen	W, LMB, B, C	Big Fork	public
Oxhide	LMB, B, C	Penguilly	public
Pancake	BKT	Goodland	public/private
Peters	BKT	Goodland	public/private
Peterson	NP, LMB	Spring Lake	public
Pickerel	W, LMB, B, C	Effie	public
Pigeon, Lower	M, W	Squaw Lake	public
Pigeon, Middle	NP, W	Squaw Lake	public
Pokegama	W, SMB, NP, B, C	Grand Rapids	public
Pokegama	BKT	Grand Rapids	public/private
Prairie	W, LMB, B, C	Grand Rapids	public
Prairie River	SMB, LMB, BRT	Grand Rapids	public/private
Pughole	M, W, B, C	Deer River	public
Raddison	NP, LMB, B	Big Fork	private
Rice	LMB, B, C	Cohasset	private
Round	W, NP	Squaw Lake	public
Ruby	W, LMB, B, C	Marcell	private

NAME	FISH SPECIES (listed by preference)	NEAREST TOWN	ACCESS
Itasca County cont.			
Rush Island	W, NP, C	Spring Lake	public
Sand	NP, W, B, C	Squaw Lake	public
Sand	NP, LMB, B, C	Warba	public
Sand, Little	NP, B, C	Calumet	private
Sand, Little	NP, W	Squaw Lake	public
Scooty	NP, W, B, C	Nashwauk ·	public
Scrapper (Wilson)	LMB, B, C	Bovey	private
Shallow	B, C, NP	Warba	public
Shallow Pond	NP, W	Northome	public
Shine	BKT	Effie	public/private
Shoal	B, NP, LMB	Nashwauk	public
Sissebakwet (Sugar)	W, NP	Grand Rapids	public
Smith	SMB, C, B	Marcell	private
Smith	BKT	Grand Rapids	public/private
Snaptail	LMB, B, C	Bovey	public
Snowball	NP, LMB, B, C	Calumet	public
Spider	W, LMB, M, C	Marcell	public
Splithand	W, NP, C	Grand Rapids	public
Splithand, Little	W, LMB, B, C	Grand Rapids	public
Stingy	W, LMB, B, C	Nashwauk	public
Sturgeon, South	NP, W, B, C	Side Lake	public
Sucker	W, NP, C	Nashwauk	private
Surprise	RBT	Grand Rapids	public
Swan	W, NP, LMB, B	Penguilly	public
Swan River	B, LMB, NP	Swan River	public/private
Tadpole	W, LMB	Marcell	public
Thistledew	W, NP, LMB, B, C	Togo	public
Tibbetts	BKT	Squaw Lake	public/private
Too Much, Big	LMB, B, C, W	Big Fork	private
Trestle (Fox)	NP, B, C	Talmoon	public
Trout	W, NP, LMB, B, C	Coleraine	public
Trout	W, NP, LMB, LKT	Grand Rapids	private
Turtle	W, LMB, NP	Big Fork	public
Turtle, Little	W, NP, B	Talmoon	public
Twin	LMB, M, B	Nashwauk	public
Twin, North	LMB, B, NP, W	Marble	private
Valley River	BKT	Togo	public/private
Wabana	W, LMB, NP, B	Grand Rapids	private
Wabana Creek	NP	Grand Rapids	public/private

NAME	FISH SPECIES (listed by preference)	NEAREST TOWN	ACCESS
Itasca County cont.			
Warba	BKT	Warba	public/private
Wasson	NP, LMB, B, C	Big Fork	private
White Swan	NP, LMB, B	Marcell	private
Whitefish	W, NP	Wirt	public
Winnibigoshish	W, M, NP	Bena	public
Winnie, Little	W, NP, B, C	Deer River	public
Wolf	NP, W, LMB, B	Nashwauk	private

Kanabec County

Ann	B, W, CTF	Ogilvie	public
Eleven	B, C NP, LMB	Kroschel	public
Fish	B, C, CTF	More	public
Five	LMB, B	Kroschel	public
Knife	W, NP, B, C	More	public
Lewis	NP, B	Braham	public
Snake River	CTF	Pine City	public/private

Koochiching County

Big Fork River	W, NP, M	Big Fork	public/private
Black River	NP, W	Loman	public/private
Caldwell Brook	NP	Northome	public/private
Clear	NP, W	Gemmel	public
Dark	NP, W	Gemmel	public
Dinner Creek	BKT	Margie	public/private
LaBree	NP, LMB, BLH	Northome	public
Littlefork River	W, NP, M	Littlefork	public/private
Moose	C, NP, LMB	Littlefork	public
Rat Root	W, NP	Ericksburg	public
Rainy	W, SMB, NP, M	International Falls	public
Seretha	W	Gemmel	public
Trout Brook	BKT	Big Falls	public/private

Lake County

Adams	W, NP	Ely	BWCA
Ahmakose	LKT	Ely	BWCA
Alice	W, RBT, B	Ely	BWCA
Alseth	BKT	Silver Bay	public
Alworth	W, NP	Ely	BWCA
Amber	W, NP	Ely	BWCA
Amoeber	SMB, LKT, W	Ely	BWCA
Angora Creek	BKT	Angora	public
Arrow, Middle	NP	Ely	BWCA
Arrow, South	NP	Ely	BWCA
Arrowhead Creek	BKT	Isabella	public

NAME	FISH SPECIES (listed by preference)	NEAREST TOWN	ACCESS
Lake County cont.			
Artlin	NP	Finland	public
Ashdick	NP, LMB	Ely	BWCA
Ashigan	SMB	Ely	BWCA
August	W, NP	Isabella	public
Bald Eagle	W, C, NP	Ely	BWCA
Bandana	W, NP, C	Isabella	private
Baptism	RBT, BRT, BKT	Silver Bay	public
Baskatong	NP	Isabella	BWCA
Basswood	W, SMB, NP, LKT	Ely	BWCA
Bean	SMB	Silver Bay	public
Bear	RBT, LKT, BKT	Silver Bay	public
Bear Island River	W, NP	Ely	public
Beaver	NP, W, B	Ely	BWCA
Beaver Hut	NP, SMB	Isabella	public
Beaver River	RBT, BKT	Beaver Bay	public
Beaver River	W, NP	Ely	public
Beetle	RBT	Isabella	public
Benson	BKT	Finland	public
Besho	NP	Isabella	public
Birch	W, NP, SMB	Ely	BWCA
Blessner Creek	BKT	Finland	public
Bluebill	NP	Isabella	public
Bog	W, NP	Isabella	BWCA
Bone	RBT	Schroeder	public
Bonga	NP	Isabella	public
Boot	W, NP	Ely	BWCA
Boulder	NP	Ely	BWCA
Budd Creek	BKT	Beaver Bay	public
Burntside River	W, NP	Ely	public
Camp	RBT	Ely	BWCA
Caribou River	RBT, BKT	Little Marais	public
Carp	W, SMB, LKT	Ely	BWCA
Cat	W, NP, B, C	Isabella	public
Cedar	NP, W	Ely	BWCA
Cedar Creek	BKT	Silver Bay	public
Cherry	LKT, W	Ely	BWCA
Chub, East	NP, W, B, C	Isabella	public
Chub, West	NP, LMB	Isabella	public
Clear	W, NP, B	Ely	BWCA
Clearwater	NP	Ely	BWCA
Cliff	RBT	Isabella	public
Cloquet	W, NP, B	Two Harbors	public
Coffee	W, NP	Schroeder	public
Comfort	W, NP	Isabella	public
Cook	NP	Schroeder	public
Crooked	W, SMB	Finland	public
Cross River	NP, W	Schroeder	public
Cypress	LKT, W, SMB	Ely	BWCA
Delay	NP	Isabella	public
Disappointment	W, NP	Ely	BWCA
Divide	RBT	Isabella	public
Dix	NP	Ely	BWCA
Dragon	W, NP, C	Isabella	public
Dumbbell	W, M, SMB	Isabella	public
Dunnigan	W, SMB, B	Isabella	public
East	NP	Schroeder	public
Echo	RBT, LKT	Finland	public

NAME	FISH SPECIES (listed by preference)	NEAREST TOWN	ACCESS
Lake County cont.			
Eddy	LKT, NP	Ely	BWCA
Egge Creek	BKT	Finland	public
Eighteen	W, SMB	Finland	public
Ensign	W, NP, SMB	Ely	BWCA
Ester	LKT, NP	Ely	BWCA
Fall	W, NP, SMB, C, B	Ely	BWCA
Farm	NP, W, B, C	Ely	BWCA
Farm, South	NP, W, B, C	Ely	BWCA
Ferne	W, NP, B	Isabella	BWCA
Finland	BKT	Finland	public
Fishdance	W, NP, B	Ely	BWCA
Found	RBT	Ely	BWCA
Fraser	W, LKT, NP	Ely	BWCA
Four	W, NP, B	Ely	BWCA
Gabbro	W, NP, C	Ely	BWCA
Gabbro, Little	W, NP	Ely	BWCA
Gander	NP	Isabella	public
Garden	NP, W, SMB	Ely	BWCA
Gegoka	W, NP, B	Isabella	public
Gijikiki	LKT	Ely	BWCA
Good	SBM, NP, W	Ely	BWCA
Gooseberry River	RBT, BKT	Two Harbors	public
Greenstone	W, NP, LMB, B	Ely	BWCA
Greenwood	W, NP	Isabella	public
Grouse	W, NP, C, B	Isabella	public
Gull	W, NP, SMB	Ely	BWCA
Hanson	LKT, NP	Ely	BWCA
Hare	BRT, BKT	Finland	public
Harriet	W, NP, C	Finland	public
Harris	M, C, B	Isabella	public
Harris Lake Creek	BKT	Ely	public
Hatchet	W, NP	Ely	BWCA
Hazel	NP, B, W	Isabella	BWCA
Heffelfinger Creek	BKT	Finland	public
Hill Creek	BKT	Isabella	public
Hogback	RBT	Isabella	public
Hogstrum	BKT	Isabella	public
Hoist	NP	Isabella	public
Homestead	BKT	Finland	public
Hope	W, NP	Ely	BWCA
Horse	W, NP, B	Ely	BWCA
Horseshoe	W, NP, B	Ely	BWCA
Houghtaling	BKT	Finland	public
Hula	NP	Ely	BWCA
Hudson	W, NP, B	Ely	BWCA
Ima	W, LKT, NP	Ely	BWCA
Indiana	SMB, NP	Ely	BWCA
Insula	W, NP, B	Ely	BWCA
Isabella	W, NP, B	Isabella	public
Isabella Creek, Little	BKT	Isabella	public
Isabella River	W, NP	Isabelle	BWCA
Jasper	W, NP, B	Ely	BWCA
Johnson Creek	BKT	Angora	public
Jordan	W, NP	Ely	BWCA
Kane	NP, W	Two Harbors	public
Kawasachong	W, NP	Isabella	BWCA

NAME	FISH SPECIES (listed by preference)	NEAREST TOWN	ACCESS
Lake County cont.			
Kawishiwi	**W, NP**	Isabella	public
Kawishiwi	**W, NP**	Ely	public
Kekekabic	**LKT**	Ely	BWCA
Kitigan	**W, NP**	Isabella	public
Knife	**LKT, W, NP, SMB**	Ely	BWCA
Knife, Little	**LKT, W, SMB**	Ely	BWCA
Knife River	**RBT**	Knife River	public
Koma	**W, NP, B**	Isabella	BWCA
Lake Superior	**LKT, RBT**	Two Harbors	public
Lax	**W, NP, B, LMB**	Silver Bay	public
Leppanen Creek	**BKT**	Finland	public
Lindstrom Creek	**BKT**	Finland	public
Longstorff River	**BKT**	Ely	public
Malberg	**W, NP, B**	Isabella	BWCA
Manitou River	**RBT, BKT**	Little Marais	public
Maniwaki	**M**	Isabella	BWCA
Marais, Little	**RBT, BKT**	Little Marais	public
Marble	**W, NP, C**	Two Harbors	public
Mike Kelly Creek	**BKT**	Babbitt	public
Missionary	**LKT**	Ely	BWCA
Mitawan	**W, NP, SMB, C**	Isabella	public
Moose	**NP, B**	Isabella	public
Moose	**W, NP, SMB**	Ely	BWCA
Moose Creek	**BKT**	Finland	public
Murphy	**BKT**	Two Harbors	public
Muskeg	**NP**	Ely	BWCA
McDougal, Middle	**W, NP, B**	Isabella	public
Newfound	**W, SMB, NP**	Ely	BWCA
Newton	**W, NP, SMB, C**	Ely	BWCA
Nicado Creek	**BKT**	Finland	public
Nine Mile Creek	**BKT**	Finland	public
Ninemik	**W, NP, C**	Finland	public
Ninemik	**W, NP, C**	Finland	public
Ogishkemuncie	**LKT, NP, W**	Ely	BWCA
Ojibway	**LKT, SMB**	Ely	BWCA
One	**W, NP, B**	Ely	BWCA
Palisade Creek	**RBT**	Silver Bay	public
Parent	**W, NP**	Ely	BWCA
Perent	**W, NP**	Isabella	BWCA
Pietro	**NP**	Ely	BWCA
Polly	**W, NP, B**	Isabella	BWCA
Quadga	**W, NP, B**	Isabella	BWCA
Rabbitt	**LKT**	Ely	BWCA
Raven	**LKT**	Ely	BWCA
Rice	**W, NP**	Isabella	BWCA
Sagus	**W, NP**	Ely	BWCA
Sand	**W, NP**	Isabella	public
Sawmille Creek	**BKT**	Finland	public
Scott Creek	**BKT**	Isabella	public
Section 30 River	**BKT**	Ely	Public
Silver Island	**W, NP**	Isabella	public
Sister	**W, NP**	Finland	public
Skull	**BKT**	Ely	BWCA
Slate	**W, NP**	Isabella	public
Snowbank	**LKT, W, SMB, NP**	Ely	BWCA/public
Split Rock River	**RBT, BKT, BRT**	Beaver Bay	public

NAME Lake County cont.	FISH SPECIES (listed by preference)	NEAREST TOWN	ACCESS
Spoon	NP	Ely	BWCA
Square	W, NP, B	Ely	BWCA
Stewart Lake	W, NP	Two Harbors	public
Stewart River	RBT	Two Harbors	public
Stony	W, NP	Isabella	public
Stony River	W, NP	Isabella	public
Sucker	W, SMB, NP	Ely	BWCA
Swallow	W, NP, B	Isabella	public
Tee	W, NP	Isabella	public
Thomas	LKT, W, NP	Ely	BWCA
Three	W, NP, B	Ely	BWCA
Thunderbird	W, NP	Finland	public
Tikkanen	BKT	Finland	public
Tin Can Mike	W, NP	Ely	BWCA
Tofte	RBT	Ely	BWCA
Topaz	LKT, W, SMB	Ely	BWCA
Tower	BKT	Finland	public
Trappers	BKT	Isabella	public

Minnesota's Arrowhead region has the perfect combination: wilderness waters and fishing action.

NAME	FISH SPECIES	NEAREST	ACCESS
Lake County cont.	(listed by preference)	TOWN	
Triangle	**SMB, LMB, NP**	Ely	BWCA
Turtle	**NP**	Ely	BWCA
Two	**W, NP, B**	Ely	BWCA
Two Island River	**BKT, BRT**	Schroeder	public
Two River, East	**BKT**	Tower	public
Two River, West	**BKT**	Tower	public
Vera	**LMB**	Ely	BWCA
Weiss Creek	**BKT**	Isabella	public
Whitefish	**W, NP**	Schroeder	public
Wilson	**W, NP**	Tofte	public
Wind	**NP, W**	Ely	BWCA
Windy	**W, NP**	Isabella	public
Wood	**W, SMB, NP, B**	Ely	BWCA

Pine County

Bangs Brook	**BKT**	St. Croix State Park	public
Bass	**C, NP**	Finlayson	public
Crooked Creek	**BRT**	St. Croix State Park	public
Crooked Creek, West Fork	**RBT**	Duxbury	public
Cross	**W, SMB, C**	Pine City	public
Grindstone	**RBT, LKT, C**	Hinckley	public
Hay Creek	**BKT**	St. Croix St. Pk.	public
Hay Creek, Little	**BKT**	St. Croix St. Pk.	public
Island	**W, C**	Sturgeon Lake	public
Kettle River	**W, CTF, SMB**	Sandstone	public
Mission Creek	**BKT**	Hinckley	public/private
Net	**B, C, BLH**	Nickerson	public
Oak	**LMB, B, C**	Kerrick	public
Pine, Big	**B, C, BLH**	Finlayson	public
Pine, Upper	**B, C**	Finlayson	public
Pokegama	**W, CTF, C**	Pine City	public
St. Croix River	**W, M, SMB, CTF**	Pine City	public
Sand	**LMB, NP, B, C, W**	Sturgeon Lake	public
Sand River	**BRT, RBT**	Askow	public/private
Snake River	**CTF**	Pine City	public
Spring Brook	**BKT**	Hinckley	public/private
Sturgeon	**W, NP, C**	Sturgeon Lake	public
Tamarak, Big	**LMB, B, C**	Duxbury	public
Tamarak, Little	**LMB, B, C**	Duxbury	public
Wilbur Creek	**BKT**	St. Croix St. Pk.	public
Willow, Big	**BRT, RBT**	Nickerson	public/private
Wolf Creek	**BKT**	Duxbury	public/private

St. Louis County

Aerie	**NP, B**	Alborn	public
Agnes	**W, NP, SMB**	Ely	BWCA
Agnes	**NP**	Ray	Voyageurs Nat'l. Park

NAME	FISH SPECIES (listed by preference)	NEAREST TOWN	ACCESS
St. Louis County cont.			
Alruss	BKT	Ely	portage
Amundsen	NP	Grace Lake	portage
Armstrong	W, NP, SMB, C	Ely	public
Ash	W, SMB, C, NP	Ash Lake	public
Ash River	BRT	Orr	public
Astrid	W, NP	Buyck	portage
Auto (Arrowhead)	LMB	Virginia	public
Balkan Creek	BRT	Chisholm	public
Ban	C, NP, SMB	Cook	portage
Barrs	W, NP, B, C	Duluth	private
Bass	B, LMB, NP	Biwabik	public
Bass	LMB, NP, B, C	Tower	public
Bass	NP, C, B	Ely	portage
Battle	W, NP, LMB, B	Ely	portage
Bear Head	W, NP, LMB	Ely	public
Bear Island	W, NP, LMB	Babbitt	public
Bear Trap	W, NP	Ely	BWCA
Beartrack	B	Crane Lake	BWCA
Beartrack, Little	B	Crane Lake	BWCA
Beast (Wilson)	RBT	Ray	Voyageurs Nat'l. Park
Beauty Creek	BKT	Orr	public
Big	W, NP, SMB, B	Ely	portage
Birch	W, NP, C, B	Babbitt	public
Blackduck	W, NP, B	Cusson	public
Blackduck River	BKT	Orr	public
Blueberry	W, NP, C, B	Ely	public
Boot	W, NP	Ely	BWCA
Boulder	NP, B	Ely	BWCA
Briar	RBT	Duluth	public
Brown	NP	International Falls	Voyageurs Nat'l. Park
Buck	W, NP	Tower	portage
Burntside	LKT, W, NP, SMB	Ely	public
Bullet	W, NP, B	Ely	BWCA
Carey	NP, W, B	Hibbing	public
Caribou	NP, B, C, W	Duluth	public
Cedar	RBT	Aurora	public
Chad	NP, LMB, B	Tower	BWCA
Chant	RBT	Ely	portage
Chester Creek	BKT	Duluth	public
Chub	W	Crane Lake	portage
Clark	W, NP, SMB, B	Ely	BWCA
Clear	LMB, B, C	Buhl	public
Cloquet River	BRT, W, NP, CTF	Independence	public
Coe	NP, C	Biwabik	public
Colby	W, NP, B, C	Hoyt Lakes	public
Coon	LMB, B, C	Hibbing	private
Crab	NP, B	Ely	portage
Cranberry	NP	Hoyt Lakes	portage
Crane	W, NP, SMB, C	Crane Lake	public
Cruiser	LKT	International Falls	Voyageurs Nat'l. Park
Cummings	NP, LMB, B	Ely	portage
Dark	NP, LMB, B, C	Buhl	public
Dark River	BKT, BRT	Sturgeon	public
Day	LMB, B, C	Chisholm	public

NAME	FISH SPECIES (listed by preference)	NEAREST TOWN	ACCESS
St. Louis County cont.			
Day Brook	NP, BKT	Nashwauk	public
Dean Creek	BKT	Bear River	private
Dewey	W, NP, C, B	Chisholm	public
Dollar	RBT	Chisholm	public
Dry	BKT	Ely	portage
Dry, Little	BKT	Ely	portage
Eagles Nest #1	W, NP, LMB, B	Ely	public
Eagles Nest #2	W, NP, SMB, B	Ely	public
Eagles Nest #3	W, NP, SMB, B	Ely	public
Eagles Nest #4	W, NP, SMB, B	Ely	public
Echo	W, NP, B	Crane Lake	public
Ed Shave	NP	Ely	public
Elbo	SMB, W, C	Cook	public
Elbow, Little	RBT	Iron	portage
Elephant	W, C, SMB	Cusson	public
Elliot	B, C, NP	Eveleth	public
Ely	W, NP, LMB, C, B	Eveleth	public
Embarrass	W, NP, C, B	Biwabik	public
Esquagama	W, NP	Biwabik	private
Eugene	C, B	Crane Lake	BWCA
Everett	W, NP, SMB, B	Ely	portage
Fairy	W, NP, B	Ely	BWCA
Fat	LKT	Crane Lake	BWCA
Fawn Creek	BKT	Orr	private
Fenske	NP, LMB, B	Ely	public
First	NP, LMB, C	Ely	portage
Fish	W, NP, B, C	Duluth	public
Floodwood	NP, LMB, B, C	Hibbing	public
Four Mile	W, NP, LMB, SMB	Tower	private
Four Town	W, NP, B	Ely	BWCA
Fourteen	W, NP, B, C	Chisholm	private
Franklin	W, NP	Crane Lake	portage
French River	BKT	Duluth	public
Gabrielson	RBT	Orr	public
Ge-be-on-e-quet	NP	Ely	BWCA
Glenmore	NP, B	Ely	BWCA
Grassy	NP, LMB, C, B	Ely	portage
Grassy (Beaver)	W, NP	Ely	portage
Green	NP, B	Ely	BWCA
Gull	NP	Ely	BWCA
Gun	W, NP, SMB, B	Ely	BWCA
Gun	LKT	Crane Lake	BWCA
Half Moon	NP, C, B	Eveleth	private
Hanson	RBT	Ely	portage
Hegman, Lower	W, NP, SMB	Ely	portage
Hegman, Upper	NP	Ely	portage
Heritage	NP, W	Crane Lake	BWCA
High	RBT	Ely	portage
Hobo	C, B, NP	Ely	portage
Hobson	LMB, B, C	Chisholm	public
Horseshoe	NP, LMB, SMB	Eveleth	private
Horseshoe	NP, C, B	Eveleth	private
Hustler	NP, B	Ely	BWCA
Isaac	W, NP, LMB, B	Babbitt	private
Island	NP, LMB, B, C	Goodland	public
Island	W, NP, C, B, M	Duluth	public
Jammer	RBT	Virginia	public

NAME	FISH SPECIES (listed by preference)	NEAREST TOWN	ACCESS
St. Louis County cont.			
Janette	W, LMB, B, C	Goodland	private
Jeanette	W, NP	Buyck	public
Johnson	W, NP, B	Ely	public
Johnson	W, NP, SMB	Crane Lake	portage
Johnson, Little	W, NP, SMB	Crane Lake	portage
Joseph	W, NP, B	Babbitt	private
Kabetogama	W, NP, SMB, C	Ray	public
Kinmount Creek	BKT	Orr	public
Kinney	NP, B, C	Buhl	public
Kjostad	W, NP, SMB, C	Orr	public
Knife River	RBT, BKT	Knife River	public
Lac La Croix	W, NP, SMB, LKT	Crane Lake	BWCA
Lake Superior	LKT, RBT	Duluth	public
Lamb	NP	Ely	BWCA
Leaf	W, NP, LMB	Gilbert	private
Leander	W, NP, B, C	Chisholm	public
Lester River	RBT, BKT	Duluth	public
Little	NP, C, B	Hoyt Lakes	portage
Little	W, NP, SMB	Ely	portage
Loaine	RBT	Duluth	public
Locator (Cranberry)	NP	International Falls	Voyageurs Nat'l. Park
Loiten	NP, SMB	International Falls	Voyageurs Nat'l. Park
Long	W, NP	Cusson	portage
Long	W, NP, LMB	Eveleth	private
Long	NP	Hoyt Lakes	portage
Long	NP, LMB, B, C	Eveleth	private
Long	LMB, B, C	Chisholm	public
Long, Little	NP, SMB, W	Ely	portage
Long Year	NP, SMB, B, C	Chisholm	public
Loon	W, NP, LKT	Crane Lake	BWCA
Loon	NP, LMB, B	Aurora	public
Lost	W, B, C	Tower	private
Lost	NP, LMB, B, C	Biwabik	public
Lost River	BKT	Orr	public
Louis (Jacob)	RBT	Ely	BWCA
Low	W, NP, LMB, C	Ely	public
Lucille	SMB	Crane Lake	Voyageurs Nat'l. Park
Lynx	W, NP	Crane Lake	BWCA
Majestic	W, NP, LMB, C	Eveleth	private
Marion	NP	Crane Lake	portage
Maude	NP	Buyck	BWCA
Meander	SMB, W, B	Ely	public
Meat (Nixon)	NP	Ely	BWCA
Merritt	NP	Tower	portage
Midway River	BRT	Esko	public
Minister	W, NP, LMB, C, B	Ely	public
Mitchell	W, NP	Ely	portage
Moose	W, NP	Cusson	portage
Moose	NP, C	Orr	portage
Moosecamp	W, NP, B	Ely	BWCA
Moran	LMB, B, C, NP	Chisholm	public
Mud	LMB, NP, W	Buhl	public

NAME	FISH SPECIES (listed by preference)	NEAREST TOWN	ACCESS
St. Louis County cont.			
Mud	B, C, NP, W	Tower	public
Mudro	W, NP, SMB, B	Ely	portage
Mukooda	LKT, W, NP	Orr	portage
Myrtle	NP, B, W, SMB	Orr	public
McCormack	B	Chislholm	public
McNiven	BKT	Buhl	public
McQuade	LMB, NP	Hibbing	public
Namakan	W, NP, SMB	Crane Lake	Voyageurs Nat'l. Park
Needle Bay	LMB, B, NP	Tower	portage
Nels	W, NP, SMB, B	Ely	public
Nichols	W, B, NP	Cotton	public
Nigh	NP	Ely	portage
Nine Mile Creek	BKT	Orr	private
Nine Moose	W, NP, SMB	Ely	BWCA
Norberg	RBT	Tower	portage
O'Leary	SMB, NP	Crane Lake	Voyageurs Nat'l. Park
One Pine	W, NP, LMB, C	Ely	public
Oriniack	W, NP	Tower	portage
O'Rourke	BRT	Toivola	public
Oyster	LKT, NP	Ely	BWCA
Paradise	B, C	Duluth	public
Pauline	NP	Ely	BWCA
Pelican	NP, C, B, SMB	Orr	public
Pelican River	NP, SMB	Orr	public
Perch	W, NP, C, B	Chisholm	public
Perch (Whisper)	LMB, B, C	Ely	portage
Pheiffer	B, LMB, SMB, C	Tower	public
Pickerel	RBT	Hibbing	public
Picket	NP, B	Buyck	portage
Pickett	W, NP, B	Ely	portage
Picketts	NP, B	Ely	portage
Pike	W, NP, C	Duluth	public
Pike River Flowage	W, NP, B	Tower	public
Pine	W, NP	Tower	portage
Pine	W, NP	Fairbanks	public
Pleasant	NP, C, B	Eveleth	private
Prairie	W, NP, C	Floodwood	public
Purvis	NP, LMB	Ely	portage
Quill	SMB, NP	International Falls	Voyageurs Nat'l. Park
Rainy	W, NP, SMB	International Falls	public
Rainy River	W, NP	International Falls	public
Ramshead	W, NP	Ely	BWCA
Rat	NP, B, C	Chisholm	public
Regenbogan	RBT	Ely	portage
Rice, Big	NP	Tower	public
Rock	NP, B, C	Chisholm	public
Rocky	NP	Ely	BWCA
Rocky Run	BKT	Esko	public
Round	W, NP	Fairbanks	portage
Ruby	NP, B	Ely	BWCA
Sabin	W, NP, C, B	Biwabik	public
Saca	W, NP, B	Ely	BWCA

NAME	FISH SPECIES (listed by preference)	NEAREST TOWN	ACCESS
St. Louis County cont.			
St. Louis River	CTF, B, W, NP	Brookston	public
St. Marys	NP, LMB, C, B	Eveleth	public
Sand	W, NP, LMB, C	Virginia	private
Sand Creek	BKT	Side Lake	public
Sand Point	W, NP, SMB	Crane Lake	Voyageurs Nat'l. Park
Sandy	NP	Virginia	public
Sandy, Little	NP	Virginia	public
Schlamn	NP, B	Ely	portage
Shagawa	W, NP, SMB, B	Ely	public
Shannon	LMB, NP	Chisholm	private
Seven Beaver	W, NP	Fairbanks	portage
Shell	W, NP	Crane Lake	Voyageurs Nat'l. Park
Shell, Little	W	Crane Lake	BWCA
Shell, Little	W, B	Buyck	BWCA
Shipman (Bass)	NP, LMB, B	Ely	portage
Shoepac	M	International Falls	Voyageurs Nat'l. Park
Shoepac, Little	M	International Falls	Voyageurs Nat'l. Park
Side	W, LMB, B, C	Chisholm	public
Silver	RBT	Biwabik	public
Six Mile	M, B, C, LMB, SMB	Tower	public
Sletten	LMB	Ely	portage
Slim	W, NP	Ely	BWCA
Slim	NP	Crane Lake	BWCA
Soroll	W, NP	Ely	portage
Spring	SMB, NP	Crane Lake	portage
Sprite	NP	Ely	BWCA
Spruce	NP, B	Ely	portage
Steep	NP	Crane Lake	BWCA
Stingy	W, NP	Chisholm	public
Stone	LMB, B, C	Zim	public
Stone, East	LMB, B, C	Zim	public
Stuart	NP	Ely	BWCA
Sturgeon	W, NP, B, C	Chisholm	public
Sucker River	RBT, BKT	Duluth	public
Susan	NP, B, C	Cook	portage
Swan, East	BRT	Hibbing	public
Swan, Little	BRT	Hibbing	public
Takumich	NP, LKT, SMB	Crane Lake	portage
Talmadge River	RBT, BKT	Duluth	public
Tamarack	NP, W, SMB	Ely	portage
Tee	NP	Ely	portage
Tesaker	LMB, B	Crane Lake	portage
Tesoker	SMB, B	Crane Lake	BWCA
Thirteen	LMB, B, C	Buhl	public
Thunder	W, NP	Ely	BWCA
Trillium	W, NP, SMB	Crane Lake	BWCA
Trout, Big	LkT, W, NP	Tower	BWCA
Trout, Little	W, NP	Tower	BWCA
Trout, Little	LKT, SMB	Crane Lake	Voyageurs Nat'l. Park
Trygg	RBT	Crane Lake	portage
Twin	W, NP, LMB, C, B	Ely	portage
Twin	C, NP	Zim	public

NAME	FISH SPECIES (listed by preference)	NEAREST TOWN	ACCESS
St. Louis County cont.			
Twin, East	W, NP, LMB	Ely	portage
Twin, North	W, NP, LMB, C, B	Aurora	public
Twin, Second	W, NP, LMB	Ely	portage
Twin, South	NP, LMB, C	Aurora	public
Vermillion	W, NP, SMB, C	Tower-Cook	public
Vermillion River	SMB, W, NP	Crane Lake	public
War Club	NP, SMB	International Falls	Voyageurs Nat'l. Park
Western	W, NP	Ely	BWCA
White Iron	W, NP, C, B	Ely	public
Whiteface	W, NP, C	Markham	public
Whitewater	W, NP, C, B	Hoyt Lakes	public
Winchester	SMB, NP	Orr	portage
Wolf	W, NP, SMB, B	Ely	public
Wynne	W, NP, C	Biwabik	public

Some of the world's finest walleye waters are found in the Heartland region.

Heartland/
Wealthy With Walleyes

No doubt, the world's greatest collection of walleye fishing lakes exists in Minnesota's mid-section.

There's famous Mille Lacs, a perfect natural walleye hatchery.

Red Lake — the largest lake within the state's boundaries and walleye rich.

Winnibigoshish — a smaller version of Mille Lacs, fondly known as "Winnie".

Leech Lake — a place where walleye fishermen get happy and muskie hunters go delirious over muskie giants.

Lake of the Woods — a massive waterland shared with Canada, an international walleye hotspot.

Those are just the big walleye waters. In between there are dozens of other walleye producers, such as Gull, Cass, Whitefish and Alexandria.

The walleye waters in the Heartland can be traced to glacial activity, which left large, shallow depressions among sand plains and gravel — perfect conditions for walleyes.

But that is not all.

The Heartland also harbors most of the state's premier muskie waters, such as Leech, Cass, Andrusia, Little Boy and others. The Mississippi River also winds through much of the Heartland, producing walleyes, smallmouth bass and occasionally trophy-sized muskies.

The bass fisherman need not weep, either. For the state's mid-section is water-rich. Those lakes that don't support walleyes usually are outstanding bass haunts — largemouth and smallmouth.

The scenery also is mixed. From farmlands and woodlots to the piney forests and man-made pits of iron ore.

The Heartland also is the center of tourism in Minnesota with a vast array of resorts, ranging from woodsy cabins to ritzy rooms in plush lakeshore surroundings complete with golf courses and swimming pools.

But the most famous natural attraction in the Heartland remains unchanged: a wealth of walleyes.

KEY			
W=Walleyes	**SMB**=Smallmouth Bass	**LKT**=Lake Trout
NP=Northern Pike	**LMB**=Largemouth Bass	**BKT**=Brook Trout
C=Crappies	**M**=Muskies	**RBT**=Rainbow Trout
B=Bluegills	**CTF**=Catfish	**BRT**=Brown Trout
P=Perch	**BLH**=Bullhead	

Waters of Heartland

NAME	FISH SPECIES (listed by preference)	NEAREST TOWN	ACCESS
Beltrami County			
Andrusia	W, M, NP	Bemidji	public
Bailey	NP, C, B	Bemidji	private
Balm	W, NP, C, B	Bemidji	public
Bass	LMB, B	Turtle River	portage
Bass	C, NP	Tenstrike	private
Bass, Big	NP, W, C	Bemidji	public
Bass, Little	NP, C, B	Bemidji	private
Battle River	BRT	Kelliher	public/private
Beltrami	W, NP, B	Turtle River	public
Bemidji	W, NP, B	Bemidji	public
Benjamin	RBT	Blackduck	public
Big	W, M, NP	Bemidji	public
Black	W, NP, C	Turtle River	private
Blackduck	W, NP	Blackduck	public
Boot	NP, W	Bemidji	public
Buzzle, Big	NP, LMB, B	Solway	private
Campbell	NP, W, B	Bemidji	public
Carter	NP, B, C	Tenstrike	public
Cass	W, M, NP, P	Cass Lake	public

NAME	FISH SPECIES (listed by preference)	NEAREST TOWN	ACCESS

Beltrami County cont.

NAME	FISH SPECIES	NEAREST TOWN	ACCESS
Clearwater	NP, W, BLH	Bemidji	public
Clearwater River	BRT, RBT	Pinewood	public/private
Dark	NP	Nebish	private
Deer	NP, W, B	Wilton	public
Delwater	NP, W, B	Bemidji	public
Fahul	NP	Nebish	private
Gilstad	W, NP, B	Blackduck	public
Grace	W, NP, BLH	Bemidji	public
Gull	NP, W, BLH	Tenstrike	public
Hoover Creek	BRT	Kelliher	public/private
Irving	W, NP, P, BLH	Bemidji	public
Julia	NP, W, P	Bemidji	public
Kitchi	W, NP, P	Pennington	public
Long	NP, W, B	Bemidji	public
Lost	NP, B	Cass Lake	public
Marquette	NP, P, BLH	Bemidji	public
Meadow	NP	Turtle River	public
Meadow Creek	BKT	Blackduck	public/private
Medicine	C, NP, W	Tenstrike	public
Moose	NP	Solway	public
Moose, Big	W, NP, B, BLH	Pennington	public
Movil	W, NP	Bemidji	public
Mud Creek	BRT	Nebish	public/private
Myrtle	NP, B	Bemidji	private
O'Brien Creek	BRT	Nebish	public/private
Pimushe	NP, W, P	Pennington	public
Rabideau	NP, W, P, BLH	Blackduck	public
Red, Upper	W, NP, P	Bemidji	public
Sandy	NP, W, C	Tenstrike	public
Sandy	NP	Wilton	public
Silver	NP, C	Bemidji	public
Spring	RBT	Pinewood	public
Spring Creek	BKT	Blackduck	public/private
Spring Lake Creek	BKT	Pinewood	public/private
Stocking	NP, P	Bemidji	public
Swenson	W, P	Bemidji	private
Three Corner	RBT	Pinewood	public
Three Island	NP, W, BLH	Turtle River	public
Turtle, Big	W, NP, B	Bemidji	public
Turtle, Little	W, NP	Bemidji	private
Turtle River Lake	NP, W	Turtle River	public
Twin, North	W, NP, B	Turtle River	public
Twin, South	C, W	Turtle River	public
Windigo	B, LMB	Star Island (Cass Lake)	public
Wolf, Big	W, NP, P	Bemidji	public

Benton County

NAME	FISH SPECIES	NEAREST TOWN	ACCESS
Mayhew	C, P, W, NP	Foley	private
Mississippi River	SMB, M	Rice	public
Rock, Little	BLH, B, NP	Rice	public
Rock, Little Creek	BRT	Rice	public/private

NAME	FISH SPECIES (listed by preference)	NEAREST TOWN	ACCESS

Cass County

NAME	FISH SPECIES	NEAREST TOWN	ACCESS
Ada	W, NP, C, LMB	Backus	public
Agate	B, BLH, LMB	Nisswa	public
Alice	NP, LMB	Walker	private
Andrus, Big	LMB, NP	Remer	public
Andrus, Little	NP, P	Outing	public
Baby	NP, M, C, LMB	Hackensack	private
Barnum	LMB, SMB, B	Longville	public
Bass, Big	NP, C, LMB	Walker	public
Bass, Big	SMB, C	Outing	public
Beauty	LMB, B	Pillager	public
Birch	NP, W, B, LMB	Hackensack	public
Birch	LMB, B, C	Remer	public
Blackwater	NP, W, LMB, B, C	Longville	public
Blind	NP, C	Backus	public
Boot	BLH	Pine River	private
Boy, Big	W, NP, M	Boy River	public
Boy, Little	W, M, P, LMB	Longville	public
Boy River	NP	Remer	public
Bungo Creek	BKT	Pine River	public/private
Cedar	NP, LMB, C	Whipholt	public
Cedar	RBT	Remer	public
Cory Creek	BKT	Pine River	public/private
Crow Wing River	NP, W, SMB	Pillager	public
Cut	NP, B, P	Pine River	public
Dead Horse	NP, LMB, B, C	Remer	public
Deep, Big	NP, W, LMB, B	Hackensack	public
Diamond	RBT	Walker	public
Egg	C, LMB	Outing	public
Fawn	NP, LMB, B	Backus	private
Five Point	NP, LMB, B, C	Hackensack	public
Gadbolt	LMB	Walker	public
George	B, NP	Outing	public
Girl	W, NP, M, LMB, B	Longville	public
Grave	NP, W, LMB, B	Remer	public
Gull	W, LMB, NP, C	Nisswa	public
Gull River	LMB, NP	Brainerd	public
Hand	W, NP, C, B	Backus	public
Hardy	NP, LMB, B	Brainerd	private
Hattie	NP, B, C	Backus	private
Hay	NP, LMB, B, C	Backus	public
Hazel	RBT	Longville	public
Horseshoe	W, NP, LMB	Backus	public
Horseshoe	LMB, BLH	Whipholt	public
Horseshoe	NP, B, LMB	Pine River	public
Hovde	W	Walker	public
Howard	W, NP, M, LMB, B, C	Walker	public
Island	LMB, B, NP, C	Outing	public
Island	NP, W, LMB, B	Longville	public
Island	NP, LMB, B	Backus	public
Johnson	NP, LMB, B	Backus	public
Kid	NP, LMB, B	Hackensack	private
Larson	NP, W, B	Hackensack	public
Lawrence	NP, LMB, C	Outing	public
Leech	W, M, NP, P, C	Walker	public
Leech River	W, NP	Deer River	public

NAME	FISH SPECIES (listed by preference)	NEAREST TOWN	ACCESS
Cass County cont.			
Lind	NP, LMB, B	Backus	public
Lizard	NP, W, C, B	Hackensack	private
Long	NP, W, LMB	Longville	public
Long	NP, W, LMB, B	Walker	public
Long	NP, LMB, B	Hackensack	private
Louise	NP, C	Backus	public
Mann	NP, W, M, LMB	Hackensack	private
Margaret	NP, B, C, LMB	Nisswa	private
Margaret	RBT	Outing	public
Marion	BKT	Outing	public
May	NP, LMB, B	Walker	public
Moccasin	NP, LMB, B, C	Longville	public
Morrison	LMB, C, B, NP	Outing	private
Mule	NP, B, LMB, W	Outing	public
Mule	NP, W, LMB, B	Longville	public
Norway	NP, B	Pine River	private
Ox Yoke	NP, LMB, B	Backus	public
Perch	BKT	Backus	public
Pike Bay	W, M, NP	Cass Lake	public
Pillager	B, C, NP, LMB	Pillager	public
Pine Mountain	NP, W, B	Backus	public
Pleasant	NP, W, C, B	Hackensack	private
Ponto	NP, W, LMB, C	Backus	public
Portage	NP, LMB, SMB	Walker	public
Portage	NP, W, LMB, B	Cass Lake	public
Portage	W, NP, C	Bena	public
Portage, Big	NP, LMB, W	Backus	public
Rock	LMB, NP, B	Pillager	public
Roosevelt	W, NP	Outing	public
Sand	NP, LMB, C, B	Backus	public
Sand, Big	W, NP, B, C	Remer	public
Sand, Little	BLH	Pine River	public
Snowshoe	BKT	Outing	public
Silver	W, P	Longville	public
Six Mile	W, NP, B, C	Bena	public
Spider	BLH, W	Pine River	public
Stocking	NP, LMB	Longville	public
Steamboat	NP, W, P	Cass Lake	public
Stevens	NP, LMB, C	Longville	public
Stoney	NP, W, B	Hackensack	private
Stoney Creek	BRT, BKT	Nisswa	public/private
Sucker	NP	Cass Lake	private
Sugar	NP, B, C	Remer	public
Swift	W, NP, B, C	Remer	private
Ten Mile	NP, W, LMB, B, C	Hackensack	public
Tepee	RBT	Whipholt	public
Thirteen	NP, W, LMB	Cass Lake	public
Three Island	NP, W, LMB, B	Longville	public
Thunder, Big	W	Remer	public
Townline	NP, W	Longville	public
Trelipe, Lower	W, B, C, NP	Longville	public
Trelipe, Upper	W, NP, B, C	Longville	public
Tripp	NP, C	Hackensack	public
Vermillion	NP, LMB, B, C	Remer	public
Wabedo	W, M, NP	Longville	public
Washburn	W, NP, P	Outing	public

NAME	FISH SPECIES (listed by preference)	NEAREST TOWN	ACCESS
Cass County cont.			
Webb	NP, W, LMB C	Hackensack	public
Welsh	NP, W	Cass Lake	public
White Oak	LMB, B, P	Outing	public
Willard	RBT	Backus	public
Wilson	NP, LMB, B, C	Remer	private
Winnibigoshish	W, NP, M	Bena	public
Wolf, Little	W, B, C	Cass Lake	public
Woman	NP, W, M, C, LMB	Longville	public

Crow Wing County

NAME	FISH SPECIES	NEAREST TOWN	ACCESS
Allen	RBT	Outing	public
Arrowhead	NP, BLH	Pine River	public
Bass	LMB, B, NP	Garrison	public
Bass (Wise)	NP, LMB	Brainerd	public
Bertha	LMB, NP	Jenkins	public
Blue	NP, LMB	Outing	private
Borden	NP, C	Garrison	private
Borden Creek	BRT	Garrison	public/private
Boy	LMB, NP, B, C	Garrison	public
Buchite	B, NP	Cross Lake	private
Clam Shell	NP, LMB	Jenkins	public
Clark	NP, LMB, BLH	Nisswa	public
Clear	NP, LMB, W	Jenkins	public
Clearwater	SMB, W	Crosby	private
Clough	NP, C	Pine River	private
Crooked	NP, LMB	Garrison	public
Cross	W, NP	Cross Lake	public
Crow Wing	NP, B, C	Ft. Ripley	public
Cullen Creek	BKT	Pequot Lake	public/private
Cullen, Lower	LMB	Nisswa	public
Cullen, Middle	LMB, C, NP	Nisswa	public
Cullen, Upper	NP, LMB, B	Nisswa	public
Daggett	NP, LMB, W	Cross Lake	private
Dean, Upper	NP	Crosby	private
Edna	NP, LMB	Nisswa	private
Edwards	W, NP, B	Nisswa	public
Emily	NP	Emily	public
Fawn	NP	Merrifield	public
Fox, East	NP	Cross Lake	public
Fox, West	NP	Cross Lake	public
Gilbert	LMB, NP, B	Brainerd	public
Gladstone	LMB, NP	Nisswa	private
Goodrich	W, NP, C	Cross Lake	private
Grass	NP	Jenkins	private
Grave	NP, B	Garrison	private
Half Moon	NP	Merrifield	private
Hardy	NP, LMB	Brainerd	private
Hay, Lower	W, NP, B	Jenkins	public
Hay, Upper	W, NP, B	Jenkins	public
Heron	NP, B	Brainerd	private
Horseshoe	W, LMB	Merrifield	public
Hubert	W, SMB, C	Nisswa	public
Indian Jack	BLH	Crosby	private

NAME	FISH SPECIES (listed by preference)	NEAREST TOWN	ACCESS
Crow Wing County cont.			
June	NP, B, C	Crosby	private
Kego	NP, B	Emily	public
Kimball	NP, M	Jenkins	public
Lizzie	NP, C	Pine River	private
Long (Tame Fish)	LMB	Garrison	public
Long, Lower	W, NP, LMB, C	Brainerd	public
Long, North	LMB, C, W	Nisswa	public
Long, Upper	W, NP, LMB, C	Brainerd	public
Loon	NP, W	Pequot Lakes	private
Lougee	LMB, NP, B	Merrifield	public
Markee	LMB, NP	Merrifield	public
Mary	NP, W	Emily	private
Mayo	NP, C	Nisswa	private
Menomin	NP, B	Crosby	private
Mille Lacs	W, NP, P	Garrison	public
Mission, Lower	NP, C, LMB	Merrifield	public
Mission, Upper	NP, W, LMB, C	Merrifield	public
Mississippi River	W, M, SMB, NP	Brainerd	public
Mitchell	NP, LMB, C, W	Emily	public
Mud	NP	Crosby	private
Nisswa	NP, LMB, C	Nisswa	public
Nokay	NP, W, C, B	Brainerd	public
O'Brien	NP	Emily	private
Ossawinnamakee	NP, C, M	Jenkins	public
Ox	LMB, B	Cross Lake	private
Partridge	NP, LMB	Garrison	public
Pelican	NP, LMB, W, C	Pequot Lakes	public
Pelican, Little	NP, LMB	Pequot Lakes	public
Pig	NP	Cross Lake	public
Pine	SMB, LMB, NP	Emily	public
Platte	B, C, W	Onamia	public
Pleasant	RBT	Cross Lake	public
Portage	NP, C	Garrison	private
Portsmouth Mine Pit	RBT	Crosby	public
Pug Hole	LMB, NP, W	Outing	private
Rabbit	B, NP, LMB	Crosby	public
Reno	NP	Deerwood	private
Rice Lake Res.	NP, M, B, C	Brainerd	public
Rogers	B, NP	Outing	private
Round	SMB	Garrison	public
Round	B, W, LMB	Nisswa	public
Round Lake Creek	BKT	Brainerd	public/private
Rush Hen	LMB, W, NP	Cross Lake	private
Ruth	NP, C, W	Emily	public
Serpent	W, NP	Crosby	public
Sibley	NP, C	Peqout Lakes	public
Smith	LMB, C, B, NP	Garrison	public
Strawberry	RBT	Jenkins	public
Sullivan	W, NP, C	Onamia	private
Twin, East	LMB, NP	Nisswa	public
Twin, West	SMB	Nisswa	public
White Sand	W, LMB	Baxter	public
Whitefish	W, NP	Pequot Lakes	public
Whitefish	LMB, C	Garrison	public
Whitleys Creek	BKT	Brainerd	public

NAME	FISH SPECIES (listed by preference)	NEAREST TOWN	ACCESS

Hubbard County

NAME	FISH SPECIES	NEAREST TOWN	ACCESS
Bad Axe	M, C, B	Park Rapids	private
Bass, Big	NP, C, B	Akeley	public
Benedict	W, NP	Laporte	public
Belle Taine	W, NP, SMB, LMB, B, C	Nevis	public
Blacksmith	RBT	Park Rapids	public
Blue	W, NP, LMB, B	Park Rapids	public
Bottle, Lower	LMB, NP, W, SMB	Park Rapids	public
Bottle, Upper	W, NP, LMB, SMB	Park Rapids	public
Boulder	W, NP, BLH	Dorset	public
Buck	LMB, B, C	Park Rapids	private
Bungashine	BRT	Bemidji	public/private
Cedar	NP, B	Two Inlets	public
Cold Creek	BKT	Bemidji	public/private
Crappie	RBT	Park Rapids	public
Crooked, East	NP, W, LMB, B, C	Nevis	public
Crooked, West	NP, LMB, B, C	Nevis	public
1st Crow Wing	W, NP	Hubbard	public
2nd Crow Wing	NP, W	Hubbard	public
3rd Crow Wing	NP, W, B, C, BLH	Hubbard	public
4th Crow Wing	NP, LMB, B	Hubbard	public
5th Crow Wing	LMB, NP, B, C	Nevis	public
6th Crow Wing	NP, LMB, B, C	Nevis	public
7th Crow Wing	NP, B, C	Nevis	public
8th Crow Wing	W, NP, LMB, B	Nevis	public
9th Crow Wing	B, C	Nevis	public
10th Crow Wing	NP, B, C	Akeley	public
11th Crow Wing	LMB, B, C, NP, W	Akeley	public
Crystal	NP, B	Akeley	public
Duck	NP, LMB, B, C	Hubbard	public
Eagle	NP, W, C, BLH	Park Rapids	public
Emma	W, NP, SMB	Park Rapids	public
Evergreen	NP, C	Lake George	public
Fish Hook	W, NP, LMB, B, C	Park Rapids	public
Fontanac	NP	Lake George	public
Garfield	NP, W, LMB, C	Laporte	public
George	W, NP, LMB, C	Lake George	public
Gillett	NP, C	Lake George	public
Gilmore	NP, LMB, B	Dorset	private
Ham	LMB	Akeley	private
Hattie	B	Lake George	private
Hinds	LMB, NP	Park Rapids	public
Island, Big	NP, W, C	Park Rapids	public
Island, Little	NP, LMB, B, C	Nevis	public
Kabekona	NP, W	Laporte	public
Kabekona Creek	BKT	Laporte	public/private
Leesburg	NP, B	Nevis	public
Long	NP, W, LMB, B, C	Nevis	public
Mantrap, Big	NP, LMB, SMB, B, C, M	Dorset	public
Mantrap, Little	NP, LMB, B	Dorset	public
Mewman	RBT	Bemidji	public
Mow	NP, LMB, B	Akeley	public
Necktie River	BKT	Bemidji	public/private

NAME	FISH SPECIES (listed by preference)	NEAREST TOWN	ACCESS
Hubbard County cont.			
Pickerel	NP	Park Rapids	public
Plantaganette	W, NP	Bemidji	public
Pockadee Creek	BKT	Laporte	public/private
Portage	NP, C	Park Rapids	public
Potato	W, NP, LMB	Park Rapids	public
Robertson	RBT	Park Rapids	public
Sand, Big	W, SMB, M	Park Rapids	public
Sand, Little	W, SMB, M	Park Rapids	public
School Craft Creek	BKT	Lake George	public/private
Schoolcraft	NP	Lake George	public
Shallow	BLH	Dorset	public
Shingobee	C, LMB	Akeley	private
Skunk	NP, B, C	Park Rapids	private
Spider	NP, LMB, M, B, C	Nevis	public
Stall Creek	BKT	Laporte	public/private
Stocking	B, LMB	Park Rapids	private
Stoney, Big	LMB, NP	Park Rapids	public
Straight River	BRT	Park Rapids	public/private

Lake of the Woods County

NAME	FISH SPECIES	NEAREST TOWN	ACCESS
Lake of the Woods	W, P, NP	Baudette	public
Rainy River	W, NP, P	Baudette	public
Tomato Creek	BKT	Baudette	public/private

Mille Lacs County

NAME	FISH SPECIES	NEAREST TOWN	ACCESS
Mille Lacs	W, NP, P	Isle	public
Ogechee	BLH	Onamia	public
Onamia	BLH	Onamia	public
Rum River	SMB	Onamia	public/private
Shokopee	BLH	Onamia	public

Morrison County

NAME	FISH SPECIES	NEAREST TOWN	ACCESS
Alexander	W, SMB, LMB, C	Pillager	public
Fish Trap	W, NP, LMB, SMB	Motley	public
Pierz	B, C, NP	Piercz	public
Placid Res.	NP	Pillager	public
Shamineau	LMB, W, M	Motley	public
Sylvan Res.	NP	Brainerd	public

Roseau County

NAME	FISH SPECIES	NEAREST TOWN	ACCESS
Bemis Hill	BKT	Warroad	public
Browns Creek	BKT	Roosevelt	public
Hayes Lake	NP	Hayes Lake State Park	public

NAME	FISH SPECIES (listed by preference)	NEAREST TOWN	ACCESS
Roseau County cont.			
Lake of the Woods	W, P, NP	Warroad	public
Roseau River	W, NP	Roseau	public/private

Sherburne County

Ann	LMB, NP, B, C	Zimmerman	public
Big	LMB, NP, B, C, W	Big Lake	public
Birch	NP, B, C	Big Lake	public
Briggs	B, NP, W, LMB	Clear Lake.	public
Briggs Creek	BRT	Becker	public
Camp	B, C, NP	Clear Lake	public
Clear	LMB, NP, B	Clear Lake	private
Eagle	NP, LMB, B	Big Lake	public
Elk, Big	B, W, NP	Clear Lake	public
Elk, Little	B, LMB, NP	Zimmerman	public
Julia	B, LMB, NP	Clear Lake	public
Long	B, C, LMB, NP	Clear Lake	public
Mississippi River	SMB, W, NP, M	Clear Lake	public/private
Mitchell	LMB, NP, B, W	Big Lake	public
Orono	B, BLH	Elk River	public
Pickerel	B, LMB, NP	Clear Lake	private
Round	B, NP, LMB	Clear Lake	private
Rush	B, NP, LMB	Clear Lake	public
Sandy	B, LMB, NP, W	Zimmerman	public
Snake	BRT	Becker	public
Thompson	B, LMB, NP	Big Lake	private

Stearns County

Achman	NP, LMB	Avon	private
Beaver	LMB, NP, B	Luxemburg	private
Black Oak	B, C, NP	Melrose	public
Browns	NP, LMB	Eden Valley	public
Carnelian	LMB, NP, B, W	Kimball	public
Cedar	B, NP	Freeport	public
Cedar Island	NP, LMB, B, C	Richmond	public
Clear	LMB, NP, B, C	Richmond	public
Cold Spring Creek	BKT	Cold Spring	public
Crooked	LMB, NP	Clearwater	private
Eden	LMB, B, C	Eden Valley	public
Fairhaven	BKT	Fairhaven	public
Fish, Big	LMB, NP, W	Cold Spring	public
Goodners	NP, B, C	Watkins	public
Grand	NP, LMB, B, W	Rockville	public
Hanson Brook	BKT	Fairhaven	public
Horseshoe	NP, LMB, B, C	Richmond	public
Island	B, C, LMB	St. Joseph	private
Kalla	LMB, NP	Avon	private
Kings	W, LMB, NP, B, C	Freeport	public
Kinzer Creek	BKT	Cold Spring	public
Kraemer	NP, B, C	St. Joseph	public
Kreigle	B, C, NP, LMB	Avon	public

NAME	FISH SPECIES (listed by preference)	NEAREST TOWN	ACCESS
Stearns County cont.			
Koronis	W, NP, LMB, B, C	Paynesville	public
Long	NP, B, C	Clearwater	public
Long	LMB, NP	Cold Spring	private
Long	NP, B, C, W, LMB	Freeport	public
Luxemburg Creek	BRT	Luxemburg	public
Maria	NP, B, C, BLH	New Munich	public
Meyer Creek	BRT	Luxemburg	public
Otter	LMB, B, NP	Fairhaven	private
Pearl	B, W, NP	Kimball	public
Pelican	W, LMB, NP, B	St. Anna	public
Pine	LMB, NP, B, C	Albany	public
Pleasant	LMB, B	Rockville	private
Pitts	NP, B	Avon	private
Rice	W, NP, B, C	Paynesville	public
Robinson Hill Creek	BRT	Luxemburg	public
Rossier	LMB, NP	St. Joseph	private
Sagatagon	LMB, NP	Avon	private
St. Anna	LMB, NP, W, B	St. Rosa	public
Sauk River	NP, B, BLH	Melrose	public/private
School Section	B, C, LMB	Kimball	public
Smarts Creek	BKT	Sartell	public
Spring Brook	BKT	Kimball	private
Spunk, Lower	LMB, B, C, NP	Avon	private
Spunk, Middle	LMB, B, NP	Avon	public
Spunk, Upper	W, LMB, B	Avon	public
Stump	NP, B, C	Avon	private
Sylvia	W, LMB, NP SMB	Melrose	public
Teal Creek	BKT	Kimball	private
Two Rivers	B, C, W, NP	St. Anna	public
Watab, Big	W, OMB, B, C	Avon	public
Watab, Long	B, BLH	St. Joseph	private
Willow Creek	BKT	Kimball	public

Todd County

NAME	FISH SPECIES	NEAREST TOWN	ACCESS
Big	B, LMB	Cushing	private
Birch, Big	W, C, NP	Gray Eagle	public
Birch, Little	W, C, NP	Gray Eagle	public
Charlotte	NP	Long Prairie	public
Coal	C, NP	Browerville	public
Crow Wing River	SMB, W	Motley	public/private
Duel Creek	BKT	Long Prairie	public/private
Horseshoe	W, NP	Browerville	public
Maple	NP, W, M	Long Prairie	public
Mound	B, LMB, NP	Gray Eagle	public
Osakis	W, C, NP	Osakis	public
Round Prairie Creek	BKT	Long Prairie	public/private
Sauk	W, NP, C, LMB	Sauk Rapids	public
Swan, Big	NP, W, LMB	Swanville	public
Swan, Little	B, C	Swanville	public
Turtle	NP	Long Prairie	public

The bubbling brooks of Hiawathaland entice the trout fisherman.

Hiawathaland/
Bluffs, Rivers and Creeks

If you marvel at babbling brooks and inspire at the sight of high-timbered hills with trout streams in the valley, this is the place — Hiawathaland.

And if your aim is to catch fish, the wrinkled terrain of Minnesota's southeast may harbor the most visible but untouched fishing grounds — the famed Mississippi.

Running along the entire eastern border of Hiawathaland, the Mississippi first blossoms into a mighty river with vast bottoms and scenic islands and waterways. As a fishing hole, the river is actually untouched. Particularly for such sporty fishes as catfish or smallmouth bass. Of course, the river holds just about every sport fish in Minnesota . . . and some not so sporty.

Tucked away in the bluff country along the Mississippi, trout streams flow out of the limestone bluffs and wind through the valleys. Brown trout are stocked in many of the streams. However, other creeks produce natural browns and brook trout.

While you're stalking the stream banks, you may be lucky enough to hear the raspy gobble of a wild turkey or the drumming beat of grouse wings. And hear it all within some of the most spectacular geology in Minnesota. It's the kind of fishing country where you almost don't mind getting skunked.

Notice I said almost.

For the southeast is kind to most of its angling visitors. The Mississippi River, particularly in the early spring, produces some of the finest walleye and sauger angling in the state.

Later, many fishermen seek their walleye fortunes elsewhere. But if you're a river rat, the Mississippi will pay off in walleyes any time of year.

This is not a fishing grounds for a lover of lakes. For lakes are few and far between in the land of bluffs, rivers and creeks.

KEY	W=Walleyes	SMB=Smallmouth Bass	LKT=Lake Trout
	NP=Northern Pike	LMB=Largemouth Bass	BKT=Brook Trout
	C=Crappies	M=Muskies	RBT=Rainbow Trout
	B=Bluegills	CTF=Catfish	BRT=Brown Trout
	P=Perch	BLH=Bullhead	

Waters of Hiawathaland

NAME	FISH SPECIES (listed by preference)	NEAREST TOWN	ACCESS
Dodge County			
Zumbro River (S. Mid. Br.)	**SMB**		public/private
Fillmore County			
Branch Creek, North	**BRT**	Forestville	public/private
Camp Creek	**BRT**	Preston	public/private
Duschee Creek	**BRT**	Lanesboro	public/private
Gribben Creek	**BRT**	Whalen	public
Root River, Main Branch	**SMB, CTF**	Lanesboro	public/private
Root River, North Fork	**SMB, CTF**	Chatfield	public/private
Root River, South Fork	**BRT**	Amherst	public
Trout Run Creek	**BRT**	Troy	public/private
Goodhue County			
Cannon River	**SMB**	Cannon Falls	public/private
Hay Creek	**BRT**	Red Wing	public/private
Mississippi River	**W, C, NP, CTF**	Red Wing	public

NAME	FISH SPECIES (listed by preference)	NEAREST TOWN	ACCESS

Houston County

Beaver Creek	BRT	Sheldon	public/private
Beaver Creek, East	BRT	Sheldon	public
Bee Creek	BRT	Spring Grove	public
Crooked Creek, Main	BRT	Freeburg	public/private
Mississippi River	W, LMB, C, B, CTF	Brownsville	public
Winnebago Creek	BRT	Caledonia	private

Mower County

Red Cedar River	NP	Blooming Prairie	private

Olmsted County

Zumbro River, South Fork	SMB	Rochester	private/public

Rice County

Dudley-Kelly	LMB, NP, B	Faribault	public
Fox	W, NP, B, C	Faribault	public
French	W, M, B	Faribault	public
General Shields	W, BLH, NP, LMB	Faribault	public
Mazaska	W, NP, B, C	Faribault	public

Steele County

Beaver	C	Ellendale	public
Straight River	NP	Owatonna	private

Wabasha County

Cold Spring	BRT	Wabasha	private/public
Indian, East	BRT	Kellogg	private
Indian, West	BRT	Kellogg	private/public
Mazeppa	BRT	Mazeppa	private/public
Mississippi River	W, NP, C, CTF, SMB	Entire stretch	public
Zumbro	LMB, CTF	Oronoco	public
Zumbro River	SMB, CTF	Zumbro Falls	public/private
Zumbro River, North Fork	SMB	Mazeppa	private/public

NAME	FISH SPECIES (listed by preference)	NEAREST TOWN	ACCESS

Waseca County

Clear	W, NP, BLH, LMB	Waseca	public
Elysian	BLH, W, NP	Elysian	public
Reeds	LMB, NP, B, C	Elysian	public

Winona County

Bear Creek	BRT	Winona	public/private
Burns, East	BRT	Winona	public/private
Cedar Valley	BRT	Winona	public/private
Gilmore	BRT	Winona	public/private
Hemmingway Creek	BKT	Rushford	private
Mississippi River	W, CTF, C, LMB, NP	Winona	public
Peterson	BRT	Winona	public/private
Pickwick	BRT	Winona	public/private
Rupprecht	BRT	Winona	public/private
Rush Creek	BRT	Rushford	private/public
Stockton Valley	BRT	Winona	public/private
Whitewater River	BRT	Whitewater St. Park	public/private

Panfish . . . everybody's first fish.

Metroland/
Fishing Among The Masses

In Minnesota, fishing is never very far away.

Even among the cement roadways, sprawling suburbs and hustle-bustle of the Twin Cities where half of the state's residents live and work.

Among those 1.9 million urban dwellers, there are rich, and poor, young and old. But no matter. Any Twin Citian with a yen to wet a line need not go far or pay much. Youngsters with no means to visit the northern waters have their own wilderness on the shores of the Mississippi as it rolls through the Twin Cities.

Elderly folks while away their angling days on the fishing docks in the city lakes in the shadow of the Minneapolis skyline.

Lake Minnetonka — a sprawling, bay-studded lake on the western outskirts of Minneapolis — is a beehive of fishing activity for folks of every economic fortune.

Lakes scattered elsewhere in the suburbs are the fishing hotspots of a neighborhood.

And some metropolitan waters are indeed hotspots.

Some fishermen think that a lake surrounded by rush hour traffic, homes, sunbathers, bikers is somehow fishless. That a lake whipped by novice canoeists or sailboaters isn't worth a fisherman's time.

Foolish assumptions.

The fishing truth is the opposite. Many lakes in metroland are ignored, underfished. There's plenty of people around, but they're sunbathing, biking, swimming, waterskiing or holding hands. That leaves plenty of fish in the water just waiting to be caught.

Some of the best largemouth bass fishing can be found within the metro area. Smallmouth bass abound in the Mississippi River and Lake Minnetonka. There are muskies in Lake Harriet and Minnetonka. And panfish all over. Northern pike, too.

Fishing among the masses can pose some problems, however. Public accesses to lakes vary. There are outboard restrictions or speed laws. Specific information pertaining to special rules on lakes is available from the Minneapolis or St. Paul Parks Departments or from the various suburb city offices that have jurisdiction over a particular lake.

The point is the Twin Cities are different from most major metropolitan centers in the nation. If you come for business or a convention, bring your fishing rod. If you forget, borrow an outfit. In Minnesota, there's always a rod and reel handy. Even in metroland.

KEY			
W=Walleyes	SMB=Smallmouth Bass	LKT=Lake Trout
NP=Northern Pike	LMB=Largemouth Bass	BKT=Brook Trout
C=Crappies	M=Muskies	RBT=Rainbow Trout
B=Bluegills	CTF=Catfish	BRT=Brown Trout
P=Perch	BLH=Bullhead	

Waters of Metroland

NAME	FISH SPECIES (listed by preference)	NEAREST TOWN	ACCESS
	Anoka County		
Coon	C, NP, B, BLH	East Bethel	public
Crooked	B, C, LMB, NP, BLH	Coon Rapids	public
George	NP, LMB	St. Francis	public
Ham	C, NP, LMB, B	Ham Lake	public
Linwood	NP, B, C	Wyoming	public
Mississippi River	SMB, W, CTF	Anoka	public
Moore	B, C, BLH	Fridley	public
Rum River	SMB	Anoka	public
Twin, East	B, C, NP	Elk River	public

NAME	FISH SPECIES (listed by preference)	NEAREST TOWN	ACCESS

Carver County

Auburn	NP, B, C	Victoria	public
Bavaria	LMB, NP, B, C	Victoria	public
Courthouse	RBT	Chaska	public
Eagle	LMB, B, NP	Young America	public
Hydes	C	Young America	public
Minnesota River	CTF, W	Chaska	public
Minnewashta	LMB, B, NP	Chaska	public
Piersons	B, C, NP	Chanhassen	public
Reitz	B, C	Waconia	public
Riley	B, C	Chanhassen	public
St. Joe	B, C	Chaska	public
Victoria	BLH, B, C	Victoria	public
Waconia	W, LMB, NP, B, C	Waconia	public
Zumbra	LMB, NP, B, C	Victoria	public

Dakota County

Byllesby	W, B, CTF	Randolph	public
Cannon River	SMB	Waterford	public/private
Crystal	LMB, NP, B	Burnsville	public
Kennaleys Creek	BKT	Hastings	public/private
Marion	LMB, NP, B, C	Lakeville	public
Minnesota River	CTF, W	Burnsville	public
Mississippi River	W, SMB, CTF	Hastings	public
Orchard	NP, B, C	Burnsville	public
Vermillion River	CTF, W, B	Farmington	public/private

Hennepin County

Brownie	B, C	Minneapolis	public
Bryant	NP, B, C	Eden Prairie	public
Bush	LMB, NP, B	Bloomington	public
Calhoun	LMB, NP, C, B	Minneapolis	public
Cedar	LMB, NP B, C	Minneapolis	public
Christmas	NP, B, C	Chanhassen	private
Crow River	SMB, W, B	Rockford	public/private
Crystal	NP, B, C	Robbinsdale	public
Eagle	LMB, NP, B, C	Maple Grove	public
Fish	B, C	Maple Grove	public
Half Moon	B, C, BLH	Medina	public
Harriet	W, LMB, M, B, C	Minneapolis	public
Hiawatha	LMB, NP, B	Minneapolis	public
Independence	B, C, M	Loretto	public
Isles, Lake of	LMB, B, NP	Minneapolis	public
Long	BLH	Long Lake	public
Long, Little	B, C	Minnetrista	public
Medicine	NP, LMB, B, C	Plymouth	public
Minnesota River	CTF, W	Bloomington	public
Minnetonka	LMB, NP, M, B, C, SMB	Excelsior	public

NAME	FISH SPECIES (listed by preference)	NEAREST TOWN	ACCESS

Hennepin County cont.

Mississippi River	SMB, CTF, W	Minneapolis	public
Nokomis	NP, B, C	Minneapolis	public
Parkers	NP, BLH	Plymouth	public
Rebecca	LMB, CTF	Rockford	public
Sarah	LMB, NP, B, C	Rockford	public
Twin	NP, B, C	Robbinsdale	public
Weaver	C, B, LMB, NP	Maple Grove	public
Whaletail	LMB, NP, B, C	Minnetrista	public
Wirth	B, NP	Minneapolis	public

Ramsey County

Bald Eagle	LMB, NP, C, B	White Bear Lake	public
Como	B, C	St. Paul	public
Gervais	NP, B, C	Little Canada	public
Johanna	LMB, C, B	Arden Hills	public
Josephine	LMB, NP, B	Arden Hills	public
Keller	NP, B, C	Maplewood	public
Long	NP, B, C	New Brighton	public
Mississippi River	CTF, W, SMB	St. Paul	public
McCarrons	B, C, BLH	Roseville	public
Owasso	LMB, NP, B, C	Roseville	public
Phalen	NP, B, C	St. Paul	public
Round	NP, B, C	Maplewood	public
Silver	W, LMB	North St. Paul	public
Silver	NP, B, BLH	Columbia Heights	public
Snail	LMB	Shoreview	public
Sucker	B, C	Vadnais Heights	public
Turtle	B, C	Shoreview	public
Vadnais	B, C	Vadnais Heights	public
Wabasso	LMB, B, C	Shoreview	public

Scott County

Carls	LMB, W, B, C	Prior Lake	public
Cedar	W, LMB, B, BLH	New Prague	public
Eagle Creek	BRT	Savage	public
Fish	NP, B, C	Prior Lake	public
Minnesota River	CTF, SMB, W	Shakopee	public
O'Dowd	W, LMB, BLH	Shakopee	public
Prior, Lower	W, LMB, NP, B, C	Prior Lake	public
Prior, Upper	W, LMB, NP, B, C	Prior Lake	public
Shakopee Mill Pond	RBT	Shakopee	public
Spring	W, B, C	Prior Lake	public
Thole	BLH, B, C	Shakopee	public

Washington County

| Alice | B, C | Wm. O'Brien St. Park | public |

NAME	FISH SPECIES (listed by preference)	NEAREST TOWN	ACCESS
Washington County cont.			
Bone	NP, B, C	Forest Lake	public
Browns Creek	BRT	Stillwater	public/private
Carnelian, Big	NP, B, C	Stillwater	public
Clear	W, B, C	Forest Lake	public
DeMontreville	BLH, B, C	Lake Elmo	public
Elmo	NP, B, C	Lake Elmo	private
Forest	W, LMB, NP, B, C	Forest Lake	public
Goose	BLH, B	Scandia	public
Jane	NP, B, C	Lake Elmo	public
Lily	NP	Stillwater	public
Long	B, C	Mahtomedi	public
Marine, Big	LMB, NP, B, C	Marine	public
Mississippi River	W, SMB, CTF	Hastings	public

In Metroland, good fishing is no farther away than downtown Minneapolis.

NAME	FISH SPECIES (listed by preference)	NEAREST TOWN	ACCESS
Washington County cont.			
St. Croix River	W, SMB, M, C, CTF	Stillwater	public
Sand	BLH	Marine	public
Square	NP, B, C	Marine	public
Tanners	NP, B, C	Landfall	public
White Bear	W, LMB, SMB, NP, M, C	White Bear Lake	public

Wright County

Bass	NP, LMB, B, W	Annandale	public
Bebee	LMB, NP, B	St. Michael	public
Birch	NP, LMB, B	Buffalo	private
Birch	NP, LMB, B, C	Monticello	public
Brooks	B, C	Cokato	public
Buffalo	NP, W, BLH, B, C	Buffalo	public
Camp	NP, LMB, B	Annandale	public
Caroline	NP, LMB, B	South Haven	private
Cedar	NP, LMB, W, B	Maple Lake	public
Charlotte	LMB, NP, B, W	Rockford	public
Clearwater	W, NP, LMB, C, B	Annandale	public
Cokato	NP, LMB, W, B, C	Cokato	public
Constance	NP, LMB, B, C	Buffalo	public
Crow River	SMB, W, NP	Dayton	public
Dean	NP, B, C	Rockford	public
Deer	NP, B, C, BLH	Buffalo	public
Eagle	NP, LMB, B, C	Monticello	public
Fish	NP, W, B, C	Clearwater	public
French	NP, LMB, W, B, C	French Lake	public
Granite	C, NP, LMB	Annandale	public
Howard	NP, LMB, B, C	Howard Lake	public
Ida	LMB, NP, B, C	Monticello	public
Indian	NP, LMB, B, C	Maple Lake	public
John	NP, LMB, B, C	Annandale	public
Limestone	NP, LMB, B, W	Silver Creek	public
Locke	NP, W, B, C	Monticello	public
Louisa	NP, LMB, B, W	South Haven	public
Maple	NP, LMB, W, B	Maple Lake	public
Maria	NP, LMB, BLH, B	South Haven	public
Mary	NP, B, W	Maple Lake	public
Mink	NP, B, BLH	Maple Lake	public
Mink	NP, B, LMB	Buffalo	public
Mississippi River	SMB, W, M, NP	Monticello	public
Nixon	NP, LMB, B	Clearwater	public
Pleasant	NP, LMB, B, W	Annandale	public
Pulaski	W, LMB, C, SMB	Buffalo	public
Ramsey	NP, LMB, B, C	Maple Lake	public
Rock	NP, LMB, B, W	Maple Lake	public
Silver	NP, B, C	Silver Creek	public
Skifstrom	NP, LMB, B	Cokato	public
Sugar	W, LMB, M, NP	Maple Lake	public
Sullivan	NP, LMB, B	Maple Lake	public
Sylvia	LMB, NP, W, B	Annandale	public
Waverly	NP, LMB, B, C	Waverly	public

Pioneerland/
Angling In Cow Pastures

If you don't mind fishing under the watchful eyes of a cud-chewing Holstein, then the waters of Minnesota's southwest are worth a visit.

Your scenic horizons will feature giant cottonwoods and barn silos, not pines and soaring eagles. But if your idea of a beautiful sight is a heavy stringer, carry a camera.

The fishing waters of the southwest consist of prairie lakes and rivers, most noticeably the Minnesota River. In general, the lakes share common characteristics. They are shallow and fertile but highly prolific as fish producers. Inter-mixed are small lakes and potholes too shallow to support fishlife but invaluable to waterfowl and fur-bearers.

Still other waters support only bullheads, which are capable of surviving Minnesota's winters with a minimum of water overhead. That makes the southwest a bullhead fisherman's paradise, including Waterville, the Bullhead Capitol of the World.

But do not be misled.

Some of Minnesota's best walleye trophy lakes can be found in the southwest far from the beaten path of tourist anglers. Consider Big Stone Lake near Ortonville, a long, shallow reservoir on the South Dakota border, known for its "hawg" walleyes.

And don't overlook such walleye producers as Big Kandiyohi or Washington Lake or Lake Koronis.

You'll not find clearer, sky blue water than that which glistens on Green Lake, a home for smallmouth bass as well as walleyes.

Northern pike also abound in many lakes of the southwest. Largemouth grow like pigs and the catfish are giants, particularly among the snags and log jams of the Minnesota River and tributaries.

Excellent bluegills and giant crappies also swim among the cow pastures.

Unfortunately, lots of folks think you've got to go "up north" to find fishing in Minnesota. That, my friends, is a lot of bull.

KEY			
W=Walleyes	SMB=Smallmouth Bass	LKT=Lake Trout
NP=Northern Pike	LMB=Largemouth Bass	BKT=Brook Trout
C=Crappies	M=Muskies	RBT=Rainbow Trout
B=Bluegills	CTF=Catfish	BRT=Brown Trout
P=Perch	BLH=Bullhead	

Waters of Pioneerland

NAME	FISH SPECIES (listed by preference)	NEAREST TOWN	ACCESS
Big Stone County			
Artichoke	NP, W, B, BLH	Correll	public
Minnesota River	CTF, BLH	Entire stretch	public
Stone, Big	W, BLH, B, C	Ortonville	public
Tom, Long	NP, B, C, W	Ortonville	public
Blue Earth County			
Ballantyne Lake	NP, LMB	Madison Lake	public
Blue Earth River	CTF, SMB, W	Rapidan	public
Duck	NP, C	Madison Lake	public
Madison	W, NP, C, B	Madison Lake	public
Brown County			
Cottonwood River	SMB	Searles	public
Minnesota River	CTF	New Ulm	public

NAME	FISH SPECIES (listed by preference)	NEAREST TOWN	ACCESS

Chippewa County

Minnesota River	**SMB, W**	Granite Falls	public

Cottonwood County

Bingham	**W, B, C**	Windom	public
Clear	**BLH**	Windom	public
Cottonwood	**W, LMB**	Windom	public
Talcott	**NP, C**	Windom	public

Faribault County

Bass	**B, C**	Winnebago	public

Jackson County

Clear	**NP, P**	Jackson	public
Fish	**W, SMB, C**	Windom	public
Loon	**W, BLH**	Lakefield	public
Round	**W, BLH**	Round Lake	public

Kandiyohi County

Andrew	**W, NP, B, C**	New London	public
Bass	**B, C**	Atwater	public
Carrie	**B, C, LMB**	Atwater	public
Diamond	**W, NP, LMB, B, C**	Atwater	public
Eagle	**W, NP, LMB, B, C**	Willmar	public
Elkhorn	**B, C**	Spicer	public
Florida	**W, NP, B, C**	New London	public
Games	**LMB, B, C**	New London	public
George	**LMB, B, C**	Spicer	public
Green	**W, NP, SMB, LMB**	Spicer	public
Henderson	**LMB, B, C**	Spicer	public
Kandiyohi, Big	**W, B, C**	Lake Lillian	public
Long	**NP, LMB, C, B**	New London	public
Nest	**W, NP, B, C**	Spicer	public
Norway	**NP, LMB, C, B**	New London	public
Point	**B, C**	Willmar	public
Solomon, East	**BLH**	Willmar	public
Swenson	**LMB**	New London	public

NAME	FISH SPECIES (listed by preference)	NEAREST TOWN	ACCESS

Lac Qui Parle County

Lac Qui Parle	W, NP, C, B	Appleton	public
Marsh	NP, W	Appleton	public

Le Sueur County

Emily	LMB, NP, B, C	St. Peter	public
German	LMB, W, NP, B, C	Cleveland	public
Jefferson	LMB, W, NP, B, C	Cleveland	public
Tetonka	BLH, W, B, C	Waterville	public
Washington	W, LMB, NP, C, B	Mankato	public

Lincoln County

Benton	W, P, BLH	Lake Benton	public
Dead Coon	W, BLH	Tyler	public
Hendricks	BLH, W	Hendricks	public
Shaokotan	BLH	Lake Benton	public

Lyon County

Brawner	LMB, B	Russell	public
Goose	W, BLH	Russell	public
Redwood River	BRT	Camden State Park	public
Schoolgrove	BLH	Cottonwood	public
Twin, West	W	Ruthton	public
Yankton	BLH	Balaton	public

Martin County

Amber	CTF, BLH, B	Fairmont	public
Budd	W, B, BLH	Fairmont	public
Cedar	P	Trimont	public
Clear	W	Ceylon	public
Fish	C, BLH	Odin	public
Fox	W, B	Sherburn	public
George	W, B	Fairmont	public
Hall	W, LMB	Fairmont	public
Iowa	BLH	Fairmont	public
Silver, South	W, NP	Fairmont	public
Sisseton	W	Fairmont	public
Temperance	BLH	Sherburn	public
Twin, Big	P, BLH	Trimont	public
Wilmert	W, NP	Fairmont	public

Famed baseball star, Carl Yastremzski, and the author, took these bass, angling among the cow pastures of Pioneerland.

NAME	FISH SPECIES (listed by preference)	NEAREST TOWN	ACCESS
	Meeker County		
Betty	B, C	Kingston	public
Clear	W, B	Watkins	public
Collinwood	LMB, B, C	Dassel	public
Crow River, North Fork	NP, BLH, W	Meeker County	public
Erie	LMB, B, C	Hutchinson	public
Francis	NP, B	Kingston	public
Jennie	W, BLH	Dassel	public
Long	LMB	Dassel	public
Manuella	SMB	Darwin	public
Minnie Belle	W, NP, B	Litchfield	public
Mud, Little	RBT	Watkins	public
Richardson	NP	Darwin	public
Ripley	NP, B, C	Litchfield	public
Star	NP	Litchfield	public
Stella	W, SMB	Dassel	public
Sucker Creek	BRT	Darwin	public
Swan, Big	NP	Kingston	public
Washington	W	Dassel	public
	Murray County		
Bloody	C, B	Currie	public
Current	BLH	Currie	public
Fox	C, BLH	Currie	public
Fulda	C	Fulda	public
Lime	P, BLH	Avoca	public
Sarah	BLH	Currie	public
Shetek	W, C	Currie	public
Summit	B	Hadley	public
	McLeod County		
Belle	W	Hutchinson	public
Marion	BLH	Hutchinson	public
	Nobles County		
Graham, West	P	Dundee	public
Indian	P, BLH	Round Lake	public
Ocheda	BLH	Worthington	public
Okabena	W	Worthington	public
	Pipestone County		
Split Rock	P, BLH	Split Rock State Park	public

NAME	FISH SPECIES (listed by preference)	NEAREST TOWN	ACCESS

Renville County

Allie	NP, C, BLH	Buffalo Lake	public
Preston	C, BLH	Buffalo Lake	public

Rock County

Blue Mound	C	Blue Mound State Park	public

Swift County

Camp	NP	Swift Falls	public
Chippewa River	BLH, B, NP	Swift County	public
Monson	W, B, C	Benson	public
Oliver	W	Appleton	public

Traverse County

Traverse Lake	NP, BLH, W	Browns Valley	public

Watonwan County

Fedji	C	Madelia	public
Kansas	W, C	St. James	public
Long	C	St. James	public

Yellow Medicine County

Canby Creek	BRT	Canby	public/private

*In Vikingland, the infinite variety of fishing for Al Lindner
included a hefty stringer of bragging-sized bass.*

Vikingland/
Infinite Variety

If you can't find the fish you're looking for in Vikingland, they don't make it.

From bluegills to whitefish, bass to walleyes, the many waters of Vikingland offer a menagerie for the angler who can't make up his mind. And that includes scenery. Call it multiple — from the piney forests to the Red River flatlands to the rolling pothole prairies.

Fishing wasn't discovered in Minnesota's northwest but the headwaters of the Mighty Mississippi were. From the tall, virgin pines of Itasca State Park, the Father of Waters begins as a small trickle on its 2,552-mile journey to the Gulf.

For the angler, Vikingland consists of infinite opportunities to fish for any of Minnesota's game fishes within close proximity. Otter Tail Lake, for example, is one of the state's finer natural walleye lakes. Down the road a few miles lies West Battle Lake, harboring a healthy supply of sporty muskies.

Northward, the community of Detroit Lakes calls itself a "Panfish Capitol" and for good reason. Among its many lakes, there are some that specialize as panfish producers.

As if that wasn't enough, Vikingland includes some of Minnesota's finest largemouth bass fishing waters, particularly around Alexandria, which calls itself a "Bass

Capitol"

However, bass fishing in the northwest is "Capitol" quality throughout the region. Not so well known is the walleye fishing available in such lakes as Osakis, Lida, Pelican, Mary and many others.

Trout waters in Vikingland are limited. Yet, the headwaters of one of the state's premier trout streams — the Straight River — is located in the western border of Becker County.

In short, Minnesota's northwest has a lot of every kind of fishing. And most of it is good.

KEY	W=Walleyes	SMB=Smallmouth Bass	LKT=Lake Trout
	NP=Northern Pike	LMB=Largemouth Bass	BKT=Brook Trout
	C=Crappies	M=Muskies	RBT=Rainbow Trout
	B=Bluegills	CTF=Catfish	BRT=Brown Trout
	P=Perch	BLH=Bullhead	

Waters of Vikingland

NAME	FISH SPECIES (listed by preference)	NEAREST TOWN	ACCESS
	Becker County		
Acorn	NP, C, B	Frazee	public
Bad Medicine	W	Park Rapids	public
Bass	LMB, C, B	Snellman	public
Bass	NP, LMB, B, C	White Earth	public
Bass	LMB, B, C	Park Rapids	public
Bejou	NP, B, C, BLH	Lake Park	public
Bemidji, Little	W, NP	Ponsford	public
Buffalo	NP, BLH, C, B	Richwood	public
Cormorant, Big	W, SMB, LMB	Audubon	public
Cormorant, Little	NP, B, C, BLH	Audubon	public
Cotton	W, NP, B, C	Detroit Lakes	public
Detroit, Big	W, NP, BLH	Detroit Lakes	public
Detroit, Little	LMB, B, C	Detroit Lakes	public
Eagle	BLH, B, C	Frazee	public
Elbow, Big	W, NP	Waubon	public
Eunice	B, C	Audubon	public
Floyd, Big	NP, C, B	Detroit Lakes	private
Floyd, Little	NP, B, C, BLH	Detroit Lakes	public
Fox	NP, LMB, B, C	Detroit Lakes	private
Hanson	RBT	Detroit Lakes	public
Height of Land	NP, BLH	Detroit Lakes	public
Hungry	BLH	Frazee	public
Ice Cracking	W, NP	Ponsford	public
Ida	W, B, C	Lake Park	public

NAME	FISH SPECIES (listed by preference)	NEAREST TOWN	ACCESS
Becker County cont.			
Island	W, BLH	Ponsford	public
Juggler	NP, B, C	Waubon	public
La Belle, East	W, B, C	Lake Park	public
Leaf	LMB, B, C	Audubon	public
Lind	NP, C, B	Detroit Lakes	private
Long	W, NP, C, B	Detroit Lakes	private
Many Point	NP, B, C	Ponsford	public
Marshall	W, BLH	Audubon	public
Maud	NP, B, C	Audubon	public
Meadow	NP, B, C	Detroit Lakes	public
Melissa	W, LMB, NP, B, C	Detroit Lakes	public
Monson	NP, C, B	Detroit Lakes	public
Murphy	NP, BLH	Frazee	private
Net	NP, B, C, BLH	White Earth	public
Pearl	NP, B, C	Detroit Lakes	private
Pickerel	B, C	Detroit Lakes	public
Reeves	NP, B, C	Detroit Lakes	private
Rock	W, B, C	Richwood	public
Round	W, LMB, C, B	Ponsford	public
Sally	W, NP, LMB, B, C	Detroit Lakes	public
Sand	NP, BLH	Lake Park	public
Sauers	NP, B, C	Detroit Lakes	public
Shell	NP, BLH	Snellman	public
Straight River	BRT	Park Rapids	public
Strawberry	W, SMB, NP	White Earth	public
Sugarbush, Big	LMB, NP, C, B	Richwood	public
Sugarbush, Little	NP, BLH	Richwood	public
Tamarack	W, NP, BLH	Richwood	public
Toad, Big	W, NP	Snellman	public
Toad, Little	W, NP	Detroit Lakes	public
Toad River	BRT	Frazee	public
Tulaby	W, NP, LMB	Waubon	public
Turtle	NP, C, B	Lake Park	public
Twin, South	B, LMB, NP, C	Snellman	public
White Earth	W	White Earth	public

Clay County

Felton Creek	BRT	Felton	off road
Lee	NP, B, C	Lake Park	public

Clearwater County

Augonash Creek	BKT	Zerkel	public
Bagley	NP	Clearbrook	public
Buckboard Creek	BKT	Zerkel	public
Bungo	W, NP, B	Waubon	public
Camp	NP	Itasca State PK.	private
Daniel	NP	Shevlin	private
Deep	NP, LMB, B	Clearbrook	public
Elbow Lake Creek	BKT	Waubon	public

NAME	FISH SPECIES (listed by preference)	NEAREST TOWN	ACCESS
Clearwater County cont.			
Elk	W, NP	Itasca State Pk.	public
Falk	W, NP	Clearbrook	public
First	NP	Bagley	public
Heart	W, NP, LMB, B	Itasca State Pk.	private
Island	RBT	Roy Lake	public
Itasca	W, NP	Itasca State Pk.	public
Jackson	NP	Zerkel	public
Johson	W, NP	Clearbrook	public
La Salle	NP, LMB, B	Bemidji	private
Lindberg	W, NP	Clearbrook	public
Lomond	NP, P, BLH	Bagley	public
Lone	LMB, NP, C	Bagley	public
Long Lost	W, LMB, NP, B	Itasca State Pk.	public
Long, South	RBT	Itasca State Pk.	public
Lost River Creek	BKT	Bagley	public
Minerva	W, P, BLH	Bagley	public
Minnow	NP	Bagley	public
Mud Creek	BKT	Itasca State Pk.	public
Pickerel	NP, W	Waubon	public
Peterson	NP, LMB, B	Clearbrook	public
Pike	NP	Gonvick	private
Pine, Big	W, NP, P	Gonvick	public
Red Lake River	CTF	Lower Stretches	public
Squaw	W, NP	Itasca St. Pk.	public
Sucker	NP	Itasca St. Pk.	public
Sucker Brook	BKT	Itasca St. Pk.	public
Walkerbrook	W, NP	Bagley	public

Douglas County

NAME	FISH SPECIES	NEAREST TOWN	ACCESS
Aaron	NP, W, C	Millerville	public
Andrews	W, NP, B, LMB	Alexandria	public
Blackwell	LMB, B, C	Holmes City	private
Brophy	LMB, B, C	Alexandria	public
Burgens	B, C, LMB	Alexandria	public
Carlos	W, LMB, B, C	Alexandria	public
Chippewa, Big	B, C, W	Brandon	public
Chippewa, Little	B, C, W	Brandon	public
Cowdry	LMB, B	Alexandria	private
Crooked	B, C, LMB	Holmes City	public
Darling	W, LMB	Alexandria	public
Devils	B, C, W, NP	Brandon	public
Freeborn	C, B, NP	Kensington	public
Geneve	LMB, B, C	Alexandria	private
Grants	B, C, LMB	Holmes City	private
Hidden	B, C, LMB	Carlos	public
Ida	W, NP, LMB	Alexandria	public
Indian	B, C	Millerville	public
Irene	B, C, LMB	Miltona	public
Jessie	B, C, LMB	Alexandria	private
Latoka	B, C, LMB, W	Alexandria	public
LeHomme Dieu	W, LMB, C	Alexandria	public
Lobster	M, LMB, C	Holmes City	public
Louise	B, C, LMB	Alexandria	public
Maple	W, LMB, B	Forada	public

NAME	FISH SPECIES (listed by preference)	NEAREST TOWN	ACCESS
Douglas County cont.			
Mary	W, NP, LMB	Alexandria	public
Mill	B, C, W, NP	Holmes City	public
Miltona	LMB, W, NP	Miltona	public
Mina	B, C, LMB	Alexandria	public
Moses	B, C, LMB	Millerville	private
Osakis	C, W, NP	Osakis	public
Oscar	NP, W	Kensington	public
Pocket	B, C, LMB	Holmes City	public
Rachel	B, C, LMB	Holmes City	public
Red Rock	NP, W	Kensington	public
Smith	B, C, LMB	Nelson	public
Stowes	B, C, NP	Evansville	public
Turtle	B, C, W	Forada	public
Union	LMB, B, C	Forada	public
Vermont	B, C, LMB	Miltona	public
Victoria	LMB, B	Alexandria	public
Whiskey	LMB, B, C	Brandon	public

Grant County

Barrett	B, C, NP	Barrett	public
Cottonwood	B, C, W	Donnelly	public
Elk	B, C, LMB	Hoffman	public
Lightning	B, C, W	Wendell	private
Mustinka	B, LMB	Herman	public
Pelican	W, B, C, NP	Ashby	public
Pomme de Terre	NP, W, C	Elbow Lake	public
Thompson	NP, W	Barrett	public

Kittson County

Bronson	W, NP, BLH	Lake Bronson St. Park	public

Mahnomen County

Bad Boy Creek	BRT	Nay-Tah-Waush	public
Bass, Big	W, SMB, LMB, B	Nay-Tah-Waush	public
Elbow Lake Creek	BRT	Waubon	public
Island	W	Langby	public
McCraney	NP, LMB	Waubon	public
Roy	BLH, W	Mahnomen	public
Snider	BLH, B, C	Nay-Tah-Waush	public
Twin, North	NP, LMB	Nay-Tah-Waush	public
Twin, South	W, B	Nay-Tah-Waush	public

NAME	FISH SPECIES (listed by preference)	NEAREST TOWN	ACCESS

Ottertail County

NAME	FISH SPECIES	NEAREST TOWN	ACCESS
Alice	LMB, B, C	Fergus Falls	public
Anderson	W	Erhardt	public
Anna	B, LMB	Underwood	private
Annie Battle	C, LMB, B	Battle Lake	private
Bahle	BLH, B	Dalton	private
Bass	BLH	Underwood	public
Bass	RBT	Maple Wood St. Park	public
Bass	LMB, B	Battle Lake	public
Battle, East	W, LMB, NP	Battle Lake	public
Battle, West	W, M, LMB, NP	Battle Lake	public
Bear	LMB, B	Perham	public
Beers	LMB, B, C	Pelican Rapids	public
Berger	W, LMB, NP	Dent	public
Blanche	W, LMB, NP	Battle Lake	public
Block	W, LMB, B	Urbank	public
Boedigheimer	B, C, LMB, NP	Ottertail City	public
Branberg Creek	RBT	Henning	public
Buchanan	W, B, C	Ottertail City	public
Clear	W, LMB, C, B	Dalton	public
Clitherall	W, NP, B, LMB	Battle Lake	public
Crystal	W, LMB, B, C	Pelican Rapids	public
Dayton's Dam Pond	W, LMB, NP	Fergus Falls	public
Dead	W, NP, LMB, C	Dent	public
Deer	W, NP, C	Underwood	public
Devils	LMB, B, C, NP	Perham	public
Donald	W, LMB, B, C	Ottertail City	public
Eagle	W, NP, LMB, B, C	Battle Lake	public
Ethel	LMB, B, C	Ottertail City	public
Five	W, NP, LMB, B, C	Frazee	private
Fladmark	LMB, B, C, NP	Pelican Rapids	public
Franklin	W, NP, B	Pelican Rapids	public
German	NP, LMB, B, C	Underwood	public
Graham	LMB, NP, C	Frazee	public
Hancock	LMB, NP, C	Urbank	public
Heilberger	NP, LMB, B, C	Erhardt	public
Hoffman	BLH, LMB, B, C	Vergas	public
Hoot	NP, LMB, B, C	Fergus Falls	public
Jewett	W, LMB, C, NP	Elizabeth	public
Jim	LMB, NP, B, C	Frazee	public
Leaf, East	W, NP, B, C	Henning	public
Leaf, Middle	W, NP, B, C	Henning	public
Leaf, West	W, NP, B, C	Henning	public
Leek	W, NP, LMB, B	Vergas	public
Lida	W, LMB, SMB, NP	Pelican Rapids	public
Lizzie	W, C, B, NP	Pelican Rapids	public
Long	LMB, B, C	Dalton	public
Long	LMB, C, NP	Ottertail City	public
Long	W, NP, LMB, C	Elizabeth	public
Long	W, NP, B, C	Vergas	public
Loon	NP, LMB, C	Vergas	public
Lost, East	LMB, NP, B, C	Underwood	public
Lost, West	LMB, B, BLH	Underwood	public
Marion	LMB, B, C, NP	Perham	public

NAME	FISH SPECIES (listed by preference)	NEAREST TOWN	ACCESS

Ottertail County cont.

NAME	FISH SPECIES	NEAREST TOWN	ACCESS
Molly Stark	LMB, NP, C	Battle Lake	public
McDonald, Big	W, NP	Dent	public
McDonald, Little	W, LMB, C, NP	Perham	public
McDonald, West	W, LMB, C, NP	Vergas	public
Olaf, West	LMB, B, NP	Pelican Rapids	public
Ottertail	W, NP	Battle Lake	public
Ottertail River	NP, B, BLH	Fergus Falls	public
Paul	W, LMB, B, C, NP	Perham	public
Pebble	LMB, RBT, NP	Fergus Falls	public
Pelican, Big	W, LMB, NP, C	Pelican Rapids	public
Pelican, Little	NP, LMB, B, C	Pelican Rapids	public
Pickerel	W, LMB, NP, B, C	Underwood	public
Pine, Big	W, LMB, NP, B, C	Perham	public
Pine, Little	W, OMB, NP, B, C	Perham	public
Pleasant	LMB, B, NP	Underwood	public
Portage	LMB, C, NP	Ottertail City	public
Rose	W, NP, LMB, C	Vergas	public
Round	LMB, NP, C	Underwood	public
Round	LMB, BLH	Perham	public
Round	LMB, B	Dent	public
Rush	W, LMB, C, NP	Perham	public
Sand	NP, LMB, C	Pelican Rapids	public
Scalp	W, NP, LMB, B	Frazee	public
Sewell	W, NP, LMB, B, C	Dalton	public
Silver	W, NP, LMB, C	Battle Lake	public
Silent, East	W, NP, C	Henning	public
Silent, West	W, NP, B, C	Henning	public
Six	W, NP, LMB, B	Frazee	public
Spirit, Big	W, NP, LMB, C	Vergas	public
Spitzer	NP, LMB, B, C	Urbank	public
Stalker	W, NP, LMB, C	Dalton	public
Star	W, NP, LMB, C, B	Dent	public
Stuart	NP, LMB, B, C	Henning	public
Swan	W, NP, LMB, B, C	Fergus Falls	public
Sybil	W, NP, LMB, B, C	Vergas	public
Ten Mile, South	W, NP, C, LMB	Dalton	public
Tenter	LMB, NP, C	Vergas	public
Townset	C, B, NP	Fergus Falls	public
Turtle, South	NP, LMB, B	Underwood	public
Twenty-One	NP, C, LMB	Pelican Rapids	public
Walker	W, LMB, NP, C	Richville	public
Wall	W, NP, LMB, C, B	Fergus Falls	public
Wimer	LMB, C, NP	Frazee	public

Pope County

NAME	FISH SPECIES	NEAREST TOWN	ACCESS
Amelia	W, NP, B, C	Villard	public
Gilchrist	NP, W, LMB	Swift Falls	public
Glacial	LMB, B, C	Starbuck	public
Grove	B, C, LMB	Sedan	public
Leven	B, C, LMB, NP	Villard	private
Links	B, C, NP	Swift Falls	public
Minnewaska	W, C, B, LMB	Glenwood	public
Pelican	B, C, W	Glenwood	public

NAME	FISH SPECIES (listed by preference)	NEAREST TOWN	ACCESS
Pope County cont.			
Reno	W, C, B, LMB	Glenwood	public
Scandinavian	B, C, LMB, NP	Swift Falls	public
Villard	C, B, LMB, NP	Villard	public

Stevens County

Hattie	NP, W, LMB	Alberta	public
Page	B, C, NP	Hancock	public
Pomme de Terre	B, C, LMB, W	Morris	public

Wadena County

Blueberry	NP, C, BLH	Menahga	public
Cat Creek	BKT	Sebeka	public
Spirit	NP, B	Menahga	public
Stocking	W, NP, B, C	Menahga	public
Twin, Lower	NP, LMB, BLH	Menahga	public

(Photo courtesy of Ray St. Ores)

Doggone, the sport of fishing is fun.

Index